Understanding India's New Approach to Spatial Planning and Development

A Salient Shift?

Sanjeev Vidyarthi
Shishir Mathur
Sandeep Agrawal

With contributions by
Neha Sami and Sudeshna Mitra

OXFORD
UNIVERSITY PRESS

OXFORD
UNIVERSITY PRESS

Oxford University Press is a department of the University of Oxford.
It furthers the University's objective of excellence in research, scholarship,
and education by publishing worldwide. Oxford is a registered trademark of
Oxford University Press in the UK and in certain other countries.

Published in India by
Oxford University Press
YMCA Library Building, 1 Jai Singh Road, New Delhi 110001, India

ISBN-13: 978-0-19-947264-2
ISBN-10: 0-19-947264-5

Typeset in Adobe Garamond Pro 11/13
by Tranistics Data Technologies, Kolkata 700091
Printed in India by Replika Press Pvt. Ltd

Contents

Tables and Figures

Tables

Figures

Abbreviations and Acronyms

ACSP	American Collegiate Schools of Planning
ADB	Asian Development Bank
AJL	Ahmedabad Janmarg Limited
AKIC	Amritsar–Kolkata Industrial Corridor
AMC	Ahmedabad Municipal Corporation
APL	Above Poverty Line
ASCI	Administrative Staff College of India
ASHA	Accredited Social Health Activist
BBMP	Bruhat Bengaluru Mahanagara Palike
BDA	Bangalore Development Authority
BEL	Bharat Electronics Limited
BESSCOM	Bangalore Electricity Supply Company
BHEL	Bharat Heavy Electricals Limited
BJP	Bharatiya Janata Party
BMPC	Bangalore Metropolitan Planning Committee
BMRCL	Bangalore Metro Rail Corporation Limited
BMRDA	Bangalore Metropolitan Region Development Authority
BMTC	Bengaluru Metropolitan Transport Corporation
BoP	Balance of Payments
BOT	Build–Operate–Transfer
BPL	Below Poverty Line
BRT	Bus Rapid Transit
BRTS	Bus Rapid Transit System
BSUP	Basic Services to the Urban Poor
BUA	Built-up Area
BWSSB	Bangalore Water Supply and Sewerage Board
CA	Census Agglomeration
CAG	Comptroller and Auditor General

CCF	City Challenge Fund
CD	Community Development
CDP	City Development Plan
CEUT	Centre for Excellence in Urban Transport
CIB	City Improvement Board
CILU	Change in Land Use
CMA	Census Metropolitan Area
CRUPO	Central Regional and Urban Planning Organization
CSD	Census Sub-division
CT	Census Town
DBFO	Design–Build–Finance–Operate
DIPP	Department of Industrial Policy and Promotion
DMIC	Delhi–Mumbai Industrial Corridor
DMP	Delhi Master Plan
DoT	Department of Telecommunications
DPC	District Planning Committee
DPEP	District Primary Education Programme
DPR	Detailed Project Report
DTA	Domestic Tariff Area
EGoM	Empowered Group of Ministers
EOU	Export Oriented Unit
EPC	Engineering–Procurement–Construction
EPZ	Export Promotion Zone
EXIM	Export–Import
FDI	Foreign Direct Investment
FIP	Financial Investment Plan
FSI	Floor Space Index
FY	Fiscal Year
GDP	Gross Domestic Product
GIS	Geographical Information Systems
GoI	Government of India
GoK	Government of Karnataka
GQ	Golden Quadrilateral
GSI	Geological Survey of India
HPEC	High Powered Expert Committee
I&A	Infrastructure and Amenities
IAS	Indian Administrative Service

ICT	Information and Communications Technology
IDSMT	Integrated Development of Small and Medium Towns
IHD	Institute for Human Development
IHSDP	Integrated Housing and Slum Development Programme
IIM	Indian Institute of Management
IIT	Indian Institute of Technology
IL&FS	Infrastructure Leasing and Finance Services
IMF	International Monetary Fund
IT	Information Technology
ITeS	Information Technology-enabled Services
ITPI	Institute of Town Planners, India
IUDP	Integrated Urban Development Programme
JDA	Jaipur Development Authority
JnNURM	Jawaharlal Nehru National Urban Renewal Mission
KSCB	Karnataka Slum Clearance Board
KSTRC	Karnataka State Road Transport Corporation
KTCP	Karnataka Town and Country Planning
KUIDFC	Karnataka Urban Infrastructure Development and Finance Corporation
KUWASIP	Karnataka Urban Water Supply Improvement Project
KUWSMP	Karnataka Urban Water Supply Modernization Project
LARR Act	Right to Fair Compensation and Transparency in Land Acquisition, Rehabilitation and Resettlement Act, 2013
MDM Scheme	Mid Day Meal Scheme
MGNREGA	Mahatma Gandhi National Rural Employment Guarantee Act
MHUPA	Ministry of Housing and Urban Poverty Alleviation
MIT	Massachusetts Institute of Technology
MIZ	Metropolitan Influence Zone
MLA	Member of the Legislative Assembly

MMRDA	Mumbai Metropolitan Region Development Authority
MoCI	Ministry of Commerce and Industry
MoF	Ministry of Finance
MoSPI	Ministry of Statistics and Programme Implementation
MoUD	Ministry of Urban Development
MP	Member of Parliament
MPC	Metropolitan Planning Committee
MRTP	Monopolies and Restrictive Trade Practices
MSDI	Metropolitan Spatial Data Infrastructure
MSRTH	Ministry of Shipping, Road Transport and Highways
MTNL	Mahanagar Telephone Nigam Limited
NASSCOM	National Association of Software and Services Companies
NCAER	National Council of Applied Economic Research
NCR	National Capital Region
NCRPB	National Capital Region Planning Board
NCU	National Commission on Urbanization
NDA	National Democratic Alliance
NDWM	National Drinking Water Mission
NGO	Non-governmental Organization
NHAI	National Highways Authority of India
NHDP	National Highways Development Project
NIDL	New International Division of Labour
NITI Aayog	National Institution for Transforming India
NIUA	National Institute of Urban Affairs
NOIDA	New Okhla Industrial Development Authority
NREGA	National Rural Employment Guarantee Act
NUTP	National Urban Transport Policy
O&M	Operations and Maintenance
OECD	Organisation for Economic Co-operation and Development
OG	Outgrowth Area
ORR	Outer Ring Road (Hyderabad)
PDS	Public Distribution System

PIL	Public Interest Litigation
PMGSY	Pradhan Mantri Gram Sadak Yojana
PPP	Public–Private Partnership
PURA	Provision of Urban Amenities in Rural Areas
PWD	Public Works Department
RAS	Rajasthan Administrative Service
RfP	Request for Proposals
RIICO	Rajasthan State Industrial Development and Investment Corporation Limited
RMC	Rajkot Municipal Corporation
RRL	Rajkot Rajpath Limited
RTI	Right to Information
RUDA	Rural and Urban Development Association
SDR	Special Drawing Right
SEZ	Special Economic Zone
SIPCOT	State Industries Promotion Council of Tamil Nadu
SIUD	The State Institute for Urban Development
SPA	School of Planning and Architecture
ST	Statutory Town
STEM	Centre for Symbiosis of Technology, Environment and Management
SUA	Standard Urban Area
TCPO	Town and Country Planning Organisation
TDSAT	Telecom Disputes Settlement and Appellate Tribunal
TIF	Tax Increment Financing
ToR	Terms of Reference
TPD	Town Planning Department
TPM	Town Planning Member
TPO	Town Planning Organization
TRAI	Telecom Regulatory Authority of India
TVA	Tennessee Valley Authority
UA	Urban Agglomeration
UI	Urban Improvement
UIDSSMT	Urban Infrastructure Development Scheme for Small and Medium Towns
UIG	Urban Infrastructure and Governance

UIT	Urban Improvement Trust
ULB	Urban Local Body
ULCRA	Urban Land (Ceiling and Regulation) Act
UN	United Nations
UN DESA	United Nations Department of Economic and Social Affairs
UPA	United Progressive Alliance
UPTPO	Uttar Pradesh Town Planning Organization
URIF	Urban Reform Incentive Fund
UK	United Kingdom
USA	United States of America
USSR	Union of Soviet Socialist Republics
VSNL	Videsh Sanchar Nigam Limited

Foreword

The publication of this book roughly coincides with the completion of the seventh decade of the Indian republic. The 'idea of India', to draw from political theorist Sunil Khilnani—that of a secular democracy and a modern state that holds together a crazy quilt of diverse ethnicities, religions, languages, customs, and castes with undercurrents of a centrifugal tendency—endures as a major triumph of collective imagination that commanded independence and nationhood from the British colonial rule. What has amazed Western observers is that while in the liberal democracies of the developed West, barely half of the eligible voters bother to vote in national elections, the turnout in national elections is always well over 60 per cent in India. Poor and starving farmers are known to get up very early in the morning and walk many kilometres to the nearest polling station to exercise their democratic right to vote. They may be poor, but they remain proud of their stake in a secular democracy and their right to vote, however evanescent or inconsequential that privilege might be in their and their children's material life experience.

Nevertheless, as we near the end of the seventh decade, the project of the Indian secular democracy remains an inchoate mix of policies, institutions, and initiatives. Nowhere that is more evident than in the evolution of spatial planning at the urban, regional, project-wide, and infrastructural scale. The idea of planning itself has always been central to the concept of the modern Indian state, although it did not necessarily come from the British who introduced the institutions of modern state in colonial India. The agency of the National Planning Commission (headed by the prime minister) and its imperatives of preparing Five Year Plans were influenced more by the Soviet Union's style of command and control planning than the legacy of the British colonial rule. In the early stages of the country's development history,

Five Year Plans set the targets for capital investments and other budget expenditures. The official mouthpiece of the Planning Commission (now the NITI Aayog) was a monthly magazine called *Yojana* (or plan), not *parikalpana* (or planning) as normally associated with territorial organizations (as in nagar parikalpana for city planning). This should not be a surprise since the entire scope of such 'planning' was seen as 'sectoral' in a macroeconomic sense. Any semblance of spatial analysis was only implicit in the dichotomy of urban versus rural sectors commonly used in the national planning efforts.

From this early beginning of very limited interest or awareness of spatial planning—other than the legacy of Town and Country Planning Act left behind by the British—urban, regional, and infrastructure planning in India have evolved significantly in these seven decades. Multiple initiatives and institutional innovations helped advance spatial planning as an apparatus of the state to guide the larger development project. While various authors have captured bits and pieces of this story over different periods, focusing on multiple localities and processes, a synoptic and penetrating overview of the planning in India had yet to be told. This volume by Sanjeev Vidyarthi, Shishir Mathur, and Sandeep Agrawal, all planning academics in American and Canadian universities, with contributions from Neha Sami and Sudeshna Mitra, planning scholars from India, is probably the very first such effort to systematically document the evolution of spatial planning efforts in India. In particular, the authors wanted to paint the entire landscape of planning nationwide—urban and rural—and not just that in big cities such as Delhi, Kolkata, and Mumbai. Accordingly, their collective gaze into this planning landscape is synoptic and comprehensive. Some of the chapters document the historiography of the phases of development from the earlier Nehruvian top–down approach to industrial development, to the most recent phase of globalization and the neo-liberal imperatives that are shaping urbanization and growth of major urban centres. Others are case-study oriented, looking at planning efforts in second order cities such as Bangalore (now Bengaluru) and Jaipur, or critically examining the neo-liberal tools such as value-capture financing and public–private partnership for implementing infrastructure development. Some of the chapters focus on special economic zones, changing urban hierarchy, and

the advent of mega projects in the wake of massive investments in infrastructure. Two chapters examine the status of rural planning, analysing the changing nature of the rural–urban continuum, and underscoring continuing infrastructure deficits even in high-density rural regions. They have demonstrated that planning in India has become much more Aristotelian involving many actors such as state agencies, real estate developers, non-governmental organizations, civil society activists, and advocacy groups. Yet seemingly the poor have not found a place at the table. The authors are quite aware of the continuing spectacle of poverty, growing inequality, and the limited effectiveness of national urban renewal and development programmes in improving the life experience of the poor.

Those of us who have often looked at China and India in a comparative perspective, would recall that since the liberalization of India's economic policies, a decade after China's embrace of the market economy, the annual gross domestic product (GDP) growth rate of India, although impressive at 5 per cent to 7 per cent, had trailed China's by 2.5 per cent to 3 per cent consistently. I would like to call this difference essentially a 'democracy discount'—the transaction costs of development in a secular democracy that China did not have to face. As China's growth rate has slowed, having proved unsustainable at the earlier pace, now India is posting a rate of growth higher than China's. At the same time economic disparity has increased. Gini index has crept up over the last decades although not as spectacularly as China's. India's billionaire count is only half that of China's (48 versus 95), but their net worth (as percentage of GDP) is four times greater than their Chinese counterparts (10.9 versus 2.6).[1] India today boasts the largest mansion of the world—a 27-storey tower in Mumbai, which at 400,000 square feet, is 1,300 times bigger than an average slum dwelling,[2] like the ones comprising Dharavi, one of the largest slums in the world that sprawls for miles in the panorama visible from this very tower. This book captures the

[1] Yanrui Wu, *Understanding Economic Growth In China And India: A Comparative Study Of Selected Issues* (Singapore: World Scientific Publishing Company, 2012).

[2] See *The Economist*, 'For Richer, For Poorer' (13–19 October 2012), pp. 3–4.

institutional complexities of Aristotelian planning but also suggests that with the imperatives of global economy and neo-liberal impulses how a Platonic tendency is emerging in India where development imperatives of the local and national state and the global capital are seemingly flouting earlier concerns for environment and social justice.

This volume is a result of rigorous scholarship, empirical research, and critical analysis, but is not necessarily judgemental. The authors see improvements in the planning process overall at different levels and scales, but they are collectively wary of the current trends and future prospects. This is a very important and timely contribution to the state of the art in spatial planning in India. It should be seen as a foundational and required reading for the students and practitioners of planning, not just in India, but the developing world more broadly.

Tridib Banerjee
Professor and the James Irvine Chair in
Urban and Regional Planning
Sol Price School of Public Policy
University of Southern California
Los Angeles, USA

Preface

Vast, diverse, and rapidly urbanizing countries like India present a range of multifarious challenges and exciting opportunities to planning scholars. Among others, investigating the nature and purpose of planning activity affecting outcomes at various spatial scales in different parts of the country is critical for comprehending how various state and non-state actors are shaping (through formal, informal, or any other kind of planning) India's settlements. Given that an increasingly urbanized population seeks city living, even as many cities fail to anticipate and prepare for social inequalities, environmental externalities, and physical hardships, the importance of catering to peoples' basic needs and promoting better places to live, work, and play cannot be understated.

Three of us, Sandeep, Sanjeev, and Shishir, began thinking about this project almost four years ago. While discussing our research interests on the sidelines of the American Collegiate Schools of Planning (ACSP) 2012 Annual Meeting organized at Cincinnati, Ohio, we noticed significant overlaps between our research agendas, including a shared interest in understanding India's contemporary approach to spatial planning and development. While the three of us study different aspects of planning work in divergent contexts— Shishir studies infrastructure finance policy in the United States of America (USA) and the Global South, including India; Sanjeev studies plan-making activity in the contexts of current debates in the global planning academia and on-the-ground outcomes in the post-colonial world, most notably urban India; and Sandeep focuses on rural–urban migration among other things—we are happy to note that this project combines our intellectual curiosities and scholarly focuses in coherent and complementary ways.

Following Shishir's initiative, we outlined the project's broad contours, divvyed-up the work, and led the efforts to write and organize the three parts of this book that fall generally in line with our study areas. As the book began to take shape, we invited Neha Sami and Sudeshna Mitra, two promising scholars of Indian urban planning, to contribute their insightful work in the form of individual chapters.

Along the way, we have accumulated a range of debts that we happily acknowledge. Sandeep would like to thank the Shastri Indo-Canadian Institute, the Institute of Human Development (IHD), and Indian Institute of Technology (IIT) Roorkee for supporting his research work; Mohammad Qadeer of Queen's University, Canada, for being an inspiration and intellectual force behind the research idea; Prakash Agrawal, his cousin in Patna, for hosting and making all the travel arrangements; students at IIT-Roorkee, especially, Neelakshi Joshi, for selfless commitment to the research; and the people of Bihar for warmly welcoming him to their homes. He would also like to thank his wife Vandna and kids, Saras and Jia, for being patient with his pursuits and idiosyncrasies. Sanjeev acknowledges the research support fellowship awarded by the Poornima Foundation, Jaipur, the camaraderie and discussions about this project with Professor Charles Hoch, and the love and affection of his parents, Pramod and Madhur, wife Priti, and daughter Anandita. Shishir would like to thank Sandeep, Sanjeev, and his father Hemendra Mathur for help with refining many arguments made in this book; Vijay Anadkat for his valuable time and insights; and his mother Mridula, wife Richa, and sons Tanmay and Anay for their love and support.

Neha would like to acknowledge the valuable research assistance provided by Geetika Anand. She is also grateful to the interview respondents for their time and candid responses. Sudeshna thanks Sandeep, Shishir, and Sanjeev for inviting her on to the book project, and for their constructive feedback and comments about her chapter. We are all grateful to the team at Oxford University Press for their continuing support and assistance in shepherding the manuscript through the review and publication process. Finally, errors of fact or interpretation are our responsibility alone.

Introduction

Tracking India's New Approach to Spatial Planning and Development

Why this Book?

Not very long ago, spatial planning and development of places was not a priority for Indian authorities. Although growing urbanization and poor upkeep of human settlements were widely perceived as important issues, a range of more pressing problems claimed the decision-makers' attention. More than any singular factor, a particularly pernicious combination of entrenched poverty,[1] rapid population growth (361 million in 1951 to 1.02 billion in 2001) (Census of India 2001), and incessant inflation in one of the poorest parts of the world meant that spatial planning and development—like many other human needs and practical conveniences such as proper sanitation and regular electricity supply—attracted genuine concern, but actually remained a low priority during the decades immediately following India's Independence in 1947.[2]

---

[1] The spread and nature of poverty that the successor states of Pakistan and India inherited from the departing British and outgoing indigenous intermediaries was absolutely appalling. In rural India, for example, the average life expectancy was 29 years, with estimates putting between 48 and 53 per cent of the population below the poverty line in 1947 which, in other words, meant that nearly half the population could not afford the basic minimum intake of food required to sustain the human body (Raychaudhuri 1999).

[2] Here it is important to note that although 'rural development' remained a high priority sector for the national government beginning from the First Five Year Plan (1951–6), the focus was on economic issues such as

Despite these concerns, and consistent with India's first prime minister Jawaharlal Nehru's modernist ideals and socialist beliefs that the central government should play a commanding role in planning the nation's future, post-Independence ruling elites attempted to shape the urban sector as part of the overall development of the nation (Dutt et al. 2016; Kalia 2004). On the one hand, they conceived a state-centred spatial planning and development model that employed the latest (but imported) concepts such as land use planning and comprehensive master plans. On the other hand, they used a combination of state power and existing institutions and routines that the colonists had left behind, such as the engineering-oriented Urban Improvement Trusts (UITs) and compulsory acquisition of private lands, to operationalize the adopted model.

However, the combination of shortage of resources and the ambitious scope of the state-led planning agenda severely constrained the chosen approach but not enough to block the institutionalization of modernist parameters and procedures in India's planning practice. Modernist projects built at the time by newly founded public sector agencies illustrate the underlying spatial imagination across the country's geography and urban order (Prakash 1969; Swamy 1966). Notable examples range from more than 65 new towns including the well-known capital cities of Chandigarh and Gandhinagar to purpose-built housing units in modernist city-extensions such as Kolkata's Salt Lake City and national capital region's (NCR's) Noida.[3]

But this 'top–down' and largely socially insensitive planning process excluded both the anticipated beneficiaries and the many poor including those that built these places. Lower rungs of the bureaucracy routinely colluded with local politicians and conniving intermediaries while paying lip service to the Nehruvian promise of modernistic urban transformation but definitely safeguarding their administrative, business, and political interests (Gupta 1995;

---

agricultural productivity and irrigation development rather than the planning and development of places.

[3] Noida is named after the parastatal authority, NOIDA, which stands for New Okhla Industrial Development Authority.

Jeffrey 2002). No wonder then, that a complex web of divides, exclusions, and contestations shaped India's settlements more than formal planning efforts.[4] Discursive policies and paper plans formulated in government secretariats and town planning departments located at the states' capital cities were relatively meaningless for smaller settlements and remote regions that often lacked the local resources and institutional capacity to implement these plans. Further, heavily focused on physical planning, these plans routinely failed to provide context-sensitive planning solutions to local problems. Like many other domains of bureaucratic purview, a particular postcolonial ennui permeated the government-sponsored urban planning and development, with the post-Independence euphoria waning rather quickly within a few decades of Independence (Frankel 2009).

Today, the situation is notably different. One simply cannot escape planning and development activity across the length and breadth of the country. Routinely encountering the postcolonial condition and the failure of comprehensive nation-wide planning, authorities in India now recognize how purposeful future-oriented efforts to improve existing conditions of both 'rural' and 'urban' human settlements (or what we identify as 'spatial planning' in this volume) can coordinate and advance the expansion of growth-oriented economic activity across the growing settlements and surrounding areas. While India's ongoing economic growth continues to provide an increasing range of resources and motivations for enlarging the scope of planning efforts in different domains of spatial development (settlements, amenities, infrastructure), larger shifts in the national polity have also begun to shape and augment the audience for spatial planning.

The move away from the exclusive government-driven development focus of the Nehruvian era, for instance, has created room for a host of planning players including the existing and new public sector agencies, emergent entrepreneurs, real estate developers, infrastructure consultants, builders of townships and special economic

---

[4] Recent literature documenting the spread and scope of informal planning practices, which is sponsored by many sections of Indian society including low-income and marginalized groups as they seek security and prosperity in the face of an uncertain future, is prolific in nature. See Benjamin (2008) for a broad overview.

zones (SEZs), environmental advocates, civil society activists, local politicians, investors, and existing and aspiring homeowners who support and sponsor a variety of spatial plans and planning initiatives targeting different policy and geographical scales.

Take, for example, the following two initiatives exemplifying ambitious efforts to cause a shift in the country's approach to spatial planning. Launched in 2005, with a first phase outlay of more than INR 60,000 crore (USD 10 billion) and an overall investment of INR 100,000 crore (about USD 66 billion in purchasing power parity, based on the 2010 dollar–rupee conversion figures), the Jawaharlal Nehru National Urban Renewal Mission (JnNURM) represents one of the largest nationally planned urban initiatives anywhere globally. Inviting the state governments' involvement and mandating local participation in the preparation of city development plans (CDPs), this central-government-sponsored programme aimed to augment basic urban services and infrastructure in the country's largest and most significant cities spread across different regions (Sivaramakrishnan 2011). In a similar vein, many national, state, and local players have worked together over the last two decades, creating a massive road network comprising a countrywide highway system that connects the largest urban centres and regional cities with the first-ever all-weather rural roads linking India's numerous remote settlements. Rarely do entire societies undertake purposeful spatial planning at this scale. So, how do we make sense of such a salient shift? What does it say about the role and nature of spatial planning and development in contemporary India?

This volume contributes to the urgent task of addressing this gap in at least three important ways. First, it tracks the shifts across the interrelated, yet rarely studied together, domains of national- and state-level infrastructure planning and development policy, local spatial plan-making practice, and empirical on-the-ground out-comes. Second, given the country's rich cultural diversity and remarkable regional variation, it deliberately chooses to move away from the largest cities, such as Kolkata, Mumbai, and Delhi, that dominate the discourse on urban India. Instead, it focuses on human settlements that frequently escape scholarly attention, including regional cities such as Jaipur and Rajkot and outlying places like remote settlements in the predominantly rural state of Bihar. Third, it locates

the contemporary shifts in the overall trajectory of independent India's planning literature and practices. Such a positioning not only helps us delineate the nature and extent of ongoing changes but also helps us uncover meaningful differences from the well-theorized Nehruvian planning and development model.

However, our examination is necessarily constrained in geographic and thematic scope by the limited number of studies that can find place in this book. We study the change in spatial planning policy and practice and not the complex political and social processes shaping local conditions, effects, and institutional practices (procedures, regulations, and decisions) that frame the making and implementation of development policies and spatial plans in each place. The shared focus of the studies on the poorly understood nature of recent settlement planning and development activity in different parts of the country—be it urban or rural—nonetheless provides useful insights for rethinking contemporary India's overall approach to spatial planning and development.

This introduction develops a framework for analysing the change in India's approach to spatial planning through a review of both the literature on post-Independence spatial planning and development and the scholarship on contemporary India that offers a detailed account of ongoing economic, social, and political changes but does not describe their impact on the field of spatial planning and development. We find that a powerful combination of diverse yet interrelated factors such as the growing availability of resources, emergence of new planning actors, and a comparatively broader focus than the Nehruvian legacy of a state-led city-level master planning approach has begun to rearticulate the cause and context of spatial planning and development at various scales, within India's new infrastructure and industrial geography, connecting corridors, as well as the vast expanse of surrounding urban peripheries, even as older ideas and entrenched practices continue to persist.

Tracking the Trajectory of Spatial Planning and Development in Independent India

This is not the first study of independent India's experience with spatial planning and development of places. We describe here

some of the extensive literature mainly to frame the context for locating the recent shift in Indian planning's overall trajectory and uncovering meaningful differences from the Nehruvian planning and development model.

The aims and purposes of independent India's approach to spatial planning and development cannot be understood without comprehending the priorities and aspirations of its national leaders and decision-makers. As the intellectual historians associated with the 'subaltern school' have noted, a new indigenous elite, spearheaded by Prime Minister Jawaharlal Nehru, took over national power after the departure of the British colonists (Guha and Spivak 1988). These elites lacked close connections with conventional sources of power such as land and religion; instead they derived their social standing and intellectual authority from formal schooling in the British education system. Chiefly employed in professional occupations such as law, medicine, bureaucracy, and teaching, these elites envisioned India's future in the image of liberal democracies found in Western Europe and North America. Perceiving India's predominately rural population and traditional society as 'backward', and like their postcolonial counterparts from other areas of the world, they aspired to create a confident and 'modern' nation.

Importantly, Indian elites visualized centralized planning as a critical tool for building the new nation.[5] Turning their gaze away from Indian planning's legacy of imperial service and colonial repressions, they sought to reconceptualize the idea of planning in terms of welfare-oriented development. In doing so, they believed that the newly independent country should purposefully employ its resources and legitimacy to pursue comprehensive improvement for people from all walks of life. This belief was in line with the mainstream theory of development planning which, emerging about the same time India gained independence, argued that, despite the ubiquity and variety of oppressions in different locales, the idea of human progress and

[5] Not discounting the significance of various critiques, a major upshot of Nehruvian faith in centralized national planning is evident in helping move the growth rate of India's GDP, from an average of 0.1 per cent for the period between 1900–47, to more than 3 per cent within the first 15 years of Independence (see Ghate 2012).

development was not only universally relevant but also entailed all-around improvement on many fronts (Huntington 1987). Depicting traditional societies like those of India as dependent, poor, violent, and oppressive, this view portrayed 'modern' societies as independent, wealthy, peaceful, and liberal—qualities requiring new political institutions (legislature, judiciary, and executive), cultural mores (for example, individualism, self-orientation), and new social structures (individual family, casteless society). Thus, it posited 'development' as both the index on which the efforts towards modernization were to be measured and the state's primary task (Sivaramakrishnan and Agrawal 2003).

But an important attribute characterized the practice of development planning in Nehruvian India. Downplaying the uncertainties associated with an unpredictable future, the tiny ruling elite (comprising elected and government officials, state bureaucrats, and technical experts) built a rhetoric that identified plans and various kinds of planning with scientific activity (Khilnani 1999). Examples of such planning included the diverse domains of national economic policy, resource allocation for different development programmes, and neighbourhood layout design. Such a discursive positioning of the idea of planning not only ignored the inherently provisional and contingent nature of planning work but also seemed to promise explicit and predictable outcomes.[6]

However, it is important to remember that in tasking themselves with pursuing such an ambitious planning agenda, as a key part of administrative duty in the uncharted territory of central-government-led development, India's new ruling elites were addressing both their constituents' eagerness for rapid national progress and their own unequivocal belief in science as a symbol of modernism that signified liberty, freedom, and universal improvement (Prakash 1999). The power and utility of planning, in this line of thinking, lay in its efficacy as a rationally applicable technology and

[6] This trend was, of course, in line with the globally dominant physical-planning-focused rational planning models, widely perceived as scientific in nature, prevalent at that time. Development of new towns and physical redevelopment of inner city areas were taking place in Europe and North America while the Soviets, and later the Chinese, were also engaging in nation-building through centralized five-year plans (Scott 1998).

not in other potential usages as a tool for identifying and evaluating alternative courses of action or for making better practical judgements suiting local political, social, and economic contexts and cultural preferences. While the central government drove the nation's economic planning, the state governments were given the responsibility for the spatial planning and development of human settlements—a responsibility explicitly enshrined in the Indian Constitution that gave the state governments, not the local governments, the power over all settlement planning and development issues in both urban and rural areas.[7]

The new capital city of Chandigarh, planned by the modernist and authoritarian architect Le Corbusier and built by the public sector, and the Ford-Foundation-sponsored Delhi master plan (DMP), the first city-level comprehensive plan with legal standing in South Asia (Banerjee 2005, 2009), perhaps best demonstrate these ideas in the realms of spatial planning and development. Supervised by Nehru himself (National Institute of Urban Affairs [NIUA] 1991), the DMP aimed to control the city's physical form and guide future development using the comprehensive planning model and the government's compulsory acquisition of peripheral lands. Chandigarh's modern architecture and segregated land uses, on the other hand, epitomized both the use of state power to translate Nehru's spatial vision for the future of urban India on the ground and a rejection of provincial sentimentalism about the colonial and precolonial heritage of

---

[7] Here, it is important to note that, in contrast with the largest cities that experienced substantial planning interventions, rural settlements have attracted relatively much lesser government attention until lately (see the next section for a detailed explanation of the recent expansion of state welfare programmes and infrastructure building in the hinterland). Literature reports the experimental Community Development (CD) programmes undertaken in the 1950s as the only notable exception to independent India's overall neglect of spatial planning for rural settlements. Aimed at comprehensive social and economic transformation, the CD programmes comprised 15 pilot projects, each covering 300 villages, across all the major states. Abandoning the CD programmes by the mid-1960s, the decision-makers, however, quickly turned their attention towards focused interventions to achieve rapid increase in foodgrain production (see Sinha 2008).

Indian cities (Kalia 2006). These ideals quickly disseminated nation-wide after the national government's Third Five Year Plan (1961–6) linked the provision of full financial aid to the states to establishing town planning departments tasked with the preparation of master plans for important cities (Institute of Town Planners, India [ITPI] 1976). Many of these first-ever master plans emulated the DMP, legitimizing the comprehensive planning approach to regional cities with distinct planning histories and identities (Ansari 1977).

Not surprisingly, a diverse range of ruptures in the adopted planning approach became evident within a few years across urban India—especially in the housing sector that comprises the bulk of city land. Colonial era institutions and governing routines contin-ued largely unabated in the newly independent nation as the central and provincial governments faced the challenges of building new institutions and practices (Subramanian 2004). Local governments and civic agencies were slow to develop regulatory frameworks and oversight mechanisms matching the new approach to spatial planning because, among other factors, they were frequently under-staffed and underfunded (Buch 1987). The potent combination of political apathy, a historic lack of government reach and capacity beyond the largest cities, and people's longstanding trust deficit in state institutions, further compounded the situation. Most impor-tantly, unforeseen circumstances—such as the wars with China in 1962 and Pakistan in 1965, Nehru's death in 1964, and the failed monsoons of 1966 and 1967—resulted in food shortages, a balance of payments (BoP) crisis, devaluation of the rupee, and runaway inflation, thereby affecting the quality of life, and leading to a loss of confidence in national pride and a constrained fiscal environment (Frankel 2009).

In the housing sector, for instance, continuing underinvestment swiftly shrank India's urban housing stock during the 1950s and 1960s (Tangri 1968). While the public and private investment in housing increased marginally from INR 11.5 to INR 15.5 billion in the first three Five Year Plans (1951–66) of the central government, overall spending on the housing sector fell significantly from 34 per cent to 15 per cent in the same period when seen as a percentage of total investment in the national economy. Consequently, accounting for an increasingly urbanized population, the available living

space contracted sharply from an already frugal 113 square feet per capita in 1921 to a paltry 70.61 square feet per capita in 1966 (Tangri 1968).

Studies document the litany of subsequent perverse effects such as subversions, informalities, encroachments, and land-market speculation that began to characterize urban India from the 1970s (see, for example, Bapat 1983; Sarin 1982). Perhaps most prominently, unanticipated developments including 'slums' and ungoverned land grabs began appropriating locations, which the first-ever city-level master plans of the 1960s and 1970s had set aside for other uses, not only blocking many of the projected future developments but also jeopardizing the very project of Nehruvian modernist planning. It is important to note that many informal settlements in India are located on state-owned lands, much of which is inherited by the government and its agencies from their pre-Independence predecessors, reflecting the bigger issue of inequitable land distribution where the predominant majority—the working class—lives on a fraction of the total settlement area (Navlakha 2000).

Yet, the 'blueprint'-oriented bureaucratic planning norms and practices spread both deep and far into official development circles, while the cities continued to expand rapidly. For instance, an evaluation study commissioned by the state of Tamil Nadu found that, even as the master plans frequently failed to meet their objectives, the idea of comprehensive planning and associated tools have remained intact as the prototypical method to make spatial development plans and policies (Centre for Symbiosis of Technology, Environment and Management [STEM] 2002). The dilemma symbolizes what Ananya Roy (2009) has provocatively called India's inability to plan its cities. Given this backdrop, how do we explain the emergence of India's new approach to spatial planning and development?

A major regime change happened in the late twentieth century, marked most famously by the liberalization of India's economic and investment policy. In contrast with prior policies, the central government allowed private sector investment and participation in a range of previously restricted sectors such as civil aviation, specialized healthcare, and general insurance. It also began to reform the tax code, lower tariff barriers, and gradually dismantle regulatory restrictions

on foreign trade and investment. Since then, India has seen steady, and in some cases dramatic, increases in a range of economic indicators including growth of the gross domestic product (GDP) and household savings rate (Government of India [GoI] 2011). Moreover, exports increased from USD 17.5 billion in 1991–2 to USD 312.6 billion in 2013–14, while imports increased from USD 19.4 billion to USD 450.1 billion during the same period (Exim Bank 2014). The next section describes how the combination of an increasing focus on economic growth and broader socio-political changes has catalysed noticeable shifts in India's approach to spatial planning and development.

Larger Shifts in India's Polity Influencing the Domains of Spatial Planning and Development

In this section, we describe the larger changes in India's polity that shaped the domains of spatial planning and development. This is important because the aims and purposes of spatial planning ultimately reflect the overall disposition and priorities of the larger society within which it takes place while the 'planning culture' of places critically shapes the work planners do (Sanyal 2005). Therefore, given the Indian elites' preoccupation with continuing economic growth, we pay particular attention to recent shifts in the country's fiscal and investment policies, while highlighting relevant changes in the social and political walks of national life when pertinent.

However, in doing so we seek to step back from the either/or framing of ideological positions and perspectives often polarized around forthright celebration or outright condemnation of India's post-liberalization polity (for example, Bhagwati and Panagariya 2013; Roy 2014). We recognize that scholars have employed two principal theoretical approaches using postcolonial and neoliberal frameworks to describe recent changes in Indian cities.[8] The postcolonial scholarship stresses on the Indian polity's uniqueness and

[8] Within these two traditions, notable works studying post-liberalization urban India include the following: Annapurna Shaw's (2007) edited volume *Indian Cities in Transition*, which is perhaps the first to document the dynamics of change in Indian cities over 30 years, from a multidisciplinary

indigenous characteristics that challenge the superiority of Western-centred approaches to study and describe it while focusing attention on cultural resistance to externally imposed political and social projects. The neoliberal scholarship, on the other hand, focuses on the convergence of India's urban political economy and spatial change with models prevalent in other capitalist societies. They highlight the adoption of neoliberal models of governance advocated by corporate interests and imposed or propagated through international and bilateral aid organizations. Studies have examined efforts to re-engineer urban governance to promote capital accumulation, most notably through the rescaling of the state and empowerment of capital within frameworks of entrepreneurial governance (for example, Gooptu 2011; Mahadevia 2011).

Thus, instead of adopting a particular ideological position, while employing useful insights from a variety of disciplinary traditions and scholarly approaches, we aim to revisit the questions that underlie both the postcolonial and neoliberal perspectives: What kinds of spatial planning is the post-liberalization period producing? How have the different central, provincial, institutional, and private actors involved in crafting a planning policy and carrying out planning work sought to finance and operationalize the spatial development agenda? What new models and approaches to spatial policy and development planning are beginning to take shape?

---

perspective. The volume *Urbanizing Citizenship*, edited by Desai and Sanyal (2012), analyses contemporary urban change through the lens of citizenship using the 'right to the city' discourse in the post-liberalization context. Anjaria and McFarlane's edited volume (2011) *Urban Navigations* also explores the dynamics of post-liberalization urban change, deploying a 'street-level emphasis on urban space-making' to highlight the complexity and contingency of post-liberalization spatial change. Gavin Shatkin's edited volume *Contesting the Indian City* (2014) shares with both of these volumes an interest in developing an understanding of urban change by using an explicit focus on shifting structures of power within frameworks of governance in Indian cities that are emerging with reform efforts and socio-spatial change. Ahmed, Kundu, and Peet (2011) examine the national adoption of international policy regimes and their implications for India's economic development policy from a regional and urban perspective.

Since India's Independence, the elites' thinking about spatial planning has been closely tied to their concerns about the nation's economic development. At some level, this was not surprising given a largely rural (81.3 per cent) and poor (almost half the population below poverty level) population, an agriculture-based economy (agriculture accounting for 47 per cent of the GDP in 1950) (Mohan and Dasgupta 2004; World Bank 1997), a very weak industrial base, and very little foreign currency for imports (Panagariya 2004). Thus, as is well documented, the national leaders chose an inward looking and strong central-government-led economic development model that focused on self-reliance and import substitution (World Bank 1997).

The adopted economic development model aimed at improving and expanding agricultural productivity and industrial activity (while protecting these sectors from external competition), and poverty alleviation through direct financial assistance and indirect subsidies to large swaths of the population (Panagariya 2004). Soft loans, debt relief, and tax exemptions to farmers, subsidies for fertilizers and fuel (kerosene and diesel), and a public distribution system through which essential food products, such as sugar, cooking oil, rice, and wheat flour, were subsidized and made available to the people that accounted for, and still account for, a large share of the state's budgetary outlay.[9]

Spatially, the adoption of these programmes and policies led to the development of large irrigation projects—such as the Bhakra Nangal Dam project that serves the northern states of Himachal Pradesh, Punjab, Haryana, and Rajasthan; and the Chambal Valley project that serves Madhya Pradesh and Rajasthan—and an extensive irrigation canal system, connecting roads, and mandi towns.[10] Similarly,

[9] For example, the central government subsidies accounted for 4.6 per cent of the GDP in the fiscal year (FY) 1998–9 (Srivastava et al. 2003), 4.2 per cent in 2003–4 (Ministry of Finance [MoF] 2004), and 2.6 per cent in 2012–13 (Schulczova 2014). Also important to note is that the central government has set a medium-term target of reducing subsidies to below 1.75 per cent of the GDP by the year 2016–17 (India Infoline News Service 2012).

[10] Mandi towns are regional hubs for trade in agricultural produce. The word 'mandi' means wholesale market in Hindi.

public-sector-led industrial projects catalysed the development and/
or expansion of several towns in different regions of the country
between the 1950s and the 1970s. Examples include Bhilai in the state
of Madhya Pradesh, Salem in Tamil Nadu, and Rourkela in Odisha.
National and state leaders also sponsored the development of new state
capitals as an economic development tool, building new towns such as
Bhubaneswar (capital of Odisha) and Gandhinagar (capital of Gujarat)
(Ansari 1977).

These programmes and policies, focused on economic
development and poverty alleviation, met with mixed success. For
example, while on the one hand the significant strides made in the
fields of agriculture and science and technology helped India become
self-sufficient in food production, on the other, the huge budgetary
expenditure on subsidies crowded out private investment in the subsidized sectors and resulted in underinvestment by the government
in other vital sectors such as education, health, and infrastructure
(US Department of State 1997). Further, the ballooning budget
deficit and the failure of economic and fiscal policies to boost exports
culminated in the BoP crisis in 1991 when the country had less than
USD 1 billion to meet its import needs and debt payment obligations
(1997). The BoP crisis led to an International Monetary Fund (IMF)
bailout that came with a few strings attached. It required the country
to undertake structural, economic, and fiscal reforms including
opening the economy to foreign investments, reducing subsidies,
and cutting red tape. These IMF-forced reforms heralded an era of
economic liberalization, causing a paradigmatic shift in the country's
political economy along with distinct implications for the country's
spatial planning and development policies.

For example, the central government opened several sectors of the
economy, such as telecommunications and insurance, after the BoP
crisis, to the private sector including foreign investors and companies.
These reforms led to higher GDP growth rates: 5.2 per cent in the
1980s, 5.6 per cent in the 1990s, and around 8 per cent in the 2000s
(Bhat 2011); and a relatively healthy foreign exchange reserve that
stood at more than USD 300 billion in 2014 compared to less than
USD 1 billion at the height of the BoP crisis (Trading Economics
2015; US Department of State 1997). An economically confident
government then also started seeking private investments in other

capital-intensive sectors such as infrastructure (roads, ports, and power) and real estate development. Here, it is important to note that the lack of infrastructure is widely acknowledged as a major bottleneck to furthering economic growth, and to reducing income inequality (Asian Development Bank [ADB] 2012), and is estimated to reduce India's GDP growth rate by as much as 2 per cent (Nataraj 2013). Further, decision-makers recognized the critical role of cities as engines of economic growth (see, for example, Sankhe et al. 2010), as the largely city-based services sector accounted for almost half of the GDP by 2000 (Mohan and Dasgupta 2004) and 60 per cent by 2014 (Ministry of Statistics and Programme Implementation [MoSPI] 2014).

Consequently, the country's economic development and finance policy frameworks were amended in incremental, but important, ways to align with these shifts in government priorities. The Eighth Five Year Plan (1992–7), for example, highlighted the need for private sector participation in urban development, including housing construction, and recommended the need to amend or repeal various regulations authorizing the state's dominant control over spatial planning and development, such as the Urban Land (Ceiling and Regulation) Act (ULCRA), rent control acts, and Land Acquisition Act (Batra 2009).[11] Similarly, the National Urban Transport Policy (NUTP) of 2006 emphasized the development of public and non-motorized transportation as the solution for cities' increasing traffic congestion and pollution problems. The NUTP helped catalyse the preparation of plans for metro rail and bus rapid transit systems (BRTSs) in several cities. In a similar vein, several policy documents such as report of the Thirteenth Finance Commission (2009) and the 2011 *Report of the High Powered Expert Committee* (HPEC), and government programmes such as the JnNURM, continue to emphasize the need for strengthening local governments' revenues and practices with an eye on the larger goal of further boosting the role of cities as engines of the country's economic growth.

There is increasing evidence that economic-growth-focused measures have benefited the city-based private industries and service sector

---

[11] The ULCRA, rent control acts, and land acquisition policies are further reviewed in Chapter 1.

more than many other segments of the national economy, turning the government's attention to city-centric development strategies and urban-based economic drivers (Kennedy and Zérah 2008). The approach is also apparent in the manner in which the new 'growth regime' has sought to strengthen the service and technological base in urban areas combined with an effort to promote large-scale capital investment in supporting and enabling infrastructure to pursue national development (Gupta and Sivaramakrishnan 2010). The central government, for example, has established more than 30 new institutes of higher learning and research including fully funded central universities, Indian Institutes of Technology (IITs), and Indian Institutes of Management (IIMs) in several regional and secondary cities over the last two decades.

Indeed, as the ruling elites position India in the world's imagination as a rising power, driven by a growing tax base and subsequently enhanced revenue receipts, they have attempted to renew nation-building efforts—only this time taking into account the increasing importance of cities. Thus, receiving wide support across the political spectrum from the communist parties to the Hindu nationalists, the policy reforms and planning efforts have gradually spread across the domains of spatial planning and development, resulting in the private development of city-extensions, industrial estates, and SEZs at the scale of urban regions (and not specific settlements) apart from the facilitation of supporting infrastructure such as toll roads and captive ports.

At this point, it is important to note that India still suffers from poor-quality basic infrastructure and services, with many parts of the country lacking access to sanitation, clean water supply, good roads, and a reliable electric supply. It has not always been clear that the capacity existed to design and implement large infrastructure projects, even with financing available (Singh 2012). The last two decades have seen some progress, with building and widening of roads; construction of new airports in Mumbai, Bangalore, and NCR; and construction of a metro system in the NCR. The government's increasing focus on infrastructure has evoked mixed reactions. On the one hand, the growing involvement of private firms in plan preparation, project development, and turnkey execution has helped authorities diverge from the Nehruvian bequest of government-led

planning and development, promoted private sector capacity, and experimented with new institutional infrastructure development arrangements such as build–operate–transfer (BOT). On the other hand, the articulation of debates around infrastructure building, mostly in terms of economic significance and in reference to urban areas, renders the constitutionally sanctioned socialist ideals less compelling as guides for policy than excuses for elite prerogatives.

In this respect, the organization of urban places as engines for economic growth challenges the legitimacy and authority of state-led development even as it improves the relevance of project development for local clientele willing and able to contribute to economic prosperity. Moreover, the combination of an expanding economy and concentration of diverse groups in urban areas generates both prosperity and exploitation even as the customary tension between the markets and democracy fosters social discontent and political protests. The tumultuous productivity in city-based economic activities, such as the rapidly expanding informal economy and real estate sector, resists control while fostering new forms of inequalities and social formations.

As discussed by Vidyarthi, Hoch, and Basmajian (2013), the national government of India has simultaneously pursued three kinds of policy in response: place-based economic development that seeks to leverage public investment and encourage civic involvement, infrastructure-building that improves the economic integration and spatial development of the nation, and welfare increases that aim to selectively target the urban and rural poor. In doing so, the post-liberalization regime not only seeks to balance the demands of economic growth and public welfare but also aims to find a way to combine these seemingly incompatible goals—the hallmark of traditional liberal policy.

First, the national government embraced the neoliberal belief that capital accumulation generates economic growth and promoted private sector investment in a range of place-based economic activities such as for-profit colleges and hospitals, industrial estates, and integrated townships—all usually situated in or near large urban areas. The national government concurrently sought to devolve several powers to local governments (from state governments) by implementing the 74th Constitutional Amendment in 1992 (Aijaz 2008), including the

power to plan and govern urban areas. However, the amendment left it up to the states to devise mechanisms for devolving these powers. Most state governments dragged their feet since the devolution of powers threatened the political status quo and their jurisdictional control over cities. Here it is important to note that the centralization/ decentralization debate is marked by the characteristically constant tension between local planning actors, usually championing decentralization of planning power and resources, and regional planning and economic development authorities, advocating closely coordinated planning for common goods such as clear air and water and productivity gains in other parts of the world, even as India's national government seeks to transfer power to local governments while promoting local planning and resource generation efforts.

The lack of progress in implementing the provisions of the 74th Amendment led the central government, for example, to offer incentives to the states by tying explicit municipal reforms with the disbursal of federal funds for building urban infrastructure and civic amenities through centrally funded programmes such as the JnNURM. Among others goals, the JnNURM also sought to reform the grossly inefficient urban taxation system, where, for example, less than 40 per cent of the approximately 2.5 million properties in Delhi are on the municipal tax register (Mathur, Thakur, and Rajadhyaksha 2009). It encouraged user-charges-based cost recovery for the provision of water supply and sewerage systems and invited private sector participation in project preparation, development, and execution. Adopting these reforms enabled access to federal grants ranging between 35 and 90 per cent of the project cost depending upon the size and location of the beneficiary city (JnNURM 2005). The programme's mandate also required stakeholder involvement in the preparation of CDPs for each participating city. This was a small but crucial part of a larger reform agenda that aimed to institutionalize and legitimize the devolution of power from the state governments to local urban institutions and to promote civic engagement by involving relevant actors (Sivaramakrishnan 2011).

Second, the increasing realization that infrastructure bottlenecks hamper the country's economic growth led to several major initiatives at the national scale. Two road-building projects—the National Highways Development Project (NHDP) and the Pradhan Mantri

Gram Sadak Yojana (PMGSY)—are noteworthy for their magnitude and impact on connecting the nation. The central government sponsored both projects. While the NHDP is highway-focused, the PMGSY seeks to improve rural India's transportation connectivity. Initiated in 1998, the NHDP seeks to upgrade and expand more than 50,000 kilometres (approximately 30,000 miles) of highways. Almost three-quarters of the road length is complete or is under construction (National Highways Authority of India [NHAI] 2014). Introduced in 2000, the PMGSY aims to connect all habitations with a population of more than 500 in the plains and 250 people in the hilly regions through all-weather roads, requiring 739,000 kilometres (469,000 miles) of new road construction or upgrades (PMGSY 2011). A fuller description and assessment of these and other relevant infrastructure projects is provided in the following chapter.

Third, even as the growing legitimacy of the private sector in spatial development projects and an expanding property market provokes fundamental changes in land regulation and transaction practices (Searle 2010), the state has attempted to augment welfare measures that aim to selectively target the urban and rural poor including marginal farmers most prone to losing their small landholdings on the urban fringe. For instance, many states, including Rajasthan, have reformed the rules for converting farms into non-agriculture uses while in 2013 the central government moved to replace the Land Acquisition Act of 1894 with new legislation, the Right to Fair Compensation and Transparency in Land Acquisition, Rehabilitation and Resettlement Act, 2013, that seeks to provide enhanced compensation to farmers and landowners.

In this respect, India's socialist legacy lives on in welfare principles—which remain a salient source of legitimacy for governing a country, where most households remain poor—and motivates the promotion of welfare-oriented public policies (Ahmed and Varshney 2012; Ruparelia et al. 2011). In a recent essay, Partha Chatterjee (2008: 56) describes the tension between the pursuit of profit and various path dependencies in the country's democratic polity: even if the growing economy justifies further reform and liberalization, local forms of resistance and the state's commitment to provide 'a culturally determined sense of what is minimally necessary for a decent life' resists the full-fledged sway of capital.

Thus, India has initiated the process of creating support services and safety nets for the poor. For example, government-sponsored welfare measures such as the National Drinking Water Mission (NDWM), the District Primary Education Programme (DPEP), and the National Rural Employment Guarantee Act (NREGA, now the Mahatma Gandhi National Rural Employment Guarantee Act or MGNREGA), rely upon the central government to fund massive employment and basic civic planning and development projects such as schools and teachers' training centres located in remote places across the country (Lalvani 2010). Here it is important to note that the concept of social responsibility for people's basic needs is beginning to take root in India's poorest regions as evidenced by the steady expansion of public facilities as per a recent authoritative study (Drèze 2013). A 2013 survey in 10 states, for instance, found that the first-ever social security pension scheme is reaching 26 million disabled, elderly, and widowed persons reasonably well (Chopra and Pudussery 2014). In other words, the neoliberal policy that favours concentrating resources for urban places funds basic infrastructure building for local players in remote areas even as parallel national interventions target the country's poor and marginalized sections.

In addition to these major changes in the economic and infrastructure sectors, scholars of contemporary India have documented significant political and social shifts that simultaneously shaped the country's polity. For instance, Pranab Bardhan (1984) argued that a coalition of the three leading proprietary classes— well-to-do farmers that benefited from the green revolution; professionals, especially those in the bureaucracy who exploited the grip over the 'license–permit raj';[12] and industrialists who profited from monopolistic controls—began to replace the ideologically oriented governing elite of Nehruvian origin. Within the urban areas, Pratap Bhanu Mehta (2003) has shown how the extension of democracy has undermined the political clientelism between the elite and marginalized groups, who increasingly utilize electoral politics to demand, and sometimes obtain, access to utilities and basic services.

---

[12] Licence or permit raj refers to the large number of permits to obtain and rules to comply with to do business in India.

Similarly, 'intermediate classes', or a loose coalition of the small-scale capitalist class, agrarian and agribusiness elites, and local officials have begun to emerge as powerful actors outside the metropolitan cities (Harriss-White 2002). On the other hand, within the largest cities, a 'new middle class', distinct from a relatively older and coherent understanding of what 'middle class' in the Indian context connoted classically (that is, a civil-service-oriented salariat), has emerged, comprising an array of occupations in new fields such as consulting and information services (Fernandes 2006). Although empirically difficult to define, the 'Indian middle class' provides a standard that other groups aspire to reach (Liechty 2003), generating both a discursive ideal and an emerging social sector tied to an urban future.

The demand for better spatial planning and development from these emergent middle and aspirant classes is routinely evident, for instance, in the wake of floods in the city of Chennai and widespread air pollution in Delhi, both during the year 2015, which appears to be evenly matched by India's vigilant civil society and environmental activists (for example, Janardhan 2015; Vishwakarma 2015). We set out to examine changes in India's approach to spatial planning and development employing the framework and insights described above as an analytical lens. Our analyses and findings are organized in the format described in the next section.

Outline of the Book

As explained earlier, this book is organized in three interrelated parts describing the shifts in the domains of infrastructure planning policy, spatial plan-making practice, and on-the-ground outcomes. Part I comprises two chapters. Dividing the post-Independence spatial planning experience into four periods—1947–67, 1968–84, 1985–91, and 1991–present—Chapter 1 provides a temporal framework for analysing and illustrating the interconnectedness between the state policy for infrastructure financing and building, and the practice of spatial planning and development. It also highlights the shift in national economic planning from a central-government-driven focus on agriculture, heavy industries, and rural poverty alleviation to a multi-actor, public–private-partnership (PPP)-based urban focus that recognizes the importance of cities as

economic generators and the key role infrastructure development plays in improving economic growth. Further, this chapter describes the failure of this urban focus to integrate infrastructure and economic development projects with spatial planning leading to reactionary and incoherent urban development.

Chapter 2 illustrates three case studies from different regional contexts in order to highlight small, yet significant efforts undertaken in contemporary India to reduce local governments' reliance on state- and central-government financial assistance by harnessing new, local, and non-traditional infrastructure finance mechanisms. The use of many of these mechanisms also requires integrating infrastructure development with spatial planning processes. The cases include the use of development charges and the infrastructure and amenities (I&A) fee in Tamil Nadu; the sale of development rights to fund the BRTS in the city of Rajkot, Gujarat; and PPP for providing water supply to three cities in Karnataka.

Part II of the book focuses on recent shifts in India's spatial plan-making practice. The first chapter of this section, Chapter 3, describes how the statutory master planning approach in the city of Jaipur, Rajasthan, has undergone gradual yet significant changes over time. Comparing and contrasting the three master plans the city has prepared so far—published in 1971, 1998, and 2011, respectively—this chapter also explains some of the salient changes in the local planning practice. These include a move towards regularization and rehabilitation of unauthorized settlements; a shift away from the outward-focused large-scale urban development model requiring state-sponsored acquisition of private lands; a recognition of the growing roles of non-state planning actors such as real estate developers, emergent entrepreneurs, and the residents of unauthorized settlements; and the oversight role of non-profits, an activist judiciary, and the media.

Chapter 4 explains how external consultants have played an important role in changing the planning practice in the southern city of Bangalore located in the state of Karnataka. Focusing on the changing roles and varied engagements that Bangalore's government has had with external experts and consultants as the lens with which to understand the transitions in planning practice in the city, this chapter uncovers several shifts. It explains how Bangalore's chief

planning agency—the Bangalore Development Authority or the BDA—has consciously moved away from developing plans in-house, preferring rather to turn to external consultants to carry out this process on the basis of a brief that the BDA provides. It also explains how the shift in Bangalore's planning approach has been both slow and strenuous, shaped in part by the state's dependence on the support of individual civil servants heading various urban local bodies (ULBs) that could easily help or hinder the planning process. The shift in the planning practice is also shaped by Karnataka's ongoing political and social dynamic: repeated regime change at the state level, incremental restructuring of the state and city relationship, and a growing demand from a rapidly expanding middle-class clientele for better planning in urban and semi-urban areas.

Part III comprises three chapters that analyse on-the-ground changes. The first chapter in this section, Chapter 5 notes how India is urbanizing differently from the conventional view of big cities becoming even bigger. Between the censuses conducted in the years 2001 and 2011, it was not the growth of big cities, smaller towns, or state capitals that drove urbanization; it was the number of census towns (CTs), which are 'urban' by definition but 'rural' in governance, that tripled. The chapter analyses various forms of contemporary settlements with a focus on census towns' challenges associated with their reclassification as statutory towns, introducing a new term 'urural' that acknowledges the emergence of urban characteristics in rural areas and vice versa. It argues that India's current method of dichotomous classification and the associated inequitable funding allocations for spatial planning and development of these places need to be revisited so that they closely align with the evolving urban–rural landscapes and better serve the people inhabiting these settlements.

Turning the focus towards some of the remotest places in the poorest Indian state of Bihar, Chapter 6 shows how the substantial shifts in the larger policy environment and plan-making practice in the largest urban centres, explained in the previous two sections, have not percolated down to these settlements. Empirically analysing the socio-economic conditions, land use, physical and social infrastructure, and state-sponsored social programmes in selected high-density rural districts, this chapter shows how these places have transformed into 'urban' communities, both demographically and economically,

but severely lack civic infrastructure. The chapter concludes by arguing that these places need to be classified as 'urban' to make them eligible to receive government support for spatial planning and for development of urban amenities.

The final chapter in this part, Chapter 7, examines the development of SEZs that emerged as a prominent and controversial policy instrument for promoting economic growth in post-liberalization India. Reviewing the spatial development of SEZs across different categories and Indian regions, the chapter shows how paper plans and discursive policies have frequently not translated into actual projects. It also highlights how, despite the lack of intended success, SEZs have fuelled imaginations of incentivized, exclusive enclaves, separated from the potentialities and barriers of local economies. Although the policies promoting SEZs currently stand de-prioritized, but the closely associated greenfield and enclaved visions have triggered off new and larger debates such as those about what land acquisition and the PPP model might mean for spatial planning and the development of places in the Indian context.

Finally, the conclusion summarizes our key findings. Among other things, we find that substantial changes in higher-level infrastructure development and spatial planning policies are fostering noticeable impacts on large urban centres, their peripheries, and along connecting corridors. These changes stand out further when compared to the dismal status of even the largest Indian cities just a couple of decades ago. But we also find that a combination of factors including the national- and state-level political dynamic, the old guard's continuing hold over planning tools and procedures, and the tensions between democratic and market-oriented impulses are shaping the planning and development of India's settlements in complex ways that are messy, uneven, and largely invisible. For instance, we find that while the spatial planning and development finance focus remains on large cities and large-scale infrastructure projects, the country is also rapidly urbanizing in the hinterland. It is ironical that despite little locally organized planning and development attention on these settlements, they prefer to continue as 'rural', even when they are turning 'urban' both in terms of economic indicators and population density—two key criteria that planners and policy

makers use to define urbanization—given the state finances available to the rural development sector.

Thus, depending upon the reader's perception, the glass may seem half full or half empty. But consistent with our belief, that spatial planning and development of places, if undertaken judiciously, can help improve the quality of life of residents and their communities, this project leaves us in little doubt that Indian planners and decision-makers have their work cut out for them.

PART I

INFRASTRUCTURE FINANCE
AND DEVELOPMENT

1

Post-Independence Infrastructure Development and Finance Initiatives

In post-Independence India, various central government policies and programmes have strived to meet the twin objectives of self-reliance and social justice through economic-growth-led poverty alleviation. In line with this overall approach, recent literature has documented the increasing recognition of urban areas as engines of economic growth and the subsequent policy shift towards the promotion of supporting infrastructure to meet national development objectives. Borrowing from Batra (2009) and Lall and Rastogi (2007), we divide the nation's post-Independence development trajectory into four phases—1947–67, 1968–84, 1985–91, and 1991–present—to provide a temporal framework for understanding both the major changes in the nation's infrastructure policy landscape and the spatial planning and development of human settlements. While the major shifts in policies for each infrastructure or service do not always neatly fit into this framework, the phases reasonably capture the contours of the major forces that have shaped the country's infrastructure policies and spatial planning and development. Such forces include the nation's political economy and needs; its ability and desire to integrate with the global trade and financial networks; the competing aspirations of its citizens; and exogenous shocks such as global economic slowdowns and oil crises. Our purpose in describing the

trajectory is to highlight both the key path dependencies (that is, a historian's way of saying that patterns from the past shape the present) as well as to underscore the significance of the move away from the Nehruvian model of state-led planning and development.

Nation-building through public-sector-led provision of basic necessities, such as food, electricity, and water, occupied the central government's attention during the first phase (1947–67). This phase was largely dominated by Jawaharlal Nehru's Fabian socialist policies that advocated techno-centric, centrally planned socialism (Dobbs 2009). In the ensuing second phase (1967–84), the central governments led by Indira Gandhi and Janta Party primarily focused on rural India to reduce poverty and food scarcity. This phase witnessed consolidation of the licence raj system,[1] which had its beginnings in the first phase. With Rajiv Gandhi as the prime minister for the majority of the third phase (1984–91), a gradual shift occurred from inward-looking, rural-development-focused policies to technology-based modernization and limited deregulation of industry, especially of the telecommunications sector. The current phase (1991–present) had its origins in the economic shock of the balance of payments (BoP) crisis of 1991. In response to this crisis, India had to seek an International Monetary Fund (IMF) bailout, which, in turn, required the country to open its economy to global trade and investment. This opening up of the economy has brought economic prosperity to a substantial section of the population, nurturing a 200-million-plus middle class[2] that is largely urban and is demanding increasingly better quality urban infrastructure and services.

Due to the close overlap and interaction between policies for economic development, infrastructure provision, and spatial planning, this chapter reviews all three of these sets of policies and initiatives for the four phases outlined above. The chapter focuses on explicating these policies and initiatives in the context of spatial planning outcomes. Compared to the first three phases, the fourth phase is discussed

---

[1] The licence or permit raj system was a complex system of regulations and approvals needed to set up and operate a business or an industry.

[2] As per the National Council of Applied Economic Research (NCAER), the middle class is estimated to reach 267 million by 2015–16 (NCAER 2011), a considerable increase over a population of fewer than 100 million in 2010.

in greater detail both due to its proximity to the present, and the perceived potential for influencing the future trajectory of the nation's infrastructure development policy and spatial development.

The First Phase (1947–67): Nation-building through Mega Projects

Mirroring the other newly independent countries of Africa and Asia at that time, India's industrial prowess was modest post-Independence. Exports primarily consisted of low-value agricultural and industrial raw materials, such as cotton, jute, and iron ore; and imports consisted of high-value finished goods such as cloth, steel, cement, machinery, radios, televisions, and refrigerators (Bhat 2011). Due to this trade composition, the country relied heavily on imports for economic growth and, in turn, on the very-scarce foreign exchange to pay for them. In response, the nation's economic planners focused on import-substitution-based industrialization (Aggarwal 2012) and used the Mahalanobis model for economic growth (Katano 1965).[3] The adoption of this model required the rapid development of the capital goods/industrial sector using several means: public sector investments in or subsidies to domestic private sector companies (as was done for the cement industry); protection of domestic industries from foreign competitors through measures such as high import duties and subsidies for domestic industry; large domestic savings that could be used to invest in and/or subsidize the capital goods sector; and discouragement of expenditure on luxury consumption goods, such as cars and televisions.[4,5]

[3] P.C. Mahalanobis was a noted Indian statistician and a member of the Planning Commission, the institution in charge of preparing India's Five Year Plans. These Plans provided the roadmap for the nation's economic growth. The Planning Commission was abolished in 2014 and was replaced by another institution, the NITI Aayog (National Institution for Transforming India).

[4] Discouraging consumption of luxury goods served two objectives: First, it incentivized households to save more, thereby allowing the government to employ the savings in the capital goods sector. Second, it allowed the government to curb imports of luxury goods, and thereby save valuable foreign exchange.

[5] Cars and televisions were considered luxury goods during this period.

The Mahalanobis model influenced India's economic development and investment policies from the Second Five Year Plan (1956–61) through the Fifth Five Year Plan (1974–9) (Guru 2014). As a result, several agro-industrial mega projects were developed during this phase. Examples include hydroelectric power and canal-based irrigation projects such as the Bhakra Nangal, Hirakud, and Chambal Valley projects; steel plants at Bhilai, Rourkela, and Durgapur; and industrial plants to manufacture tools and equipment for these mega projects, such as the plants operated by Bharat Heavy Electricals Limited (BHEL) and Bharat Electronics Limited (BEL).

India's development during this period was also affected by foreign relations; in order to sidestep cold-war-generated tensions and to focus on the country's development, the ruling elites adopted a policy of non-alignment—that is, a decision not to side with either of the two cold-war-era superpowers—the United States of America (USA) and the Union of Soviet Socialist Republics (USSR). Under this policy, India was able to partner with both the USA and the USSR (and their allies) as required. For example, five Indian Institutes of Technology (IITs) were developed during this phase, with the aim of training high-quality engineers to power the country's agro-industrial development. The IITs at Bombay (now Mumbai), Madras (now Chennai), Kanpur, and Delhi were set up in collaboration with the USSR, Germany, the USA, and the United Kingdom (UK), respectively (IIT Delhi 2014). Similarly, the Bhilai and Durgapur steel plants were developed with assistance from the USSR and the UK, respectively (Reference for Business 2014).

The development of mega projects had at least two significant spatial planning and development outcomes. First, these efforts required large-scale sub-national and regional planning. Such plans were prepared for large irrigation projects such as the Rajasthan Canal project[6] and the Damodar Valley project. The plans were similar to those prepared in the USA, for example, by the Tennessee Valley Authority (TVA). Indeed, W.L. Vourduin, a leading expert with the TVA, prepared the first conceptual plan for the Damodar Valley project. This plan aimed to control flooding of the Damodar

---

[6] This was later renamed the Indira Gandhi Canal project.

River, and to harness the river for navigation, power generation, and irrigation (Hussain 2011).[7]

Second, the development of industrial towns such as Bhilai and Rourkela provided an opportunity to introduce the latest town-planning principles and practices, and to develop a road map for planned urban development. Indeed, as early as 1955, the Town Planning Organization (TPO) was set up with the assistance of the Ford Foundation to formulate the first master plan for Delhi. Later, the Central Regional and Urban Planning Organization (CRUPO) was set up to assist with Delhi's regional plan, and to advice on the development of steel towns and river-valley projects. In 1962, the TPO and CRUPO were merged to form the Town and Country Planning Organization (TCPO). Among other functions, the TCPO provides technical urban planning assistance to the Ministry of Urban Development (MoUD) and serves as the nodal agency for several MoUD schemes (TCPO 2014).

India faced a significant foreign exchange crisis in the early 1960s despite its focus on import-substitution industrialization. As a result, several tools were employed to earn valuable foreign exchange, including the establishment of export promotion zones (EPZs). With the development of the Kandla EPZ in 1965, India became the first Asian country with an EPZ. While industries had to comply with a plethora of regulations in the rest of the country, these regulations were relaxed in the EPZs to facilitate the development of export-oriented industries. Because only one EPZ was developed prior to the end of the first phase (the aforementioned Kandla EPZ in 1965), the economic and spatial impacts of the EPZ policy were modest in this phase. However, these impacts have become significant in magnitude and complexity in the current phase, as the EPZ policy and the number of EPZs (now called SEZs—special economic zones) has expanded.[8] The cumulative spatial and policy impacts of SEZs are reviewed in greater detail later in this chapter in the section titled

---

[7] Historically, the Damodar River was called the 'sorrow of Bengal' due to its frequent devastating floods.

[8] The Santa Cruz EPZ was developed in 1974, and the Madras (now Chennai), Cochin (now Kochi), and Falta EPZs in 1984. The more recent SEZs include Surat SEZ (2000), Mahindra City SEZ (Chennai) in 2002, Dahez SEZ in 2006.

'The Current Phase (1991–Present): The Post-liberalization Era', and in Chapter 7.

The creation of new states from the reorganization of the provinces of British India and erstwhile princely states was another event with significant spatial impacts. The States Reorganisation Act of 1956 modified the boundaries of existing states and carved out new states. The reorganization was done primarily along linguistic lines (Cohen 2014). For example, three new states—Andhra Pradesh,[9] Gujarat, and Haryana—were created, the first by carving out the Telugu-speaking region of the Madras state; the second, the Gujarati-speaking region of the Bombay state; and the third, the Hindi-speaking region of the Punjab state (haryana-online.com 2009). Boundaries of several other states were modified, too. For example, Rajasthan subsumed the Ajmer state and included parts of the Bombay and Madhya Bharat states (Indian Kanoon 2014).

The creation and reorganization of states had two major spatial development impacts. First, in several cases it led to the construction of new state capitals, such as Chandigarh (the joint capital of Haryana and Punjab), Bhubaneswar (the capital of Orissa [now Odisha]), and Gandhinagar (the capital of Gujarat). The spatial layout and urban design of these cities combined the latest ideas about modernist architecture, urban design, and the planning of new towns, such as those espoused by Le Corbusier in Chandigarh, Otto Koenigsberger in Bhubaneswar, and the town planners trained under Le Corbusier—Prakash M. Apte and H.K. Mewada—in Gandhinagar (Gandhinagaronline 2014). A second major impact resulted from existing cities being newly designated as state capitals, such as Jaipur in Rajasthan. This designation led to the outward-oriented development of these new capital cities, and in some cases (such as Jaipur), this development turned its back on the cities' rich architectural patrimony and built heritage.

From an urban planning perspective, this phase saw an acute realization of the need to plan urban areas. Indeed, the Third Five Year Plan (1961–6) encouraged state governments to set up state town planning departments and to prepare city master plans. Further, this

[9] Andhra Pradesh was further subdivided into Telangana and Andhra Pradesh in 2014 by the Andhra Pradesh Reorganisation Act, 2014.

Plan identified the speculation-led increase in land value as the main reason for urban ills such as slums and the inability to undertake development projects.[10] Therefore, the Third Five Year Plan called for freezing land values and identified pre-emptive bulk land acquisition as one solution (Planning Commission 2010a) that would allow urban areas to be planned in an orderly fashion. The First (1951–6) and the Second (1956–61) Five Year Plans focused on large-scale government-led construction of houses for low-income households[11] and on slum clearance. However, the burgeoning gap between the housing need and supply encouraged the policymakers writing the Third Five Year Plan to seek other solutions, such as, locating industries away from large urban centres in the hope that the development of the hinterland would not only balance urban–rural development but also slow the population growth of cities, thereby mitigating the urban slum problem (Basu 1988).

In summary, several new urban areas developed or expanded during this phase. However, the heavy-industry- and mega-project-focused economic planning which, at worst, neglected humans settlements, and at best treated them as mere inputs for industrialization,[12] resulted in a failure on the part of the central government to focus on developing a coherent vision for settlement planning and development. This lack of attention to urban areas resulted in underinvestment in civic infrastructure and services, a pattern that entrenched itself over the next two phases, and which the nation is trying to break in small steps in the current phase (1991–present). Worse still in terms of spatial planning and development, the Indian Constitution assigned authority to the individual states over administration of all matters related to urban and rural settlements, including spatial planning and governance (MoUD 2015).

---

[10] The Plan noted: 'The most important element in raising housing and other costs and in restricting the scale on which improvements can be undertaken in the interests of low income groups is high land prices' (Planning Commission 2010a).

[11] This task was taken up by the state housing boards. The central government provided aid for the large-scale land acquisition required to undertake such housing projects.

[12] For example, industrial towns were seen as labour inputs.

As a result, the state governments had (and still mostly retain) the sole authority to legislate, plan, and develop the settlements under their jurisdiction, and the central government has had little leverage with which to influence human settlement policy. Furthermore, the Indian Constitution did not confer a formal status on local governments (either rural or urban).[13] They were, and to a large extent still are, dependent on their state governments for administrative powers and financial resources. Such a situation, wherein both the central and the local governments exercise little influence over spatial planning and development issues and the state governments (especially compared to the central government) are financially weak, has led to a gradual neglect of and underinvestment in India's human settlements. Over time, this neglect had visible spatial impacts, in the form of rising informal housing and commercial sectors, illegal land grabs, and the decay and inadequacy of water supply, sewerage, transportation, and other urban infrastructure and services. This neglect of human settlements, especially evident in the urban sector, deepened in the second phase.

The Second Phase (1968–84): Rural-India-focused Populism

The demise of two prime ministers in quick succession—Jawaharlal Nehru in 1964 and Lal Bahadur Shastri in 1966—led to a power struggle within the ruling Congress party. Indira Gandhi, the daughter of Jawaharlal Nehru, wrested control, serving as the country's prime minister for the majority of the second phase, until her assassination in 1984. Political exigencies, external shocks (such as the 1971 war with Pakistan[14] and the oil crisis of 1973), and on-the-ground

---

[13] The 73rd and 74th Constitutional Amendments formally recognize rural and urban local bodies as the third tier of government. These constitutional amendments are discussed in greater detail in the section titled 'The Current Phase (1991–Present): The Post-liberalization Era'.

[14] The USA's anti-India bias during the 1971 war with Pakistan (Gandhi 2002) exemplified by the stationing of the *USS Enterprise* in the Bay of Bengal, unauthorized arms transfer to Pakistan, and the cutting off of developmental aid (Schaffer 2009) highlighted the need for self-sufficiency.

realities[15] led Indira Gandhi to focus on rural development, poverty alleviation, and self-reliance.

Jawaharlal Nehru's popularity among the masses had ensured that he was the undisputed leader of his political party and the country; he had had to worry little about winning elections. Indira Gandhi was not so politically fortunate. She had to thwart strong competition not only from leaders within her party to become prime minister but also from opposition parties, such as the Jan Sangh, that had a strong urban middle-class base. The first political reality led Indira Gandhi to consolidate power in her hands (Vohra 2012) and the second, to cultivate rural India as her electoral base. Therefore, Indira Gandhi decided to focus on populist rural development projects that had small gestation periods (Lall and Rastogi 2007). For example, as opposed to the mega projects with long gestation periods undertaken in the first phase, such as the canal-based irrigation projects, the projects of the second phase included installation of tube wells for irrigation and the electrification of farms to provide electricity to operate these tube wells. The electricity was provided either free of cost or highly subsidized. Furthermore, farmers were provided loans on very lenient terms, and these loans were often forgiven.[16] The rural-development focus arguably helped improve India's food security (Kotwal and Ramaswami 1999), reduce poverty (World Bank 1997), and build a network of rural roads; at the same time, however, the populist policies (such as loan write-offs and subsidized electricity, water, and fertilizers) were a big drain on the country's finances. Explicit subsidies by the central government increased four fold, rising from 0.3 per cent of the GDP in Fiscal Year (FY) 1970–1 to 1.2 per cent of the GDP by FY 1980–1 (MoF 2004). The large subsidies also hampered private sector participation in these basic infrastructure sectors and provided little incentive to be efficient to the public sector providers of such infrastructure and services.

---

[15] These realities included rampant inflation and the devastating famines of the mid-1960s.

[16] Indian banks were nationalized in 1968 (Austin 1999), providing the central government significant leverage over their functioning and role in the Indian economy.

The socialist platform inherited from the first phase (1947–67) was used in this phase to weave a policy web that served to concentrate power at the level of central government, and was anti-big-business and anti-urban in character. The licence raj system stifled private enterprise and helped to develop a nexus between bureaucrats and elected officials that had the power to confer or deny economic favours (Lall and Rastogi 2007). This phase saw graft, or rent-seeking, proliferate through India's governing structure (Ghosh 1997).

The Monopolies and Restrictive Trade Practices (MRTP) Act of 1969 imposed further controls on expansion and investments by large private sector companies (Ahluwalia 1994). Anti-big-business and anti-urban biases were further deepened by the Industrial Policy Resolution of 1977. This policy resolution criticized the earlier governments for their bias in favour of large industries and increased the number of industrial products reserved for small-scale industries. It also argued for locating these labour-intensive cottage and small-scale industries in rural areas and small towns, away from the big cities. The policy discouraged banks and other public sector financial institutions from providing credit to large private sector businesses; furthermore, it opposed foreign investment in private industries that produced non-critical consumption goods (Department of Industrial Policy and Promotion [DIPP] 2002).[17] Finally, various government policies required banks to focus on rural areas and agriculture (Banerjee, Cole, and Duflo 2004), reducing the availability of credit for the urban economy.

Regulations such as the Urban Land (Ceiling and Regulation) Act (ULCRA) of 1976 had significant spatial urban development impacts.[18] The ULCRA was intended to reduce land speculation and ensure the availability of urban land for social purposes, such as low-income housing, by preventing concentration of vacant urban land in the hands of a few. The ULCRA required landlords to register their land parcels with a competent authority, and if their vacant land was more than the specified limit for that city (for example, more than 500 square metres in the case of New Delhi or Mumbai), the

[17] This phase was marked by the exit of Coca-Cola and IBM from India.
[18] The ULCRA came into force in 64 urban agglomerations spread over 17 states and union territories.

landlord was required to surrender the excess vacant land to the state government at a government-determined price (Batra 2009).

However, the enforcement of the ULCRA was uneven. Establishing landownership was often not possible due to poor-quality property records. Further, states differed regarding the methodology for calculating the amount of land an owner could retain and the compensation to be paid to the landowner for the excess vacant land acquired by the government. The compensation was often considered too little, which led to considerable litigation (Jawaharlal Nehru National Urban Renewal Mission [JnNURM] 2010) or to the landlords evading registration of their lands with the government—both practices impeded the development of sizable amounts of urban land. Moreover, the land parcels acquired by the state governments were often fragmented, odd-shaped, or small in size, rendering them unsuitable for developing large projects. All these factors had the perverse effect of creating an artificial scarcity of urban land, which, in turn, arguably contributed to a sharp increase in land prices across the nation. The act failed miserably in its primary goal of making urban land available for development.[19] As Batra (2009: 14–15) notes, 'only about 8 percent of 166,162 hectares of surplus land identified was acquired and only 2 percent was physically taken possession of. Moreover, only 0.37 percent of the total surplus land was used for construction of low income housing which was ostensibly the main reason given for the enactment of the Act.'

Land scarcity was further exacerbated by rent control acts enacted by many states. These acts froze rents of commercial and residential properties. Therefore, property owners were unable to extract market value by raising rents or selling property. Thus, the owners had little incentive to maintain their properties and consequently, many let their properties deteriorate. Finally, the prevalent populism led the state and local governments not to charge property taxes, or to keep them very low. This practice encouraged investment in land for speculative purposes; indirectly encouraged graft by providing a safe haven for unaccounted for, or black, money; drew capital away from productive sectors such as manufacturing and directed

---

[19] Indeed, the repeal of the ULCRA is one of the mandatory reforms under the JnNURM, as explained later in this chapter.

it towards unproductive sectors such as land (Kumar 2002); and discouraged efficient use of land overall. Furthermore, it financially weakened urban local bodies (ULBs) due to unrealized property tax revenues. The provision of urban infrastructure and services suffering as a result. Finally, the artificial urban land scarcity created by the ULCRA, rent control acts, and the various development-control rules led to unplanned suburban sprawl and the development of unauthorized colonies.

The urban housing policies of the period continued to focus on constructing housing for the urban poor in small- and medium-sized towns. However, for larger towns, the policy focus shifted from slum clearance to slum upgrade by providing basic infrastructure and services in the slums. The policy to develop the rural hinterland and small towns to stem in-migration to large urban areas also continued. For example, one MoUD scheme, the Integrated Development of Small and Medium Towns (IDSMT), sought to strengthen cities having populations under 0.5 million by providing capital grants and soft loans for infrastructure and services projects such as roads, water, and sewer systems. The scheme was introduced in the Sixth Five Year Plan (1980–6) in the hope that such improvement projects would make small and medium towns regional centres, thereby reducing migration to large cities. However, extremely limited funds were allocated for this scheme. The central government assistance to the IDSMT totalled INR 4.9 billion over a 23-year period (1980–2002), benefiting 1,005 towns at an average annual assistance of a meagre INR 200,000 (Ministry of Housing and Urban Poverty Alleviation [MHUPA] 2004). As a result, the IDSMT failed to have any significant impact on small towns' urban infrastructure and services or on reducing migration into large cities (Sridharan 2014).

Despite the rural and small-town focus of this phase, some attempts were made to strengthen large cities. For example, the Integrated Urban Development Programme (IUDP) was launched in the Fifth Five Year Plan (1974–9).[20] Under the IUDP, the central government provided financial assistance to the state governments in the form

[20] All state capitals, all cities with a population greater than 300,000, and those deemed to be of national importance were eligible to be included in the IUDP (Shaw 2013).

of seed grants to create revolving funds for urban development. The creation of a revolving fund and the absence of specific guidelines regarding eligible projects led the bulk of the funds to be spent on land acquisition and development of housing and retail to serve middle- and high-income households. This 'self-sustaining' urban development model focused primarily on the physical planning and development of new areas and neglected the needs of already existing areas of cities and of the urban poor (Basu 1988). New urban areas were largely planned and developed by development authorities and parastatal organizations under the control of state governments. These resource-rich development authorities had, and still have, little incentive to coordinate with resource-poor ULBs, such as municipal corporations. Further, this two-organization system created over-lapping, and often contentious, jurisdictional and governance issues (Weinstein, Sami, and Shatkin 2014). For example, when residential colonies developed by the development authorities are transferred to municipal corporations, the latter often complain of low-quality infrastructure and services in these newly developed areas, and that the provision of adequate infrastructure and services becomes their responsibility after the transfer.

While a myriad of rules distorted land and property markets and weakened governments' financial ability to deliver urban services, urbanization continued at a brisk pace during this period. The urban population almost doubled, increasing from 103 million in 1968 to 184 million in 1984 (United Nations Department of Economic and Social Affairs [UN DESA] 2014). In terms of spatial development, underinvest-ment in urban infrastructure and services and the failure of housing policies were the leading causes of the growth of informal urban hous-ing during this phase. The urban slum population was 29.8 million in 1981, or 18.75 per cent of the 159 million urban people (Bose 1992), a number that would go up over the next two phases.

The Third Phase (1985–91): The Beginning of Industrial Deregulation

The assassination of Indira Gandhi in 1984 propelled her son, Rajiv Gandhi, to the political centre stage. The Rajiv-Gandhi-led Congress party won an overwhelming three-quarters of all seats in the

1985 parliamentary elections. Rajiv Gandhi served as the country's prime minister until 1989, after the next parliamentary elections, when the National Front—a coalition of several smaller parties with Vishwanath Pratap Singh (V.P. Singh) as the prime minister—formed a minority government. This government lasted one year, till 1990, and was followed by the Chandra-Shekhar-led Samajwadi Janta Party government that lasted another year, until March of 1991.[21]

Two major policy pronouncements made during this phase have had significant spatial development impacts in the years since. First, the National Commission on Urbanization (NCU) emphasized the close link between urbanization and economic development, and thus highlighted the need to strengthen existing urban centres. This was a distinct shift from the earlier, rural- and backward-area-focused, economic development policies. Second, the National Housing Policy of 1988 argued that the government's direct role should be restricted to housing the poorest and the most vulnerable urban population, and that the government should only 'facilitate' housing for middle- and high-income groups by removing barriers to private-sector-led housing development and by providing infrastructure and services (Batra 2009).

The shift in housing policy from the government as a developer to the government as a facilitator of housing for middle- and high-income groups had been advocated earlier in the Seventh Five Year Plan (1985–90). That plan advised the state housing boards to focus only on providing developed land for middle- and higher-income housing and not on constructing housing units (Planning Commission 2010b). Indeed, this third phase witnessed the beginning of large-scale land development by private real estate developers, marked by the construction of DLF City in Gurgaon, at the periphery of New Delhi, and later, in the form of private townships across the country. The entry of real estate developers into the urban development arena was not without its pitfalls, however. Private real estate development has been blamed for increasing graft

---

[21] Neither the V.P. Singh nor the Chandra Shekhar governments had the majority of the seats in the Lok Sabha. The former was supported from outside by the Bharatiya Janata Party (BJP) and the Left parties, while the latter was supported by the Congress party.

and for providing a safe haven for unaccounted or black money (Hiro 2014).[22]

The Seventh Five Year Plan continued the urban development policies of the past plans, including the continuation and expansion of the IDSMT scheme and support for pro-active bulk land acquisition to reduce land-price speculation. The plan was novel in a couple of ways, however. First, it highlighted the need for providing credit to individual households and to housing cooperatives and building societies for the construction of housing units. Second, noting the inability of ULBs to provide basic infrastructure and services, the Plan called for improving the ULBs' financial capacity and for reforming the property tax system (both these reforms were undertaken in the current phase (1991–present)). The first policy pronouncement led to the expansion of credit for the housing sector, and the second led to various Central Government incentives for urban reforms through programmes such as the Jawaharlal Nehru National Urban Renewal Mission (JnNURM).

While several populist schemes from the previous (second) phase continued, and even expanded during the third phase, the seeds of the post-1991 economic liberalization were being sown. Rajiv Gandhi's government realized the need to make industries globally competitive through enhanced productivity and efficiency, and sought to do so through, among other strategies, fostering technological advancements and selectively relaxing the licence raj system (DIPP 2002; Lall and Rastogi 2007), especially for the telecom industry.[23] Although modest, the telecom reforms introduced the ideas of privatization, liberalization, and corporatization into the public sector. Privatization was limited to allowing the private sector to manufacture telecom equipment; liberalization was restricted to

---

[22] Hiro (2014) argues that it was easier to purchase an apartment using black money from a private developer than purchasing from a state housing board. Also feeding the likelihood of corruption was the fact that a private developer had to seek approvals from several government agencies and was forced to pay 'speed money' for these approvals.

[23] The government was also concerned about the precarious BoP situation. Therefore, enhanced productivity and efficiency were deemed critical for boosting exports (Planning Commission 2010b).

the expansion of manufacturing licences and to the relaxation of the import regime (Lall and Rastogi 2007); and corporatization was carried out by carving separate corporate entities out of the Department of Telecommunications (DoT)—the Mahanagar Telephone Nigam Limited (MTNL) for telephone services in the large cities of Delhi and Mumbai, and the Videsh Sanchar Nigam Limited (VSNL) for international telephony.[24] Finally, the March 1991 report of the Telecommunications Restructuring Committee recommended the entry of the private sector into the provision of telephone services, the separation of the service-provision and policymaking functions of the DoT, and the need for an independent regulator (Mukherji 2010). The committee's report helped seed the ground for what came next; it provided the roadmap for the post-1991 economic liberalization of not just the telecommunications sector, but also of other sectors such as electricity, ports, railways, and roads.

The Current Phase (1991–Present): The Post-liberalization Era

The BoP crisis of mid-1991 marked the beginning of the current phase. A multitude of factors came together to create a perfect fiscal storm, one that led the country to seek an IMF bailout to meet its debt and import obligations.

The populist and subsidy-heavy policies of the previous two phases had already strained the nation's fiscal health. Several other factors also contributed to the 1991 crisis. The industrial deregulation that began in the third phase (1985–91) led to a faster increase in imports compared to exports. The import–export gap widened further because oil imports rose sharply during this phase. This rise was due to the increases in global oil prices and domestic demand for oil coupled with stagnation in domestic oil production. Moreover, global economic growth contracted significantly between 1988 and 1990, including that of the USA, then India's largest export destination. Another one of India's export destinations, the USSR, was breaking apart. The current account deficit rose higher. The government tried to fill the deficit through high-cost, short-term commercial borrowing and by using the remittances from non-resident Indians.

---

[24] The DoT was earlier carved out of the Department of Posts.

The political uncertainty, the unstable domestic situation, and the downgrade of India's credit rating led to the flight of short-term capital, however. The non-resident remittances shifted to outflows and the creditors were reluctant to roll their short-term loans into long-term loans (Cerra and Saxena 2000). By mid-1991, the country had less than USD 1 billion to meet its import needs and debt payment obligations (US Department of State 1997), forcing it to seek a USD 4.8 billion IMF bailout (IMF 2002).[25] The bailout terms required fiscal and economic reforms including delicensing of industries, trade liberalization through lowered restrictions on imports and foreign investments, and tax reforms.

These reforms immediately had favourable economic outcomes. The country's GDP grew at 6.8 per cent against a target of 5.6 per cent during the Eighth Five Year Plan period (1992–7) (Ministry of Statistics and Programme Implementation [MoSPI] 2013). More notably, since this growth was achieved at a time of declining private sector investments, it heralded a paradigm shift from the public-sector-driven, inward looking socialist economy to a private-sector-driven, globally connected, market-based economy. A prominent symbol of the licence raj system, the MRTP Act, was repealed.[26] Further, the notion that the infrastructure sector is an important enabler of economic growth began to gain currency during this phase (High Powered Expert Committee [HPEC] 2011; Nataraj 2013). Many services that were previously considered luxury goods, such as telephony and aviation, were now considered essential for economic growth and, thus were opened for private sector participation. Similarly, transportation mobility was deemed critical for trade and commerce. Therefore, two nation-wide road-building projects were initiated—the National Highways Development Project (NHDP) and the Pradhan Mantri Gram Sadak Yojana (PMGSY). However, the economic liberalization process was gradual and often uneven, as illustrated in the subsequent sections that review the reforms

[25] The bailout amounted to 3.6 billion special drawing rights (SDRs), or approximately USD 4.8 billion at the 30 July 1991 rate of 1 SDR = USD 1.33 (IMF 2015).

[26] The MRTP Act was amended as early as 1991 to loosen the licence raj system and was repealed in 2009 (Rajkumar and Hanley 2007).

undertaken in the telecommunications (telecom) and roads sectors, land acquisition policies, and in urban governance (through JnNURM).

Telecommunications Sector

As mentioned earlier, the seeds of telecom sector reforms were sown in the preceding phase (1985–91), notably through partial deregulation and the creation of MTNL and VSNL. The pro-private-sector headwinds originating from the post-1991 crisis resulted in the gradual implementation of the Telecommunications Restructuring Committee recommendations. The National Telecom Policy of 1994 allowed the private sector entry into the basic fixed telephony sector. However, fixed telephony was the least profitable sector for private investors; further, the private sector companies had to contend with public sector competitors on an unequal financial footing. The bidding process that began in 1995 for awarding licences to telephone service providers was highly litigious and resulted in the creation of a telecom regulator—the Telecom Regulatory Authority of India (TRAI)—in 1997. However, TRAI has limited regulatory and enforcement powers. It can only make non-binding recommendations to the DoT. Further, a separate appellate body—the Telecom Disputes Settlement and Appellate Tribunal (TDSAT)—was created in 2000, with the power to arbitrate disputes between the DoT and service providers (Mukherji 2010). In spite of the evolving policy and regulatory environments and cases of financial impropriety,[27] the telecom sector is among India's most remarkable infrastructure success stories, with a subscriber base of 958 million and a teledensity of 76.75 telephone connections for every 100 people (as of September 2014) (TRAI 2014). This success is largely credited to the advancements in cellular technology and to the entrepreneurship of private sector companies (Mukherji 2010).

The most visible spatial impacts of the telecommunications sector are indirect. This sector aided the development of the information technology (IT) industry in cities such as Bangalore by providing the backbone communications infrastructure. Further,

[27] The notorious '2G Scam' forced the central government to cancel all the licences through which the 2G-frequency spectrum was allocated to private mobile telephone companies.

in the nascent growth phase of the IT industry, skilled labour was often recruited from the telecommunications sector (Aranya 2003). The spatial impacts of the IT industry, especially the growth of IT parks, are discussed in greater detail in Chapter 7.

Roads Sector

Among all the infrastructure sectors in India, the roads sector has contributed the most to the nation's economy (PricewaterhouseCoopers [PwC] 2012)—4.8 per cent of the GDP, by some estimates (Kumar 2011). The 3.3-million-kilometre road network in the country carries 65 per cent of all freight and 80 per cent of all passenger traffic. Within the roads sector, the national highways play an extremely significant role. They comprise just 1.7 per cent of the road length but carry 40 per cent of all road traffic (National Highways Authority of India [NHAI] 2014a).

The critical role of the roads sector in the nation's economy is widely recognized and empirically established (Datta 2012). However, the beginnings of the highway development effort were humble. India inherited 21,440 kilometres of national highways from the British in 1947. Over the next four decades (1947–90), the highway length increased by a mere 57 per cent to 33,612 kilometres (Ministry of Shipping, Road Transport and Highways [MSRTH] 2007). After the 1991 BoP crisis, the central government was pre-occupied with macroeconomic stabilization and structural economic reforms, and did not pay immediate attention to road development. The economy continued to grow and so did highway congestion. By the second half of the 1990s, the urgency to expand the highway capacity was deemed critical for the country's continued economic growth. In response, the NHDP was initiated in 1998. Divided into seven phases, the NHDP seeks to upgrade and expand more than 50,000 kilometres (approximately 30,000 miles) of national highways. The total national highway length doubled in the next 15 years (1992–2006) (MSRTH 2007); at present almost three-quarters of the road improvements have been completed or are underway (NHAI 2014b).

Among other projects, the NHDP upgraded the national highways connecting the four major metropolitan cities—Delhi, Mumbai, Chennai, and Kolkata—through the Golden Quadrilateral (GQ)

project.[28] Other major upgrades include the four or six laning of the North–South and East–West Corridors (NS–EW) connecting Srinagar to Kanyakumari and Silchar to Porbandar, the six laning of 6,500 kilometres of existing four-lane highways, and the two-laning of 20,000 kilometres of existing one-lane highways (Lok Sabha Secretariat 2013). Unable to upgrade the highway system solely through its own funds, the government has actively sought a wide array of private sector partnerships ranging from the traditional engineering–procurement–construction (EPC) contract to the more innovative build–operate–transfer (BOT) and design–build–finance–operate (DBFO) contracts. Apart from spurring highway development, these innovative contractual arrangements have provided a roadmap for inviting the private sector into the development of state highways and other infrastructure sectors.

The highway upgrades have had significant economic development and spatial impacts—both desirable and undesirable. For example, an evaluation of the GQ project shows that the highway upgrades led to a significant increase in manufacturing activity within 0–10 kilometres of the upgraded highway compared to 10–50 kilometres away (Ghani, Goswami, and Kerr 2014). On the other hand, highway upgrades have often spurred unplanned, sprawling, ribbon-like informal developments that have effectively relegated some sections of national highways to serve as intra-city roads. For example, due to residential, industrial, and commercial developments along several sections of National Highway 8 (NH-8), that highway serves as a city road in those sections, thereby hindering the interstate flow of trade, commerce, and passengers—the primary function of national highways. Further, since the majority of the national highways are not access-restricted, these developments pose a significant security risk for the highway traffic. Rigorous coordination of land use and transportation planning and end-use supervision of formal plans are, therefore, critical. Such coordination assumes even greater importance because the next major wave of economic and spatial development is envisaged through industrial corridors that would be developed primarily along existing national and state highways.

---

[28] The GQ scheme was initiated in 2000 and was substantially completed by 2003.

For example, the 150-kilometre-wide, 1,483-kilometre-long Delhi–Mumbai Industrial Corridor (DMIC) would significantly overlap with NH-8 (DMIC 2014); likewise the 150–200-kilometre-wide, 1,839-kilometre-long Amritsar–Kolkata Industrial Corridor (AKIC) would overlap with NH-1 and NH-2 (World Bank 2015). These industrial corridors are in the advanced planning and preliminary development stages. They will include the development of a large number of new cities and industrial townships (including SEZs), thereby offering spatial planning and development opportunities at an unprecedented scale at various levels, from local to sub-national. However, these corridors pose significant planning and implementation challenges, too. First, it is feared that these new cities and townships would primarily serve the economic needs of the manufacturing and services economy, not of the poor. This fear is further compounded by the often-contentious land acquisition process employed to secure land for these cities/townships. Finally, it is feared that these cities and townships would be governed by state-level parastatal organizations such as industrial development corporations or development authorities, with little control retained by the residents.

The Jawaharlal Nehru National Urban Renewal Mission (JnNURM)

Economic growth, infrastructure provision, and spatial development in the current phase have been influenced by the lack of effective urban governance, and by recent efforts to address this inadequacy. As discussed earlier, the Indian Constitution gave states power over all urban issues, including city planning and development. Further, the Constitution did not formally recognize ULBs; therefore, states exert direct control over them. As a result, the vast majority of ULBs have a very limited capacity to plan and govern urban areas. This limited capacity, over time, has been a leading cause of the deterioration of urban areas. The central government, through the 74th Constitutional Amendment of 1992, sought to address this problem by formally recognizing ULBs as the third tier of the government, and by directing states to devolve power to the ULBs to perform city planning and development functions. In the years following the 74th Amendment, the states have hesitated to devolve these powers. Unable to directly intervene, the central government launched several

schemes to incentivize power devolution. For example, in 2003, an Urban Reform Incentive Fund (URIF) was set up to link financial assistance to urban reforms mandated by the 74th Amendment. The major mandated reforms included the following: (a) state-level ratification of the repeal of the ULCRA;[29] (b) a reduction in stamp duty; (c) reform of rent control laws; (d) the introduction of computerized processes of registration; (e) property tax reforms; (f) the levy of reasonable user charges; and (g) the introduction of double-entry system of accounting (National Institute of Urban Affairs [NIUA] 2004). Other such incentive programmes included the City Challenge Fund (CCF) and the National Urban Renewal Mission/Fund (Mohanty 2005). Finally, several existing programmes for urban development and slum upgrade/removal were merged in 2005 into the JnNURM.

The JnNURM had two sub-missions and two sub-schemes. The two sub-missions—Urban Infrastructure and Governance (UIG) and Basic Services to the Urban Poor (BSUP)—targeted 65 mission cities. The mission cities included those with million-plus populations, all state capitals, and cities of tourist or religious importance. The two sub-schemes—the Urban Infrastructure Development Scheme for Small and Medium Towns (UIDSSMT) and the Integrated Housing and Slum Development Programme (IHSDP)—could focus on any urban area chosen by the state governments. A grant of INR 406 billion was provided by the central government in the first seven years (2005–12) against a total commitment of INR 661 billion. The JnNURM was extended to FY 2013–14 to allow completion of projects sanctioned up to FY 2011–12 (Comptroller and Auditor General [CAG] 2012).

The mission cities were able to access JnNURM funds if they prepared a city development plan (CDP) and detailed project reports (DPRs), and committed to a timeline for completing all the mandatory reforms as well as a set of optional reforms. Such reforms included devolution of city planning and development functions to the ULBs, repeal of the ULCRA, rent control act reforms, the bolstering of ULB finances through property tax reforms, the levy of user charges to cover operation and maintenance costs of providing

---

[29] The central government repealed the ULCRA in 1999.

infrastructure and services, and the strengthening of democratic local governance through regular elections for the ULBs.

The JnNURM's effectiveness has been moderate at best. It has been criticized for its large-city bias, uneven distribution of funds across states, a focus on stand-alone infrastructure projects rather than on projects conceptualized through an integrated urban and infrastructure planning process, and for its inability to effect ULB reforms such as the 74th-Amendment-mandated devolution of city planning and development functions to the ULBs.

The JnNURM was designed to target both big and small cities. The two sub-missions specifically targeted large cities and the two sub-schemes, smaller cities. However, in practice, the sub-missions received more funds than did the sub-schemes (around 70 per cent of the funds committed by the central government), and within the sub-schemes, the larger cities received more funds (Ahluwalia and Mohanty 2014; Khan 2014).

Most CDPs and DPRs were of poor quality. With a time horizon of 20–25 years, to be developed through an extensive stakeholder participation process (including participation by the urban poor), the CDPs were to serve as a comprehensive planning and infrastructure development roadmap for a city. The DPRs were to implement the CDPs by providing the infrastructure projects' design, development, and implementation details such as construction drawings, financing plans, and socio-economic and environmental impact reports. In practice, many CDPs were hastily developed and were a mere wish list of all the infrastructure projects desired by the state governments. The DPRs seldom had a robust financing plan, and the linkages between the CDP and the DPR were often missing. Moreover, it became difficult to withhold project-level funding despite the state and local governments' failure to implement the promised reforms (Ahluwalia and Mohanty 2014; CAG 2012).

On a positive note, the JnNURM's reform-centric approach led a few progressive states to innovate, and these projects show the potential to have a contagion effect. These innovations include the JnNURM-funded bus rapid transit system (BRTS) in Ahmedabad (Ahmedabad Janmarg Limited [AJL] 2012); deployment of IT for property tax collection and building permits (Ahluwalia and Mohanty

2014); and experimenting with public–private partnerships (PPPs) for developing infrastructure projects.

Special Economic Zone and Land Acquisition Policies

Two policies—SEZ and land acquisition—had, and continue to have, significant direct and combined impacts on infrastructure and spatial development during this phase. As mentioned earlier, the first SEZ (then known as an EPZ) was developed in 1965 at Kandla, Gujarat. Very few SEZs were developed over the next three decades, however, until the adoption of the SEZ Act of 2005 and the SEZ Rules of 2006 (rules for the implementation of the 2005 Act).[30] The post-2006 SEZs differ from the earlier EPZs. The EPZs were primarily export-oriented central-government-developed industrial estates engaged in manufacturing, with little supporting physical and social infrastructure. The SEZs are more diversified in their economic (manufacturing, services, or a combination of both) and market (export or internal consumption) orientations, and are envisioned to have comprehensive supporting logistics and physical and social infrastructure. Indeed, the post-2006 period witnessed a sharp upsurge in SEZs in terms of absolute numbers—196 operational SEZs in 2014[31] compared to 19 in 2005–6 (Ministry of Commerce and Industry 2014a)—and economic impact—exports from SEZs grew from INR 220 billion in 2005 to INR 4.25 trillion in 2014 and investments grew from INR 4 billion to INR 2.84 trillion during the same period (CAG 2014).

Spatially, the 491 approved SEZs occupy 113,464 hectares, with an average size of 231 hectares, or 2.31 square kilometres. A large majority of SEZs (72 per cent by number and 84 per cent by area) are concentrated in seven states.[32] Measurement of the success of the SEZ strategy is complicated by the fact that only about one-third of the approved SEZs are functional, of which a majority (60 per cent

---

[30] An SEZ policy was formulated in 2000. However, it failed to instil investor confidence, due to legal and administrative uncertainties.

[31] By May 2014, 491 SEZs were formally approved and an additional 32 had in-principle approval.

[32] Authors' analysis of data retrieved from the Ministry of Commerce and Industry (2014b).

of the operational SEZs) are in the IT/information technology enabled services (ITeS) sector (CAG 2014).

From an urban planning perspective, the SEZs are encouraged to be located far from urban agglomerations; to be environmentally sustainable; to be self-contained with respect to basic infrastructure and services; and to be located preferably on barren land. However, a review of operational SEZs by the Comptroller and Auditor General (CAG) of India found that a majority of them are located in close proximity to a major metropolitan city; several SEZs are operating without adequate environmental clearances; and approximately 3,000 hectares of SEZs are on defence, forest, agricultural, irrigated, or environmentally sensitive land (CAG 2014). Further, SEZs have been accused of being tantamount to land-grabs in the garb of economic development. For example, the same CAG report found that 5,400 hectares of SEZ land was diverted for non-SEZ commercial purposes by their promoters and that more than half of the land allotted for SEZs remains idle. The history, growth, political economy, and spatial impacts of SEZs overall, and of IT parks, specifically, are discussed in greater detail in Chapter 7.

State governments often use the power of 'eminent domain' to acquire land for SEZs. Some such acquisitions—for example, Nandigram and Singur in West Bengal—have become lighting rods for popular resistance against compulsory land acquisition. This resistance has negatively affected SEZs and other infrastructure development projects, such as highway upgrades. While compulsory land acquisition for public purposes has been the norm for the colonial and postcolonial Indian governments,[33] the recent popular resistance has its roots largely in the landowners' belief that their land is being acquired for private benefit (SEZ promoters in the case of SEZs, or developers in the case of townships); or that they are not compensated fairly for their land. The 2014 CAG report found evidence for the latter belief when it noted that the price at which land was allotted to SEZ developers in several cases was five to twenty times the price paid to the original landowners for acquiring the land (CAG 2014: 14). Further, many landowners and populations have

---

[33] Pandit Jawaharlal Nehru had famously asked landowners to give up their land for mega-projects as service to the nation (Chakravorty 2013: 131).

lived off the land for generations.[34] Often, therefore, once the land is acquired, they have no employable skills that could be useful for the manufacturing or service economy.

Implications for the Future

From the mega-project orientation of the first phase to the rural focus of the second and the seeds of change in the third, the country's economic, infrastructure, and spatial development landscape has virtually come full circle in the fourth phase. There is a renewed focus on mega projects, exemplified by the industrial corridor projects such as the DMIC, and the smart cities initiative from the Narendra Modi government but with two crucial differences this time around: First, many actors are involved in the process rather than the state carrying the solitary burden of nation-building. Second, there is a clear recognition that cities are engines of economic growth, and that infrastructure development is critical for sustained economic growth. While this urban focus should have ideally led to serious conversations about ways to better integrate infrastructure and economic development with urban planning, presently the focus seems largely on individual infrastructure and economic development projects, and not on linking them with city planning. This lack of linkage is exemplified in JnNURM's focus on individual projects. For example, in the case of New Delhi, many JnNURM-funded projects were geared towards the 2010 Commonwealth Games and were not included in the city's CDP or master plan (CAG 2012). Further, the failure to devolve city planning functions to the ULBs and to establish District Planning Committees (DPCs) and Metropolitan Planning Committees (MPCs) has resulted in rather incoherent, reactionary spatial urban development.

On a more positive note, the sizable, growing, and increasingly globally connected middle class is demanding better-quality infrastructure, services, and environmental stewardship. The popular resistance to compulsory land acquisition and the empowerment of

---

[34] Many tribal people, or adivasis, have lived off the land for centuries. Many have no concept of private land ownership, and are often not even eligible for compensation when public land is used for economic or urban development.

the hitherto-suppressed socio-economic classes have sustained the focus on the urban poor and on the rural–urban economic divide. A few states have devolved city planning functions to the ULBs and have undertaken urban financing, infrastructure provision, and service delivery reforms. The next chapter analyses three such cases—the sale of development rights to fund the BRTS in Rajkot, Gujarat; use of an impact fee to fund infrastructure development in Tamil Nadu; and PPP to provide water in three cities in Karnataka. These cases, and their possible contagion effect, provide key inspirational insights into the potential for the nation's spatial landscape.

2

Innovative Infrastructure Funding Mechanisms

Use of Impact Fee, Public–Private Partnership, and Sale of Development Rights to Fund Infrastructure

Traditionally, urban local bodies (ULBs) in India have relied primarily on grants and loans from central and state governments and, to a lesser extent, on land use conversion charges, development charges, and local taxes such as house and property taxes to fund infrastructure and services. The funds received through these loans, grants, charges, and taxes are often woefully inadequate. This gap in infrastructure funding has encouraged the exploration of more innovative local funding mechanisms. Three such novel infrastructure funding mechanisms are explored in this chapter. We examine the use of the infrastructure and amenities (I&A) fee in Tamil Nadu; the sale of development rights along the bus rapid transit system (BRTS) in Rajkot, Gujarat; and the public–private partnership (PPP) established to provide water to three cities in the state of Karnataka.

The Tamil Nadu I&A fee is a promising sign of change and a significant step towards covering the cost of urban-level infrastructure and basic utilities, marking a noteworthy shift from the traditional state-aid-based financing model. It is important to note that the fee rates are much higher than the traditional development charges.

Further, the fee varies by urban development type and intensity of use.

The case study of Rajkot, Gujarat, highlights a ULB's successful attempt to capture a part of the infrastructure-generated property value increase through the sale of development rights along the infrastructure corridor—in this case, the BRTS. Finally, Karnataka's PPP model for water delivery tests an alternative to government-funded, operated, and managed urban water supply systems by harnessing the private sector's managerial and technical efficiencies to plan and operate such systems.

As mentioned in Chapter 1, several central government programmes and policies have stressed the need to encourage private sector participation and to explore financially sustainable ways to develop urban infrastructure. While the overall performance of such measures at the national level has been mixed, the potential signalled by the contagion effect of a few successful examples gives hope. For example, the Rajkot BRTS case study exemplifies a model adopted by several cities—among them Ahmedabad and Surat in Gujarat, and Jaipur in Rajasthan—that are using or planning to use the sale of development rights to fund public transportation projects. Similarly, the PPP model for water supply employed by three cities in Karnataka has encouraged water delivery reforms in other cities, such as Nagpur in Maharashtra.

In addition to this section, this chapter is divided into four parts. The first three review the innovative infrastructure finance mechanisms, and the final section explores the spatial planning and development implications of each mechanism.

Tamil Nadu Infrastructure and Amenities Fee

Background

Local governments throughout the world face fiscal constraints. At the same time, they face strong opposition to tax increases from their residents, who also demand an increasingly higher quality of public infrastructure and services. The situation is further exacerbated in rapidly urbanizing developing countries that need to provide urban infrastructure at a fast pace. As of 2010, 76 per cent (2.64 billion out of 3.49 billion) of the global urban population lived in Asia,

Africa, and Latin America. This proportion is estimated to increase to 81 per cent by 2030 (3.95 billion out of 4.9 billion people) (UN DESA 2011). Furthermore, developing countries, such as India, suffer from weak bond markets and property tax systems, and the centralization of tax-based revenue at the national level (Mathur 2013). This situation has led cities and towns in many countries to actively seek new sources of local non-tax-based revenue, such as the impact fee.

Impact fees are a popular revenue source in the United States of America (USA). They have been used for several decades by virtually all local governments to fund public infrastructure and services. Potable water, sanitation, and sewerage facilities; transportation projects such as roads and highways; and libraries, parks, schools, and police and fire facilities are all commonly funded through impact fees (Nelson et al. 2008; Smith 2008). Recently, the use of the impact fee mechanism has spread to other parts of the world including India, China, the United Kingdom (UK), and Australia.

An impact fee is a type of development exaction—a mechanism by which governments require real estate developers to contribute public facilities, infrastructure, and/or services, either financially or in kind (for example, through land donation). The term *impact fee* is strictly used to describe financial exactions (Altshuler and Gomez-Ibanez 1993). Standardized rather than negotiated (Nelson, Nicholas, and Juergensmeyer 2009), an impact fee is charged to recoup the capital costs of providing services and infrastructure (Smith 2008). The fee has various names depending upon its purpose, including 'capacity fee', 'facility fee', 'impact development fee', 'infrastructure charges', and 'development charges'. However, the basic principle behind all types of impact fees is the same—a developer pays money to a government entity for the development of infrastructure and services that will serve a new project. From a legal standpoint, an impact fee is not a tax, but a fee. To be characterized as such, it is required that the impact fee paid by a developer should be used to provide services or amenities that are directly related to the development. In legal terms, the fee must have a *nexus* (that is, there must be a direct relationship between the development and the impact-fee-funded infrastructure/services) as well as *rough proportionality* (that is, the fee must be proportional to the infrastructure/services impacts or needs generated by the development) (Altshuler and Gomez-Ibanez 1993).

Impact Fee Use in India

Variants of the impact fee—land use conversion charges, development charges, and I&A fee—exist throughout India. Although these mechanisms seek to fund the infrastructure needs generated by new developments, they are often levied upon change of land use, rather than at (or in addition to) the building permit approval or the building construction stage. In some ways, then, these charges capture the zoning-change-led increase in land value and, therefore, are akin to betterment levies. For example, in Haryana, owners of residential and commercial land pay up to approximately USD 7 and USD 78, respectively, per square metre of land area at the time of land use change (*Haryana Government Gazette* 2014).[1] Furthermore, in some parts of the state, the charges vary by the development potential of the land, with the assumption being that areas designated as having high development potential—that is, those deemed likely to be developed more intensively—will require a greater amount of infrastructure and other public facilities, as compared to areas with low development potential, and therefore, merit higher charges. Rajasthan, on the other hand, varies development charges by city size. Thus we see that broad proxies, such as development potential and city size, are often used to formulate fee rates, rather than the actual cost of development. The case of Tamil Nadu, one of the larger and more prosperous states situated in India's southern peninsula, helps understand the scope and nature of some of these new sources of revenue.

Development Charges and the Infrastructure and Amenities Fee in Tamil Nadu

Local jurisdictions in Tamil Nadu levy two types of charges: development charges and (more recently) I&A fee. Both types of charges are used to fund the cost of new-development-generated needs for infrastructure and public facilities; the I&A fee was instituted because the traditional development charges have proved inadequate (they were last updated in 1996), especially in regard to funding infrastructure and public facilities related to multi-family housing and non-residential uses. Single-family residences pay only development

---

[1] Values given at conversion the rate of USD 1 = INR 60.

charges, not the I&A fee, because they are deemed to have a smaller impact on public infrastructure and facilities than does high-rise multi-family housing.

The Tamil Nadu Town and Country Planning Act of 1971 ('Planning Act') and the Planning Authority (Levy of Development Charges) Rules of 1975 provide the state-level framework that enables local governments to levy development charges. Similarly, the Planning Act and the Tamil Nadu Levy of Infrastructure and Amenities Charges Rules, enacted in 2008, provide the state-level enabling framework to levy the I&A fee. These enabling acts and rules also establish the charges and fee rates. Because in most parts of India, including Tamil Nadu, urban planning and development is controlled directly by the state government through its planning department, additional local-level enabling ordinances or resolutions are not required to levy development charges. However, in a few cases where the local planning and urban development function has been delegated to an autonomous government agency (often a development authority), a separate resolution may be required to set or levy development charges. For all other local jurisdictions, the Tamil Nadu Town and Country Planning Department sets the charges.

In Tamil Nadu, development charges are levied at various points in time: first, at the time of change of land use from agriculture to urban use; second, at the time of any subsequent change from one urban use to another; and third, at the time of building construction. For example, the city of Kagithapuram levies a USD 0.02 per square metre (INR 10,000 per hectare) development charge for a change of land use from agriculture to residential; this is called the residential rate. The city charges twice the residential rate, or USD 0.04 per square metre, for a change of land use from agriculture to commercial (*Tamil Nadu Government Gazette* 2013). A rate of USD 0.02 per square metre (USD 0.04 minus USD 0.02) is payable at the time of conversion from residential to commercial use. It is noteworthy that the Tamil Nadu Planning Authority (Levy of Development Charges) Rules, 1975, advise that the residential rate should be based on the value of the property (City of Kanchipuram 2014a), not on the actual cost to mitigate the impact of the new developments on public infrastructure and facilities.

Tables 2.1 and 2.2 list the development charges and the I&A fee charged by one major city in Tamil Nadu, Tiruchirappalli. As mentioned

Table 2.1   Development Charges: Tiruchirappalli, Tamil Nadu, India

Type of Development	Rate for Site (per square metre)	Rate for Building (per square metre)
Residential	INR 1.50	INR 5.00
Commercial	INR 3.00	INR 10.00
Institutional	INR 1.00	INR 3.40

Source: http://www.trichy.tn.nic.in/tlpa/Fees_and_charges/developmentcharges.htm (accessed 7 January 2015).
Note: As of 12 June 2014, USD 1 = INR 60.

Table 2.2   Infrastructure and Amenities Fee: Tiruchirappalli, Tamil Nadu, India

Category	Type of Development	Rate (per square metre)
1	Multi-storey building	INR 250
	Commercial or IT building	
	Industrial	
	Institutional	
	Combination of such buildings	
2	Multi-storey residential	INR 250
3	Other than multi-storey buildings	INR 125
	Commercial buildings/IT buildings	
	Group Development and special building	
4	Institutional building	INR 50
	Not covered under Category 1	
5	Industrial building	INR 75
	Not covered under category 1	

Source: http://www.tn.gov.in/tcp/gos/hud_e_86_2012.pdf (accessed 7 January 2015).
Notes: (a) As of 12 June 2014, USD 1 = INR 60. (b) Multi-storey building is defined as a building with more than four floors including the ground floor; if the ground floor is used for parking, then a building with a height of 15 metres or more (*Tamil Nadu Government Gazette* 2008).

earlier, the development charges were last updated in 1996. The I&A fee was instituted in 2008, and was uniformly increased by 50 per cent in 2012. In summary, the charges and the I&A fee can be updated through government orders but are not indexed to inflation, nor are they periodically updated. This is in contrast to other parts of

the country, where state laws provide for automatic annual increases to adjust for inflation (for example, 10 per cent per year in the Haryana). In Tamil Nadu, the charges and the fee may be used to purchase land and develop capital facilities; it is unclear whether they can be used to fund operations and maintenance (O&M) expenses. With the exception of government properties, no development is exempt from paying the charge and the fee; however, the state government has the power to exempt any class of development from these charges (City of Kanchipuram 2014a, 2014b). Furthermore, the charges and the fee need to be paid in a lump sum at the permit approval stage. When the I&A fee was initially instituted in 2008, it could be paid in instalments, but a 2012 amendment to the enabling regulation removed this provision (Government of Tamil Nadu 2012).

Design Features that Fulfil the 'Nexus' and 'Rough Proportionality' Principles

Since development charges and the I&A fee are 'fees', legally speaking, the *nexus* and *rough proportionality* principles apply. At present, however, the nexus principle is only partially met. The development charges are not adequately tracked to ensure that they are spent on public infrastructure or facilities that serve the charges-generating projects.

In the case of the I&A fee, there is an attempt to track the inflow and outflow of fee revenues by requiring that the revenues accrue to a state-level fund (called the Tamil Nadu Infrastructure and Amenities Fund), with the Commissioner of the Tamil Nadu Town and Country Planning Department being the overall fund in charge. This arrangement is, at best, a very weak attempt at meeting the *nexus* principle, in our opinion. The cities that generate the fee revenue have no control over the fund. Furthermore, the infrastructure projects on which the fee revenues can be spent are not identified by the state. Indeed, the 2009 Tamil Nadu Government Order that created the fund provides broad powers to the state-level committee to administer the fund; for example, the committee may spend the fee revenues on any projects that comprise 'essential infrastructure schemes'. (For committee composition and powers/functions, see Government of Tamil Nadu 2009.) Essentially, the revenues generated from the charges and fee can be spent anywhere in the state, and there is no time limit within which the charges and fee need to be spent.

Developers do not receive credits for new-development-generated tax revenues. The only relief is that developers can appeal the charges if they believe that their development does not impact public infrastructure and facilities. Finally, it is not clear how double counting, due to the levy of both development charges and the I&A fee, might be avoided. Indeed, the concept of I&A fee was challenged in court (*D. Manikandan* v. *State of Tamil Nadu*)[2] on the ground that it does not meet the principle of rational nexus, and therefore is a tax, not a fee. The challengers also alleged that the fee leads to double counting because development charges are already collected for the provision of infrastructure. The Madras High Court (the highest court in the state of Tamil Nadu, and the equivalent of a state supreme court in the USA) ruled that the I&A fee does not constitute double counting because the fee is levied on projects that have significant infrastructure impacts, while development charges are levied on all uses (LegalCrystal 2014). In our opinion, the court thus implicitly acknowledged that the basic development charges are inadequate to meet existing infrastructure needs, and that, therefore, the I&A fee is valid. The court found further that the mere establishment of the state infrastructure and amenities fund, and the mention of other safeguards in the enabling act and regulations, were adequate to meet the nexus principle—a very low threshold by any measure.

The rough proportionality principle is not fully met either. While development charges and the I&A fee vary by land use and by the intensity of use (see Tables 2.1 and 2.2), there is one charge and fee per land use and these are not defined by the type of infrastructure or public facility to be funded. This could be because the charges and the fee are not based on detailed infrastructure plans, nor are they tied to level-of-service standards. Consequently, they are not tied to specific capital improvement projects.

Insights from the Case Study and Suggestions for Improvement

The Tamil Nadu I&A fee exemplifies the innovations that have begun to emerge in urban India as the state and local governments seek new

---

[2] See http://indiankanoon.org/doc/86012970/?type=print, last accessed in February 2017.

revenue sources to fund urban infrastructure and services. It is likely that other states in India will also employ an impact fee in the future. But when they do so, they will face one major question: How can they develop high-quality public infrastructure and facilities using impact fees? A high fee rate might be required to fund fully high-quality infrastructure. The need for a high fee rate is much easier to justify if the *nexus* and *rough proportionality* principles are clearly met.

An examination of how development charges and I&A fees in Tiruchirappalli compare with those levied in highly developed cities with high-quality infrastructure provides useful insights. We estimate that a 100-square-metre apartment in Tiruchirappalli would generate USD 634 in development charges and fees. The developer of a similarly sized apartment would pay several times more in developed countries—for example, 28 times more in Brisbane, Australia (USD 18,000), and 40 times more (approximately USD 24,000) in Fremont, California, USA. Even after controlling for a purchasing power parity of 0.3 (World Bank 2014a), the total amount generated by the development charges and I&A fee in Tiruchirappalli is, respectively, 10 and 13 times smaller than that in Brisbane and Fremont. If Tiruchirappalli wishes to provide infrastructure and services of the developed-world quality, it would need to increase the fee amount. The city will have to justify the increase, which it could do using several strategies employed by Brisbane and Fremont. These include: basing the fee on a clear level of service standards; varying the fee by infrastructure/service; and preparing detailed infrastructure plans (similar to Brisbane's Planning Scheme Policies or Fremont's Capital Improvement Plan) that clearly detail the projects needed to serve new growth. In fact, the Tamil Nadu I&A fee rules already note that the fee can be used to fund infrastructure investment plans and infrastructure projects proposed in a city's development plans, an indication that local governments are expected to engage in detailed planning.

The fee should adjust for inflation. This is especially critical for countries such as India that often experience high inflation rates. Such a step would have an immediate and positive effect on local infrastructure funding efforts. In addition, the impact fee rate should be revisited at regular intervals to ensure that it is adequate to meet the current infrastructure/service funding needs. Finally, the purchase of the land needed for the development of public infrastructure and

facilities should be a permitted use of impact fee revenues. The ability to purchase land is especially critical for land-consuming facilities such as public parks and outdoor recreation areas, and for the construction of roads where the right of way needs to be purchased.

Sale of Development Rights: Bus Rapid Transit System in Rajkot, Gujarat

Background

A rapidly increasing urban population, worsening traffic congestion and environmental pollution, and the high cost of gasoline have all lent urgency to the development of public transportation systems in Indian cities. The Jawaharlal Nehru National Urban Renewal Mission (JnNURM) and National Urban Transport Policy (NUTP) have provided further impetus. As a result, several megacities such as Delhi, Kolkata, Mumbai, and Chennai are focusing on building capital-intensive, heavy-rail-based Metro Rail systems. Others, including 'second-tier' large cities (those with one million plus populations), are exploring the utilization of a BRTS, either as a complement or an alternative to the more expensive Metro system.

Indeed, buoyed by the success of the 88-kilometre-long Ahmedabad BRTS (Centre of Excellence in Urban Transport [CEUT] 2015), cities such as Rajkot and Surat are actively developing their own BRTS. These next generation BRTS projects are exploring non-traditional financing models, including the sale of development rights along the bus rapid transit (BRT) corridors.

In the field of transportation, the sale of development rights is one of the several value-capture-based infrastructure finance mechanisms. Other such mechanisms include the sale or joint development of public land in proximity to transit stations, lease or sale of air rights above transit stations, levy of special assessments, land-value taxation, and capture of property-tax increments through tax increment financing (TIF).

Value capture is based on the 'benefits received' principle—that is, those who benefit from a particular infrastructure or service should also pay for it. Simply put, since nearby properties benefit from the transportation infrastructure, they should contribute towards funding it (Smith and Gihring 2009). A well-established stream of literature

has empirically substantiated the positive land/property value impacts of transportation infrastructure—both of auto-oriented infrastructure[3] and of public transportation.[4]

While Indian cities have generated revenue through the sale or transfer of development rights before,[5] their use for funding public transportation projects is new. This section explains how the city of Rajkot, situated in the western state of Gujarat, is selling development rights along a BRTS corridor.

Rajkot Bus Rapid Transit System

The Rajkot Municipal Corporation (RMC) began planning for a BRTS in the early 2000s. In 2006, the RMC took over the operation of the city bus system from the state government. Rajkot's city development plan (CDP) (a document required to apply for JnNURM funding) had envisaged an efficient public transportation system by the year 2008, much needed because the city of 1.2 million had a virtually non-existent public transportation system—a mere 13 buses operated by the state transport corporation.[6] The city residents' transport needs were being met by a slew of unregulated, accident-prone, para-transit vehicles that mostly comprised three- and four-wheeled auto-rickshaws (RMC 2007).

Following this, in 2007, the RMC submitted a detailed project report (DPR) to the central government seeking JnNURM funding. The DPR envisages three BRT corridors. The 29-kilometre-long first corridor, the Blue Corridor, is planned along the existing ring road, which, as the name suggests, rings the city of Rajkot. The second corridor, the 16.5-kilometre-long Green Corridor, is planned along the city's north–south axis, and the third, the 18-kilometre-long Red Corridor, is planned along the city's east–west axis. The combined length of

[3] See Boarnet and Chalermpong (2001); Mathur (2008); Vadali (2008); and Voith (1993).

[4] See Armstrong and Rodriguez (2006); Debrezion, Pels, and Rietveld (2006); Gibbons and Machin (2006); Henneberry (1998); Lochl and Axhausen (2010); McMillen and McDonald (2004); Redfearn (2009).

[5] For example, Mumbai has used grant of extra floor space index (FSI) to incentivize developers to construct affordable housing units.

[6] Against the norm of 370 buses per million population (RMC 2007).

these corridors is 63.5 kilometres. The entire BRTS is envisioned as comprising three phases of development, with Phase 1 being further subdivided into three parts (see Table 2.3). Land for a 10.7-kilometre stretch of the proposed Blue Corridor was already owned by the RMC at the time of the DPR preparation; this stretch was, therefore, planned as Phase 1, Part 1, to be developed first. The DPR focuses on this stretch for cost and financing estimates, including the potential for the sale of development rights. The total project cost was estimated at the time to be INR 1.1 billion (RMC 2007), or USD 18 million.[7]

Sale of Development Rights

Compact, high-density development along the BRTS corridor was deemed desirable by the RMC for successful coordination between land use and transportation, as well as to ensure adequate ridership on the BRTS. It was argued that the introduction of high-quality public transportation would spur real estate development, especially within the 250 metres along either side of the BRTS corridor, since properties in this distance band were likely to accrue most benefit from the BRTS. Therefore, these properties were targeted for revenue generation through the sale of additional floor space. In Rajkot, in addition to building height and setback restrictions, the floor space index (FSI) is a key parameter used by the ULB to control building form and intensity of development. The properties along the Blue Corridor in the RMC area were already allowed a maximum FSI of 1.5,[8] of which 0.68 was utilized on average, leaving an average unutilized capacity of 0.82.

The RMC conducted a survey of buildings along this corridor, examined the existing land uses and the prevalent land prices, and conducted a development impact analysis. It concluded that, given the locational desirability and the forecasted impact of the BRTS, this corridor would need an FSI of 1.5 to 1.7 over the existing 0.68 FSI, resulting in a potential additional demand for approximately 0.7 to 0.9 FSI (1.5 to 1.7 minus the current unutilized capacity of 0.82). Therefore, three options for sale of the extra FSI were

[7] At a dollar-to-rupee conversion rate of USD 1 = INR 60 as of 2014.

[8] FSI = building area/land parcel area. Therefore, with an FSI of 1.5, a building with a floor area of up to 1,500 square metres may be constructed on a 1,000-square-metre parcel of land (1,500/1,000 = 1.5).

Table 2.3 Rajkot BRTS Corridor Phasing

Phases	Description	Length in Kilometres	Period of Implementation as per the DPR	Actual Period of Implementation
Phase 1 (Part 1)	Development of Blue Corridor in RMC area	10.7	2007–9	2007–12
Phase 2	Development of Red Corridor	16.5	2008–9	Implementation not started due to lack of funds
Phase 3	Development of Green Corridor	18	2008–9	Implementation not started due to lack of funds
Phase 1 (Part 2)	Development of Blue Corridor in RUDA area	9.26	2008–10	Implementation not started due to lack of funds
Phase 1 (Part 3)	Development of remaining part of Blue Corridor—National Highway Portion	9.14	2009–11	Implementation not started due to lack of funds

Source: Authors; RMC (2007); Anadkat (2015).
Note: RUDA refers to Rajkot Urban Development Authority.

considered—sale of 0.50, 0.75, and 1.0 FSI. It was assumed that only one-quarter of the existing residential and commercial land parcels would purchase additional FSI, and that only half of the currently vacant land zoned for mixed-use would be developed, of which only one-fifth would purchase additional FSI. Finally, two price levels were assumed for the sale of FSI. The FSI for residential, commercial, and mixed land uses would be sold at a per-metre rate of INR 750, INR 1,000, and INR 800, respectively, under the first price-level option; and at a per-metre rate of INR 1,500, INR 2,000, and INR 1,750, respectively, under the second price-level option (RMC 2007). Table 2.4 shows all the revenue-generation alternatives considered.

The RMC opted for the sale of 0.75 FSI at the second price-level option, resulting in an estimated revenue of just over INR 1.2 billion—a little more than the estimated project cost of INR 1.1 billion (see the shaded portion of Table 2.4). It is noteworthy that even the most conservative option—sale of 0.50 FSI at the first price-level option—was estimated to generate a considerable amount of money, INR 413.3 million, or approximately 38 per cent of the project cost.

Current Status of the Project

The 10.7-kilometre-long Phase 1, Part 1, opened for trial service in 2012 (RRL 2012) and for commercial operation in May 2013 (Communicate Karo 2013). Eleven buses operate on this route at four-minute intervals (Anadkat 2013). The final total project cost was INR 1.75 billion, INR 650 million over the DPR's estimate of INR 1.1 billion, an increase primarily due to the need to construct a 1.5-kilometre-long overpass at a cost of INR 530 million (RMC 2010). In 2012, the government of Gujarat approved a 0.45 FSI increase in the parts of the city that were deemed to have a good public transportation system. Additionally, the state government allowed the RMC to sell 0.75 FSI within a distance of 250 metres along either side of the BRTS corridor (Anadkat 2015). The FSI sale began in 2013; as of mid-March 2015, the FSI sale had generated INR 310 million. Owners of an estimated 25 per cent of the total eligible land parcels have purchased additional FSI. With 75 per cent of the land parcels still remaining, it is estimated that FSI sales could generate revenue

Table 2.4 Estimated Revenue from FSI Sale by RMC

FSI	Residential	Commercial	Vacant Mixed-use	Total (in INR million)	Revenue as Percentage of Estimated Project Cost of INR 1100 Million	Revenue as Percentage of Final Project Cost of INR 1750 Million
	INR 750	INR 1000	INR 800			
			Option 1			
0.50	224.1	133.8	55.5	413.3	38%	24%
0.75	336.1	200.6	83.3	620.0	56%	35%
1.00	448.1	267.5	110.0	826.6	75%	47%
	INR 1500	INR 2000	INR 1750			
			Option 2			
0.50	448.1	267.5	97.1	812.8	74.0%	46%
0.75	672.2	401.3	145.7	1219.1	111.0%	70%
1.00	896.3	535.0	194.3	1625.5	148.0%	93%
0.45 (State-government-approved FSI sale)	403.3	240.8	87.4	731.5	66.5%	42%

Source: Authors' Analysis and RMC (2007).

Note: Revenue generated is based on per-square-metre rate for additional FSI (in INR million).

in excess of INR 2 billion (Anadkat 2015), well exceeding the total project cost of INR 1.75 billion, and far greater than the RMC's projected estimate of INR 1.2 billion.

The FSI is sold at the *Jantri*[9] rate (Anadkat 2015), which is the value of a square metre of land as assessed for the purposes of levying registration tax at the time of transfer or sale of land or real estate (AMC 2011). The Gujarat state government divides each city within the state into several zones and then determines the Jantri rate for each major use within each zone. The state government revises Jantri rates only sporadically (the rates were last revised in 2011); therefore, these rates might not equal market prices. Rajkot is able to generate significant revenues from FSI sales as compared to the estimate because that estimate was based on much lower rates—for example, INR 1,500 per square metre for residential use and INR 2,000 for commercial use (see Table 2.4)—while the Jantri rates for various zones that fall within the 250-metre-distance-band along the Ring Road are often well above INR 10,000 per square metre (Government of Gujarat 2011).

Insights from the Case Study and Suggestions for Improvement

The sale of FSI has the potential to generate significant funds for infrastructure development. Without appropriate strategic implementation, revenues may disappoint, however. The following is a list of the most crucial steps and strategies:

1. The FSI sales must be calibrated to the existing or planned capacity of infrastructure and services. Is there enough existing capacity within the transportation, water, sewerage, and electricity systems to serve the new users of the additional FSI? If not, are there infrastructure projects in the pipeline that will augment capacity enough to meet the projected needs?
2. The ULBs should conduct micro-level demand analysis to estimate the real estate demand likely to be generated by a new infrastructure project. A BRTS passing through a neighbourhood zoned for low-density residential development, where adequate

---

[9] Jantri refers to the government document that specifies the value of land and building for revenue collection purposes (for example, for levying stamp duty).

transportation capacity already exists, might not accrue the same monetary benefit to the neighbouring properties, as would a BRTS that passes through a high-density area with constrained transportation capacity.

3. The FSI sale price must be indexed to inflation. Because FSI sales are likely to take place over several years, if the price is not adjusted for inflation, the value of the revenue from the FSI sale will decrease in constant money terms. This is especially important for a high-inflation country such as India.

4. The ULBs relying primarily on FSI sales for funding of projects would benefit from accurate project cost estimates and from an accurate knowledge of the precise amount of extra FSI capacity that they will be allowed to sell. For example, the cost of the Rajkot BRTS increased from INR 1.1 billion to INR 1.75 billion, primarily due to the unanticipated need to construct an overpass. Luckily for the RMC, two factors helped recoup this cost: First, the state government allowed the city to sell an additional 0.75 FSI, not a lower value. Second, the Jantri rates are higher than the FSI sale rates assumed in the DPR. These two factors combined have resulted in robust revenues from FSI sales.

5. The majority of the revenues from FSI sales are likely to accrue *after* the infrastructure project has been developed, while funds are needed *beforehand* to develop the project. This revenue–expenditure mismatch needs to be addressed for each project. It is noteworthy that the development of the remaining phases of the Rajkot BRTS has not begun due to a lack of funding (Anadkat 2015). The JnNURM funded Phase 1, Part 1. However, no new funding is forthcoming at present to develop subsequent phases.

ULBs in developed countries such as the USA often address this revenue–expenditure mismatch by issuing municipal bonds. However, the municipal bond market is weak in developing countries such as India, meaning other financing mechanisms must be explored. For example, the state governments or the central government could provide low-interest loans to the ULBs on the condition that the loans would be repaid from FSI-generated revenues.

6. Where multiple agencies are likely to stake a claim on the FSI-generated revenues—for example, if one agency had developed the BRTS in Rajkot, and another the Ring Road—the demand for the additional FSI generated by them would need to be separately estimated in order for the FSI-generated revenue to accrue to the two agencies proportionally.
7. Finally, services impacts must be assessed. Increased FSI might require a ULB to augment other services, such as water supply and sewerage. Monetary impacts of such augmentation need to be considered while developing a model for sharing FSI-generated revenues.

Karnataka Urban Water Supply Improvement Project

Background

Water scarcity and poor water quality are arguably among the most pressing problems facing urban India, especially the 25 per cent of the urban population that lives in slums. Overall, only 64 per cent of India's population has access to individual water connections or to water stand posts (public spigots or posts shared by community members). Water supply ranges from one to six hours per day, with a per capita supply of as little as 39 litres per day (High Powered Expert Committee [HPEC] 2011). Further exacerbating the situation, theft, leakages, and unbilled water use account for 74 per cent of non-revenue water supplied in urban areas; only 4 per cent of water use is metered (ASCI 2010); and finally, only 30 to 35 per cent of water-supply-related O&M expenses are recovered from user charges (HPEC 2011). All these performance indicators fall well short of the service benchmarks developed by the Government of India, that is, 100 per cent water coverage, a 24×7 water supply of 135 litres per capita per day, 100 per cent cost recovery, 100 per cent metering, and a maximum of 15 per cent non-revenue water (Ministry of Urban Development [MoUD] 2010a).

Taking into account the current backlog in water delivery projects as well as future population increases, a USD 174 billion funding need for a 20-year period (2012–31) is estimated—USD 64 billion for capital expenses and USD 110 billion for O&M (HPEC 2011).

Expenditures are projected to be, on average, USD 8.5 billion per year.[10] In addition to the heavy financial burden, and chronic shortfall, at least two other sets of factors—political and institutional—have contributed to poor-quality water service.

Owing to the dynamics of electoral politics, decision-makers at the state and local levels have shown a marked proclivity either not to charge for water, or to undercharge. This has led to a lack of funds for developing and maintaining water infrastructure, resulting in severe negative impacts mainly borne by low-income people—the very constituency the undercharging purportedly benefits—since they have to pay a disproportionately large percentage of their income for privately supplied water in order to have the reliable access that ought to be provided by civic entities. Institutional dysfunction—including a fragmented administrative structure and poor technical and managerial capacity of many organizations responsible for water delivery—also plays a role.

To meet water delivery challenges, experts have suggested a variety of approaches, such as decreasing the proportion of non-revenue water, covering 100 per cent of O&M expenses through user charges,[11] and the use of PPPs (HPEC 2011; Sankhe et al. 2010). The PPP model for infrastructure delivery is often employed for one or more of the following reasons: (a) to attract private investment for developing a project (capital funding); (b) to benefit from private sector technical expertise; and (c) to realize gains from private sector operational and management efficiencies.

Various kinds of PPP models exist on a continuum of low to high private sector participation. The degree of participation depends primarily on which entity—public sector or private sector—is responsible for the following: (a) asset ownership; and (b) commercial risk. Table 2.5 illustrates various PPP models. Hybrid PPP models exist. For example, an operations contract where the asset is public-sector-owned; or a work and services, management, and operations contract where the public sector owns the asset, and the private sector augments, operates, and manages it.

[10]   At 2009–10 prices, at the rate of USD 1 = INR 50.
[11]   One-hundred-per-cent recovery of O&M expenses for water supply was one of the JnNURM's mandatory reforms (MoUD 2010b).

Table 2.5 Various Kinds of PPP Models

	Works and Services Contracts	Management Contracts	Operations Contracts	Build–Operate–Transfer (BOT), Design–Build–Operate–Transfer (DBFO), and Similar Contracts	Full Privatization
Asset Ownership	Public	Public	Public	Public or Private	Private
Commercial Risk	Public	Public	Private	Private	Private
Examples	Road engineering–procurement–construction (EPC) contract	Toll stations	City bus service	Highways; Bus terminals	Telephone service; Power generation and/or supply

Source: Authors' compilation.

Evolution of Water PPPs in India

The evolution of water PPPs in India can be divided into two phases. The first phase (1991–2000) began immediately after economic liberalization. During this phase, PPP projects focused on securing private sector funding for public water infrastructure capital projects. Most such projects failed due to poor design, lack of financial viability, and strong public opposition to the 'privatization' of a basic need—water. The present phase, which began in 2001, has witnessed a shift in focus—from persuading private partners to fund and own capital-intensive bulk water augmentation projects to focusing on gains in efficiency and coverage of water distribution (Aziz and Shah 2012; World Bank 2014b). This shift in focus—from water infrastructure funded and owned by private sector to a more limited private sector participation where the sector only manages and operates water infrastructure—unsurprisingly, has resulted in a critical lack of private investment in the capital projects needed in the public water sector. There have, however, been measurable benefits from tapping the private sector's technological, operational, and management expertise: cost savings, better revenue collection, and service delivery improvements. Further, since the water infrastructure is still public-sector-owned, these second phase projects are not opposed for attempting to 'privatize' water.

The PPP project discussed next—the three-city Karnataka Urban Water Supply Improvement Project (KUWASIP)—is a promising example of a second-phase PPP project. As mentioned earlier, the project is also notable for its contagion effect; it has inspired several cities (such as Nagpur) to explore the PPP model to improve water service (World Bank 2014b).

Karnataka Urban Water Supply Improvement Project

The KUWASIP covers three cities—Belgaum, Gulbarga, and Hubli-Dharwad. These cities have a total population of around two million (World Bank 2010). Typical of the situation in cities across Karnataka, these three cities suffer from intermittent and inadequate water supply. For example, in the first half of the 2000s, city residents received water for only a few hours once every three to

five days (Government of Karnataka 2011). The situation was worse in Hubli-Dharwad, where water was supplied for only two hours every 15 days in the summer of 2002 (Sangameswaran, Madhav, and D'Rozario 2008). During this period, the Government of Karnataka formulated the Karnataka Urban Drinking Water and Sanitation Policy, 2002. The policy encouraged the state government to work with ULBs to provide universal water coverage in all urban areas in the state, and to promote private sector participation in enhancing the public water sector in the form of PPPs (Government of Karnataka 2010).

In 2003, the Government of Karnataka partnered with the World Bank to commence the design and implementation of a demonstration project—the KUWASIP—to ensure continuous water supply (24×7) to selected zones of the three cities of Gulbarga, Hubli-Dharwad, and Belgaum. These zones covered more than 10 per cent of the cities' population, with a total coverage of approximately 230,000 people (World Bank 2015). The KUWASIP's main objectives included demonstrating: (a) the feasibility of providing adequate, continuous, and good-quality water to all segments of the population and (b) the advantages of 24×7 water supply over intermittent water supply (World Bank 2010).[12] It was hoped that the KUWASIP's success in meeting these objectives would provide a roadmap for addressing the water needs of all urban areas.

---

[12] The critics of 24×7 water supply argue that continuous water supply leads to wasteful over-consumption of water, loss of water through leakage, and very high water charges for consumers. They also argue that this method strains the already-limited water resources because more bulk water is needed for a 24×7 water-supply system. The proponents of 24×7 supply highlight several advantages, including better quality water resulting from continuous high pressure in the pipes, which reduces seepage from the surrounding soil. Further, they argue, a 24×7 water supply *reduces* water consumption because consumers do not have to store water; a significant proportion of stored water is thrown away. Finally, in the absence of adequate municipal water supply, consumers rely on dubious-quality, privately supplied, expensive water, and/or pay high electricity charges to pump groundwater (often illegally).

Implementation Process

The INR 2.37 billion KUWASIP was funded jointly by the Government of Karnataka (INR 550 million) and the World Bank (INR 1.82 billion). The project was structured as a PPP between state agencies, the three cities' ULBs, a private concessionaire (Compagnie Générale des Eaux, or Veolia), and non-governmental organizations (NGOs) such as the Rural and Urban Development Association (RUDA), with the Karnataka Urban Infrastructure Development and Finance Corporation (KUIDFC), a state-level public sector company, serving as the nodal agency (The State Institute for Urban Development [SIUD] 2012).

The state agencies were responsible for ensuring adequate supply of bulk water to the private concessionaire, Veolia. Towards that end, these agencies undertook projects such as the replacement of water mains, construction of pump stations, and upgrades to water treatment plants. The three ULBs allowed Veolia access to their water distribution systems, and transferred the management and operations of the water supply system in the demonstration zones to Veolia. The ULBs retained the power to set tariffs, collect bills, and connect or disconnect water connections. Veolia developed a financial investment plan (FIP) for rehabilitating the water distribution network in the demonstration zones, implemented the rehabilitation projects, and ran water supply operations for four years,[13] which included addressing consumer complaints in a time-bound manner; establishing a billing system; and training the ULB staff deputed to Veolia. In collaboration with the KUIDFC, the three ULBs and the NGOs ran a communications campaign that aimed to address consumers' concerns about water tariffs and about the role of the foreign private concessionaire, Veolia (World Bank 2010).

Successes and Challenges

Initial reports about the KUWASIP have been mixed. The project has been successful on several fronts, including water delivery and

[13] Veolia was awarded the contract in 2005. The rehabilitation projects were undertaken in 2006 and 2007. The 24×7 water distribution commenced in April 2008, and the two-year operation period ended in March 2010. Thereafter, Veolia won a two-year extension contract (World Bank 2010).

tariff revenue collection. The demonstration zones benefit from 24×7 water supply, whereas areas outside the demonstration zones have an average of 10 hours' supply per week. At the same time, bulk water consumption has decreased more than 10 per cent, and water loss has decreased from 50 per cent to 3 per cent. Furthermore, the water pressure has increased enough to supply water up to an elevation of 20 feet, thereby obviating the need to pump water for several households. Coverage has increased more than 50 per cent, from 16,399 connections to 25,172. Moreover, for households that consume less water, water bills have been reduced by almost half—from a fixed water bill of INR 90 per month for all households to INR 48 for households consuming 8,000 litres or less water per month (at the rate of INR 6 per 1,000 litres).[14] At the same time, 100 per cent metering and 80 per cent billing efficiency have resulted in a sevenfold increase in revenues (SIUD 2012; World Bank 2010).

The objective of providing residents access to water free of cost through public hand pumps has not been met. Violating the assurances given to the residents, all hand pumps and public stand posts have been closed. Further, non-payment of water bills remains a serious issue, primarily because Hubli-Dharwad has chosen to carry forward old arrears (Burt and Ray 2014).[15] Finally, scaling-up remains a significant challenge for this project and for others like it. The capital needs for the KUWASIP were funded entirely by the Government of Karnataka and the World Bank, a financing model that is fiscally unsustainable. Indeed, buoyed by the success of the KUWASIP, the Government of Karnataka and the World Bank are moving ahead with the Karnataka Urban Water Supply Modernization Project (KUWSMP). This project seeks to extend the geographical coverage of 24×7 water supply to the entire area of

---

[14] The actual savings could be much larger for three reasons: First, households save on electricity costs since they no longer need to pump water from underground tube wells or pump low-pressure municipal water to storage tanks on rooftops. Second, households do not have to rely on expensive private water supplied through water tankers. Third, householders can use their time more efficiently because they do not have to spend time obtaining water, a special benefit to those engaged in hourly-wage work.

[15] Gulbarga wrote-off all the old arrears and started their KUWASIP tariff collections from zero (Burt and Ray 2014: 115).

Gulbarga, Belgaum, and Hubli-Dharwad—a fiscally challenging task because, as per the KUWSMP's funding formula, the three ULBs will be required to fund 26 per cent of the capital expenditure (World Bank 2015). Even if these three ULBs are able to bear their share of the capital expenditure, it is likely that a large proportion of ULBs across the country would not have a similar financial capacity.

Spatial Planning and Development Implications

The three case studies reviewed in this chapter highlight the small, yet significant shift away from the state-led Nehruvian model of development described in the preceding chapters, towards a model in which multiple actors, including the private sector, participate in urban development. The active role of these cities' ULBs is of special interest, as exemplified by the Rajkot BRTS project, where the RMC conceptualized, designed, and implemented the project. Further, these case studies illuminate the progressive steps being taken towards reducing ULBs' reliance on state- and central-government financial assistance by harnessing new, own-source revenue sources in different parts of the country—the sale of development rights in Gujarat, the impact fee in Tamil Nadu, and water user charges in Karnataka.

From a spatial planning and development perspective, the sustainable and local nature of these revenue sources portends well for the rapid spatial development and upkeep of urban areas. Financially sustainable urban development models would facilitate the provision of basic civic amenities such as water supply and public transport. Furthermore, these revenue streams link city planning with infrastructure development, and instil fiscal discipline in public sector decision-making—a significant shift from the dominant approach in India, where plan-making is often disconnected with finances and infrastructure provision. However, a growing body of literature that focuses on urban water supply, notes that the use of these market-based infrastructure finance mechanisms is leading to the marginalization, even criminalization, of the urban poor who often live in slums and squatter settlements, or at the periphery of urban areas; their right to live in cities is being questioned (Anand 2012; Bjorkman 2014; Graham, Desai, and McFarlane 2013; Ranganathan 2014); and their wishes, concerns, and suggestions are being sidestepped (Anand 2015;

Gopakumar 2014). Further, often the local political economy and the history of the infrastructure system make it difficult to measure the success of market-based financing mechanisms. For example, Anand (2015) highlights the difficulty in accurately estimating the proportion of non-revenue water in Mumbai's water supply system because an unknown amount of water is supplied 'illegally' (though with the connivance of local engineers and politicians) to the city residents. In conclusion, although with varying degrees of success, all three case study projects strive to enhance the quality of basic urban infrastructure and services—an important prerequisite for fulfilling the city residents' aspirations for a high-quality urban environment.

PART II

LOCAL SPATIAL PLAN-MAKING PRACTICE

3

Marginal Shifts or Significant Changes?

Tracking Jaipur's Three Master Plans: 1971–2025

Why Study Master Plans?

The literature describes the enduring employment of a master-plan-based comprehensive planning approach in Indian cities even as many scholars highlight long-standing concerns, such as the lack of social equity and growth of informal settlements, that the master planning approach has failed to address (for example, Adhvaryu 2011; Benjamin 2008). But, on the other hand, the literature also reports notable shifts in India's polity. For instance, the changes as described in the 'Introduction' to this book include the ongoing growth of city-based economic activity that creates new formations and social groups like a globally oriented middle class even as the ever-deepening democracy and the continuation of an older patronage politics facilitate the rise of marginalized groups and intermediate classes (Harriss-White 2002). What impact have these broader shifts had on the nature and scope of master plans for Indian cities? Have the focus and purpose of master plans changed at all or do these continue to offer more of the same?

This chapter aims to answer these questions by comparing and contrasting the three master plans that the city of Jaipur has had so far. Published in 1971, 1998, and 2011, respectively, these plans

are important for several reasons. First, despite the many critiques of modernist frameworks and bureaucratic modes of governance that the idea of master planning ostensibly signifies, these plans are formally adopted statutory documents that not only represent state policy but also distribute sizable resources. Not discounting their socially insensitive and 'top–down' disposition, these plans also hold certain legitimacy in the popular imagination. The educated classes, for example, continue to perceive these efforts as meaningful expressions of future intentions about a place, with the local media routinely discussing master-plan-related issues in considerable detail (see *Rajasthan Patrika* 2009, for instance). The courts of law take more than a cursory interest as well, frequently admitting public interest litigation (PIL) in master-plan-related matters and often intervening directly, especially when the plan proposals are not being followed or are flouted brazenly (Bhan 2010).

While there is little doubt that 'instruments of state', such as legislative mandates, official rules, and legal oversight, scaffold the making and application of master plans, ultimately these documents are cultural artefacts symbolizing the climate of opinion prevalent at the time of their creation. Not only do these plans embody the values and ideals of their makers shaped in the context of a larger social sphere and the contemporary system of the political economy but they also shed light on the thinking and working of the larger society that produced these artefacts. In this sense, these plans constitute a small yet significant part of the history of city planning, of the life of Jaipur city, and of the larger intellectual domain that produced these documents. They exemplify prevalent ideas and ideological beliefs that, in all likelihood, would have emerged before a given plan and are likely to have survived it as well. Encapsulating diverse practical influences and discursive themes dominant at the time, these texts describe the manner in which their makers understood the existing city and imagined its future.

Moreover, studying changing plans for a single city like Jaipur provides a window for visualizing how the expectations and actions of plan-makers have changed over time as the city has continued to grow at a rapid pace (see Figure 3.1). As officials expedite the preparation of spatial plans in post-liberalization India (see the 'Introduction'), comparing recent and earlier plans provides a unique opportunity for *reading* the nature and focus of the changing planning regimes

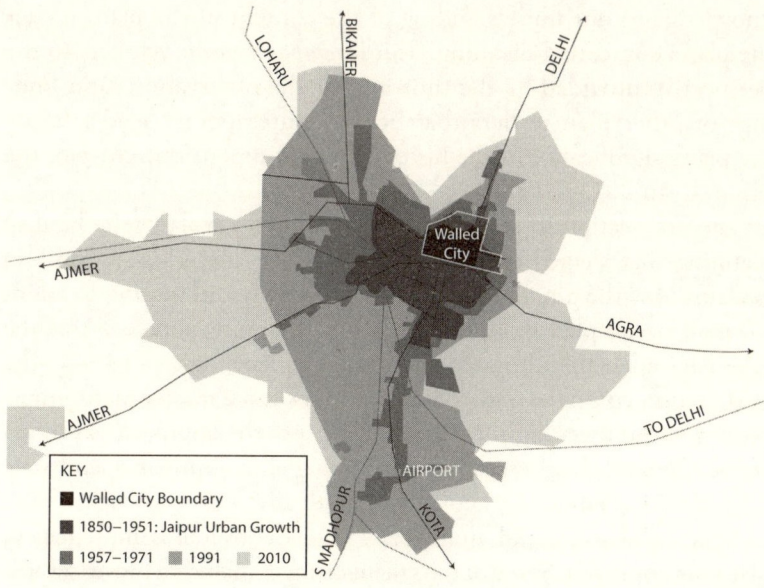

Figure 3.1   Urban Growth of Jaipur, India (1850–2010)
Source: Authors.

in India's many cities characterized by diverse cultural settings and varying historical trajectories.

We borrow the idea of *reading* a plan from Brent Ryan (2011) who suggests that a reader should formally 'read through' a plan, not just to grasp its rich content, essential ideas, or the means of implementing those ideas, but also to comprehend the additional levels of meaning contained within the plan document. Drawing insights from the literature on the interpretation of the visual arts, Ryan distinguishes three kinds of meaning that spatial plans typically contain: First, *factual meaning*, which describes information about raw data and its interpretation, which we accept, true or not, as being what it purports to be. Relevant facts and information may be found in diverse aspects of the plan document including its graphic design, content organization, and plan recommendations. Second, *contextual meaning*, which may or may not be explicitly stated but reflects the larger social, political, economic, and physical settings that collectively influence the plan document at the time of its creation. Understanding a plan's many contexts, and applying this

knowledge to our understanding of the content of the plan, reveals the plan's contextual meaning. Third, *temporal meaning* refers to the perspective provided by the time and by the observations and findings of other plan readers that help a contemporary reader locate the plan's significance in the historical development trajectory of the place (Ryan 2011: 313).

The first section introduces Jaipur and briefly explains the kind of planning that shaped the city under princely rule. This section also explains how the planning regime shifted slowly, attempting to adopt the new master-plan-based comprehensive planning approach that the national leadership promoted after India's Independence in 1947. The next section compares and contrasts Jaipur's three master plans, interpreting and illustrating their meanings as per the approach explained above. We find that despite the continuing elite dominance and state control, city planners in Jaipur have gradually begun to engage with a wider set of issues and audiences within the overall comprehensive planning approach. Some of the salient changes include a move towards regularization and rehabilitation of unauthorized settlements; a shift away from the outward focused large-scale urban development model requiring state-sponsored acquisition of private lands; and a growing recognition of the role of non-state planning actors such as real estate developers, emergent entrepreneurs, and the residents of unauthorized settlements. The last section discusses these findings reflecting upon broader transitions in India's post-liberalization polity.

The Master-plan-based Comprehensive Planning Approach at Jaipur

The origin and application of master plans within the field of urban planning is well documented.[1] Our purpose in this section is to

---

[1] The idea of a master plan, or the notion that a singular plan can anticipate forthcoming events and shape the city's physical form and supporting systems, often with state's backing, to fit the envisaged future, has roots in the rational-comprehensive planning model, and a long-standing legacy in the planning field. See, for instance, Keeble (1959) for a historical discussion about the nature and role of master plans in the planning profession and Godschalk and Anderson (2012) for an updated view of the comprehensive planning model. Also see Banerjee (2009) for a description of how these ideas came to postcolonial India.

provide a quick overview of Jaipur's planning trajectory, helpful both in framing the context for comprehending the introduction of the master planning approach in the post-Independence period, and situating the shift to this new kind of planning within the overall development history of the city.

Located at the heart of 'princely India', or the area comprising two-fifths of the Indian subcontinent, ruled by indigenous kings and chiefs until the departure of the British colonists, Jaipur occupies a special place in the modern planning history of South Asia. Comparatively a recent city by Indian standards, Jaipur was founded by Maharaja Sawai Jai Singh in 1727, that is, only about 60 years before L'Enfant started planning Washington, DC. Popularly perceived as the exemplar of indigenously designed city in India, Jaipur's plan demonstrates a formally conceived consistency with distinct physical features, such as the division of the city into nine squares, a gridiron pattern with hierarchal and wide roads, and Cartesian orientation.

The plan's regularity attracted a steady stream of colonial visitors, who reported its deviance from the 'chaotic' layout of other Indian cities and identified Jaipur as a superlative example of city building in this part of the world (Karatchkova 2007). Several scholars have argued that the plan, its proportions and orientation, and the layout of major buildings are based upon the treatises on *Vastu Vidya*, or the traditional knowledge about city-building and architecture (Sachdev and Tillotson 2002).[2] Notwithstanding the merit of these assertions, it is important to note that a small group of elite (and mostly old) men, comprising select members of trusted feudal families, hand-picked building experts, and career colonial officials, led by Jaipur's kings conceived and controlled the city's overall development.

The hereditary maharajas of Jaipur, like the chiefs of the more than 550 princely states of pre-Independence India, were sovereign rulers of their territories. Although formally subservient to the 'paramount power' of the British colonists through subsidiary alliances, these native rulers exercised almost unbridled authority in their states (Singh 1998). Land was typically perceived as the kingdom's foremost productive asset and thus related issues occupied a prominent place

[2] Also see Chakrabarti (1998).

on the royal agenda. Many kings customarily paid close attention to the entire gamut of land planning and landscape management activities including the siting and building of human settlements, public works, and the conservation of the local ecology. Since *lagaan* (or the various forms of taxes on the peasants) generated a major part of state income (almost two-thirds in the case of Jaipur state), regulating land ownership and land use constituted a key part of government work (Bayley 1879).

In the Jaipur state, for example, even if all the land ultimately belonged to the *darbar* or the king himself, land revenue officials kept detailed records distinguishing between *khalsa* or state-owned properties and *jagir* or alienated lands awarded to members of the feudal order including nobles, ministers, priests, and courtiers in lieu of services rendered, annual taxes, or as a gift from the royal court (Bayley 1879). The revenue officials mapped and classified lands based on soil quality and uses, and utilized detailed records of individual landholdings to document annual productivity and calculate long-term averages for different fields. They also fixed corresponding tax rates, collected cash or in-kind tributes, and resolved and reconciled minor issues and petty disputes while seeking to maintain the land's productive usage and wield the state's authority on the ground. In line with the royal predilection for hunting and outdoor living, these officials looked after other elements of the natural landscape such as water bodies, forests, hills, pastures, and open lands as well (Gold and Gujar 2002).

Such a sharp gaze upon the territorial landscape combined with the predominant authority of the feudal court meant that land acquisition and official coordination required for building development projects and new settlements were not an issue under the king's authoritarian rule. As in other high-ranking princely states—such as Hyderabad, Baroda (now Vadodra), Gwalior, and Mysore—hereditary monarchs took pride in Jaipur's distinctive civic identity and up-to-date infrastructure. The city was known for impressive palaces and monuments as much as for modern amenities such as street lighting, trash removal, and piped water supply that arrived in the late nineteenth century with the colonial influence (Sarkar 1984).

Thus, the Jaipur state was no stranger to modernization, employing both British-trained Indians and colonial officials to superintend

a range of progressive projects such as schools, colleges, hospitals, museums, and new city extensions funded by the royal treasury, over the course of the nineteenth and the first half of the twentieth century. At a certain level, these developments were not unusual and conformed with the largesse native kings routinely exhibited towards their subjects. For example, the rulers commonly granted state servants cash awards and lands for faithful and loyal service, aided community groups and philanthropic individuals providing public services, and granted land titles to the poor, who often built dwellings in unoccupied and marginal locations (Ismail 1954).

Here, it is important to note that, despite the development of modern amenities and public facilities, the society's overall disposition remained comparatively conservative with the *purdah* system (segregation of the sexes) being widespread, and the education of girls not very common until well after India's Independence.[3] Similarly, occupational communities and identity-based social groups continued to inhabit specific localities, patronize particular shrines, maintain traditional forms of living, and pursue customary practices and rituals while the urban economy remained largely centred upon the local bazaars.

Moreover, unlike British India, where a range of urban actors were increasingly involved in local governance and the shaping of public culture (Haynes 1991), in Jaipur, the king, his courtiers, and a handful of state officials controlled civic and public affairs until the mid-twentieth century. For instance, apart from the ex-officio city engineer and health official, the royal court nominated all 26 members of the municipality's executive council (Roy 1978). In these respects, and however ambiguously, Jaipur's king-led and elite-supported 'indigenous modernity' and attendant forms of closely-supervised princely planning bridged the society's conservative

---

[3] Maharani Gayatri Devi, the princess of Cooch Behar and later the third and youngest wife of Jaipur's last reigning ruler, pioneered the education of girls by promoting the first girls' education centres (named MGD school and Maharani College in her honour) at Jaipur during the early 1940s. Her autobiography, *A Princess Remembers: The Memoirs of the Maharani of Jaipur*, provides an insightful account of the changes in Jaipur during the second half of the twentieth century. See Devi (1996).

and progressive impulses in deeply symbolic and meaningful ways that were critical to the city's spatial organization and social functioning.

Institutional arrangements and power relations, however, began to change after the merger of Jaipur state with independent India in 1949 (Rudolph and Rudolph 1984). From the seat of a relatively small princely state, Jaipur became the capital of India's second largest state, Rajasthan, which came into existence in 1950. The transfer of power from the princely courts to a new ruling elite—comprising political leaders, elected officials, state bureaucrats, and technical experts (see the 'Introduction' describing the rise of indigenous elites)—gradually initiated a string of fundamental changes in all walks of life. The next section takes up that story describing how, in the relatively short span of 60 years in the city's rather long life, Jaipur experienced significant social and spatial changes.

Pressing concerns, however—such as the unification of the former princely states, the formation of basic administrative structures, and the transition to democracy—meant that the newly formed governments had little attention and few resources to deal with the many demanding issues (Wilcox 1965). On the one hand, given the resource constraints and restricted attention to urban affairs, the Rajasthan state government largely permitted, and actively co-opted, many practices from the princely period.[4] On the other hand, it focused on reconciling and streamlining administrative procedures for the previously princely entities, and creating standardized organizations in line with those of postcolonial India.

For instance, the state government did not alter the organizational structure or function of Jaipur's main development agency, the City Improvement Board (CIB), which was formed during the princely period in 1942. The CIB continued to develop new city extensions, conceptualized during the princely period, until its amalgamation with the newly formed Urban Improvement Trust (UIT) in 1961. Similarly, the authorities not only retained the revenue department's supremacy over land classification and ownership issues but also extended the scope of revenue officials' duties to include the entire range of development works. So, the erstwhile colonial revenue

---

[4] The trend was not peculiar to Jaipur but prevalent in other parts of India as well. See for instance, Fahim (2009).

collectors became general duty administrators in postcolonial India (as evident in the new nomenclature of the Indian Administrative Service [IAS] and Rajasthan Administrative Service [RAS]). Transferable across different departments, these state bureaucrats with permanent jobs came to occupy many of the highest positions in the central and provincial officialdom entrusted with the task of developing the newly independent nation (Subramanian 2004).

Against this background of institutional continuity and incremental change, professional planners found a toehold in the state bureaucracy when the Rajasthan government created a town planning section within the Public Works Department (PWD) in the early 1950s. The new cadre of town planners succeeded in delineating its own domain in 1959, when the state enacted the Urban Improvement (UI) Act, enabling legislation for public-sector-led planning activities, including the preparation of master plans (Institute of Town Planners, India [ITPI] 1976). Shortly afterwards, funded by the Third Five Year Plan (1961–6) of the central government, the planning section separated from the PWD as a statutory department of the state, and was rechristened the Town Planning Department (TPD) in 1963. Headquartered at Jaipur, the professional planners (civil servant planner hereafter) and supporting staff employed by the TPD worked on various in-house projects such as master plans for large cities. They were also deputed out on ex-cadre posts to other departments and public agencies such as the Rajasthan Housing Board and the Rajasthan State Industrial Development and Investment Corporation Limited (RIICO), and later, the Jaipur Development Authority (JDA).

The TPD began working on the first master plan for Jaipur from the mid-1960s, using the Delhi Master Plan (DMP) protocol. Sponsored by the Ford Foundation, a joint team of American consultants and young Indian planners, who had recently returned from graduate schools abroad, had conceived the DMP as a comprehensive plan for the Delhi region during the late 1950s (Staples 1992). Supervised by Prime Minster Jawaharlal Nehru himself, the DMP had legal standing and authorized compulsory acquisition of lands followed by formally planned development in the target area (Ansari 1977).

The motivation behind the adopted approach stemmed from the comprehensive plan's perceived ability to simultaneously tackle many intertwined issues that characterize urban areas worldwide (such as

jobs, housing, transport, utilities, environment, social services, and more). The unique mix of factors prevalent in the post-War period helped as well. These included robust confidence in the ability of the social sciences to solve complex human problems; rise of the mainstream development theory which argued that modern political, cultural, and spatial contexts, such as those promised by the master plans, were needed to pursue widespread social and economic trans-formation in the recently decolonized nations; and Nehru's posi-tioning of the Indian state at the centre of the national imagination (Khilnani 1999).

Perhaps most prominently pursued in the domain of national eco-nomic planning through the legendary Five Year Plans espoused by the Delhi-based Planning Commission (see Chapter 1 for a detailed explanation), this kind of state-centred planning spread rapidly to other walks of government work such as irrigation, agriculture, and public health as well. Identifying plans with explicit and predictable outcomes and ignoring the inherently provisional and contingent nature of planning work, the adopted approach was facilitated by liberal use of state power and a certain confidence stemming from the faith in scientific knowledge and technical expertise (Khilnani 1999).

The domain of city planning was little different, where this new kind of planning aimed to acquire a multidimensional knowledge of the city in question (such as spatial and economic locations of households, sizes and configuration of demographic cohorts, composition of social groups, nature of occupations, etc.). The planners then, in theory at least, could analyse and comprehend this vast information, and apply that knowledge in order to balance the interaction effects between the functional elements of the urban system (labour and housing markets, natural systems, utilities and modes of transportation, etc.) through land use proposals and development projects while promoting general public welfare and contributing to the project of nation-building.

The latter was important because in line with the contemporary nationalistic fervour, decision-makers imagined planning as a tool to pursue national development (National Institute of Urban Affairs [NIUA] 1991). Civil-servant planners played along, eliciting the state's patronage by underscoring the significance of their own trade: 'Planning is necessary not only for the sake of our physical environ-ment but also to build our nation, to put in the citizens of the state

that spirit, health and outlook which free citizens must have' (Uttar Pradesh Town Planning Organization [UPTPO] 1952: 4). Calling for a comprehensive land use planning policy '[that requires] setting up of a suitable planning machinery at all levels [of governance]' (ITPI 1955: 9), planners sought the consent of other groups as well, by associating planning with high moral principles: 'What makes our new planning system different from the old is not only the change of scale from the patronage of the few to the services of working millions but also the fact that we are making a conscious and concerted effort to control our environment. We are, in fact, submitting to a voluntary, self-imposed discipline' (UPTPO 1952: 3).

Operationalizing this kind of state-centred planning that is full of patriotic rhetoric and public promises, however, depended on legislative mandates and bureaucratic procedures. The master-plan-making process as per Rajasthan's UI Act of 1959, for example, stipulated the following sequential steps. After the government's approval to proceed, civil servant planners would conduct a civic survey, collecting diverse information about existing land uses and socio-economic phenomena in consultation with experts from relevant government departments and agencies such as traffic and transport, industry and business, utilities, environment, and housing; analyse this data to formulate relevant projections for the horizon year; and then recommend land use allocations and pertinent projects to meet the projected requirements. After inviting comments and objections from the public, but not requiring their actual involvement at any stage, the expert collective would fine-tune and submit the draft master plan to the state government. Keeping political expediency and bureaucratic convenience in mind, the state officials would then notify the master plan at some opportune time in the future. How did this rhetoric and process play out in practice? What meanings can we derive from a formal reading of Jaipur's three master plans that followed this procedure? That is the focus of next section.

Reading the Master Plans

This section compares and contrasts the three master development plans of Jaipur and presents the analyses along the factual, contextual, and temporal dimensions.

Master Plan for Jaipur 1976–91 (Town Planning Organization)

A Factual Reading

Authored by a team of professional planners, aided by technical staff, and headed by the state's chief town planner and architectural adviser, the first master plan for Jaipur is a thin volume of 66 pages published in May 1976. Hardbound with a simple cover, the black-and-white document is printed on ordinary paper and comprises three grey-scale maps folded in the back pocket. These maps include an existing land use plan for the year 1971, a proposed land use plan for 1991, and a general city map showing the extent of the urban area and its division into eight planning districts surrounded by a periphery control belt. The plan's overall composition is austere, relying heavily on text and containing few graphics and tables to communicate ideas and advice.

B. Kambo headed the planning team. He had first trained as an architect at the Delhi Polytechnic, the precursor to the School of Planning and Architecture (SPA), New Delhi and then as a planner at the Massachusetts Institute of Technology (MIT), Cambridge, Massachusetts. Before coming to Rajasthan as the state's chief town planner and architectural adviser in 1967, Kambo had served as a member of the DMP team and then headed the team designing the new steel city of Bokaro in Eastern Bihar, both of which constituted the foremost plan-making efforts that formalized the comprehensive approach in Indian planning practice (Town and Country Planning Organization [TCPO] 1962: 85). Not surprisingly, Kambo's professional confidence and practical experience, gained while working with state bureaucrats, mark the opening master plan of post-Independence Jaipur.

To begin with, the plan speaks in a tone that 'knows'. The plan content reflects the authors' confidence as well, with four clearly defined chapters: Introduction (8 pages), Planning Concept (6 pages), Land Use Plan (37 pages), and Plan Summary (5 pages). The authors also make a point of displaying official support at prominent locations in the plan document—both setting precedent for later efforts and becoming a ritual over time. The front matter, for instance, comprises a foreword written by the minister for town planning, a preamble penned by the secretary of the urban development and

housing department, the list of state bureaucrats and official nominees comprising the advisory council that guided the plan-making effort, and Kambo's acknowledgement of planning officials who worked on the master plan. The back matter, on the other hand, includes official paperwork establishing the legal standing of the master plan. It contains relevant excerpts from the UI Act of 1959, which empowers the state government to prepare and implement master plans, and three appendices that include a list of the 125 revenue villages notified as part of Jaipur's urban area, and pertinent government notifications issued in pursuance of the UI Act during the years 1964, 1972, and 1976 respectively. In this sense, the master plan is a self-contained document that leaves little doubt in the readers' mind about the legal credentials and official backing for Jaipur's first-ever master plan.

In contrast with the prominent display of state support at the 'top and tail' of the plan, the plan authors do not dwell much on plan formulation, background, rationale, and methodology in the document. They, however, briefly describe the process of data collection and projection of the population, from 615,000 in 1971 to 1,250,000 in the horizon year of 1991, right at the beginning of the Introduction chapter. The authors next explain key planning concepts including the rationalization of the population density across the urban area by measures such as the decongestion of the central business district and development of district-level work centres, outward oriented development for accommodating urban growth, and the hierarchically conceived organization of self-sufficient planned areas at various spatial scales ranging from the smallest unit of 'housing clusters' containing 15–200 families to the eight planning districts comprising the entire city. However, as is clear from the length of the individual chapters, plan authors devote the bulk of the document to explaining land use proposals that outline downstream plans and development projects recommended to meet future urban growth.

A Contextual Reading

Such a reading of the plan requires a comprehension of larger developments at the local, state, and national levels. The TPD was first

asked in 1964 to initiate the work on the Jaipur master plan, which the state government eventually approved in 1976 as per the official notification enclosed with the plan document. Twelve long years taken by the authorities to complete the due process and approve the plan stand testimony to the strenuous transition from the princely planning model powered by the sovereign's command to the post-Independence approach predicated upon civil-servant-led master plans and bureaucratic paperwork.

On the one hand, governments of newly formed states such as Rajasthan were preoccupied with pressing tasks like the creation of basic government machinery that spared little attention for urban affairs and accumulating housing shortages. On the other hand, planners were yet to earn professional standing among civil service peers, many of whom belonged to well-established cadres of colonial vintage such as those of the revenue department's officials and PWD engineers. Not surprisingly, the main audience of Jaipur's first master plan comprised state bureaucrats and fellow civil servants from the different branches of government service. Thus, the plan authors employ both an assertive tone, for example, when explaining the planning concept (for example, *Master Plan for Jaipur*: 10) and emphasizing the magnitude of impending urban growth and a voice of solidarity, for instance, when underscoring the importance of assuming the plan's collective ownership and calling for follow-up action (for example, *Master Plan for Jaipur*: 16).

In line with the tumultuous changes in the national polity taking place around the time Jaipur's first master plan was being prepared—such as Nehru's death in 1964, the two wars with Pakistan in 1965 and 1971, failed monsoons of 1966 and 1967 accompanied by severe food shortages, substantial devaluation of the Indian Rupee in 1966, and the nationalization of India's largest private banks in 1969—the plan demonstrates both utopian and practical impulses. On the one hand, and in tune with the Nehruvian tradition, the authors imagine the state in the driver's seat, trusting its developmental impulse with the ultimate responsibility for implementing the master plan. Such a positioning is both by default (for example, the authors do not name any alternative actor who may pursue the plan) and explicit (for instance, the idea of state-centred development runs throughout the document).

Similarly, non-state actors and private property rights find little mention in the plan that posits urban land as a community resource and describes the role of city planning as 'regulation of and control on the use of this primary resource to the optimum as well as the best benefit of the community' (*Master Plan for Jaipur*: 8). In a similar vein, the authors attempt to evoke the clienteles' goodwill because the image presented in the plan does not 'claim to be an exact prediction of WHAT WILL BE nor it is intended to be a prescription of WHAT SHALL BE. It is an image of WHAT IS LIKELY TO BE if the public organizations and private individuals responsible for the development of the area pursue their interests in a proper way' (capitalization for emphasis in original, *Master Plan for Jaipur*: 16).

On the other hand, and in sharp contrast with the DMP, the master plan for Jaipur does not recommend mandatory acquisition of private lands within the urban area—although the authors do expect the development agencies to acquire private lands as per the need and location of the project at hand. Apparently aware of the courts' sympathetic stance towards private property rights, and inordinate delays due to associated litigation, the authors refrain from recommending liberal employment of 'eminent domain', or the use of the state's police power to acquire private property. Similarly, and like many other master plans of Indian cities prepared around the same time, the plan does pay homage to the city's distinct patrimony and historical quarters but focuses on practically easier-to-build outward-oriented development projects.

A Temporal Reading

By reading the plan against the backdrop of the city's overall development trajectory, and taking advantage of hindsight, it is easy to see that Jaipur's first master plan played a crucial role in attempting the shift to the new kind of comprehensive planning approach that the national leadership promoted in the post-Independence period.[5]

---

[5] This attempt was in line with the contemporary trend where metropolitan and regional plans prepared in both developed and developing countries followed a comprehensive approach and exhibited a physical bias.

The plan authors not only exemplified the abstract comprehensive planning model by making an actual plan but, in doing so, also sought to create a constituency among the state bureaucrats and official colleagues working in other departments. This becomes clear both in the many pedagogical efforts the plan authors make to clarify the meaning and purpose of comprehensive planning in the plan document (for example, *Master Plan for Jaipur*: 13) and in the manner in which they explicate an entirely new vocabulary of attendant planning terms such as 'land use plan', 'long-range planning', and 'work centre–living area relationship' throughout the plan document (for example, *Master Plan for Jaipur*: 10, 12, and 37).

Since the future is difficult to predict, the authors of Jaipur's first master plan, like those of comprehensive long-term plans anywhere, could not anticipate and prepare for unforeseen events—many of which were considerably beyond their scope of work. These included a sustained lack of state support for city planning that, perhaps most famously, resulted in the extension of the plan horizon from the year 1991 to 1998 because the state bureaucracy could not get its act together for preparing the next master plan on time; impending emergence of unauthorized subdividers and real estate developers motivated by housing shortages that the concerned government agencies failed to meet; and the failure of development authorities to prepare and pursue downstream plans such as zonal development plans and implementation tools such as zoning regulations.

Nonetheless, the plan's basic tenets such as the planned development of self-sufficient areas comprising civic amenities such as parks and open spaces and decongestion of dense urban quarters became accepted wisdom and continue to be evoked today. More importantly, development agencies pursued several of the plan proposals and projects with salutary effects. Notable examples include the Jhalana planning district that contains two industrial areas providing many jobs, the city's airport, and the institutional zone that houses many public and government offices. Similarly, the Jhotwara planning district provides the new Vishwakarma industrial area with corresponding housing and civic facilities along with many other development projects undertaken by public sector agencies such as the Rajasthan Housing Board and the JDA.

Master Development Plan 2011, Jaipur Region 1998–2011
(Jaipur Development Authority)

A Factual Reading

Prepared by the town planning wing of the JDA, the statutory agency constituted in 1982 for the city's spatial planning and development, the second master plan for Jaipur is a sizeable document of two volumes published in September 1998. Unlike the preceding master plan comprising a single volume, the term 'plan' refers both to Part I (policy document) of the master plan that comprises 123 pages and three main maps and Part II (land use plan) comprising 81 pages and one folded map and six land use maps (see Table 3.1). The three main maps include the drawings of the existing developed area, proposed urbanizable limits, and different planning zones constituting the urban region, while the seven land use maps for the horizon year 2011 include those for the central city and nearby settlements, deemed important by the authors. Hardbound with a colourful cover featuring the popular tourist landmark of Hawa Mahal, or the palace of the winds, the graphic-rich document is printed on fine paper and contains many data tables and charts.

Part I (policy document) opens with the 'scope of work' describing the mandated nature and official scope of the master plan, reasons for which are described later. The next section outlines the natural settings and manmade features of the Jaipur region (27 pages) followed by an analysis of existing conditions (5 pages), and plan projections for the horizon year 2011 (2 pages). Plan policies and proposals dominate the remainder of the volume (41 pages), which concludes with recommendations for plan implementation (2 pages) and important annexures and drawings (28 pages). Part II (land use plan) is designed to operationalize the master plan policies and proposals (described in Part I) on the ground. The volume begins with a review of the preceding master plan (18 pages), explaining the various shortcomings in the implementation mechanisms and the host of unforeseen developments that followed in their wake. The next section explains the detailed classification of proposed land uses (18 pages) and envisaged activities in Jaipur's satellite settlements (19 pages). The bulk of the remaining document (32 pages) elucidates the 'land use zoning code' that lists compatible uses and permitted

Table 3.1   A Summary of the Characteristics of the Three Master Plans of Jaipur

	Master Plan for Jaipur (1976–91, Extended up to 1998)	Master Development Plan-2011, Jaipur Region (1998–2011)	Master Development Plan-2025, Jaipur Region (2011–25)
Authorship	Town Planning Department.	Town planning wing of the Jaipur Development Authority.	Master plan cell of the Jaipur Development Authority.
Plan document	Single volume of 66 pages and three folded maps.	Part-I (policy document) comprising 123 pages and three folded maps and part-II (land use plan) comprising 81 pages and one folded map and six land use maps.	Five volumes comprising more than 830 pages and numerous maps and a separate map-book with detailed GIS maps for the urban region.
Public input	Draft plan and drawings displayed over 60 days generating nearly 500 comments from the public.	Draft plan displayed for over 120 days receiving 70 comments from the public.	Draft plan displayed for 180 days receiving more than 700 comments from the public. More than 20 interactive sessions held with public representatives and professional and industry associations.
Audience	State bureaucrats and fellow civil servants in other departments.	Officialdom.	State officials and educated classes.

(Cont'd)

Table 3.1 (*Cont'd*)

	Master Plan for Jaipur (1976–91, Extended up to 1998)	Master Development Plan-2011, Jaipur Region (1998–2011)	Master Development Plan-2025, Jaipur Region (2011–25)
Plan sponsor and supporters	Civil-servant planners.	Civil-servant planners, progressive officials, and local media.	Civil-servant planners, progressive officials, state leadership, higher judiciary, and local media.
Prominent planning ideas	Hierarchically organized and self-sufficient planned areas, outward-focused development, de-densification of central business district.	Regional planning focus, development of satellite settlements, flexible approach towards unanticipated developments of the past and future land uses.	Focus on environment (depleting groundwater, diminishing green cover, and quality of life, etc.), transportation issues, development of regional settlements and city heritage and tourism.
Detractors	State bureaucrats and real estate developers.	Real estate developers and lower-level political functionaries.	Lower-level political functionaries.
Implementation	Implemented only piecemeal, but basic tenets of plan continue to be evoked.	Implemented only piecemeal, but successfully shifted the planning and development focus to the regional scale.	Ongoing.

Source: Authors.

activities in each land use category. The document concludes with seven maps illustrating the proposed land use for the horizon year 2011 in the central city and surrounding settlements.

Several planning principles of Jaipur's second master plan differ from the preceding effort. For instance, plan-makers conceive Jaipur's spatial future in terms of the overall urban region unlike the first master plan that focused on the central city and its immediate surroundings. Both the plan title, namely the *Master Development Plan 2011 Jaipur Region*, and the plan content, which pays significant attention to proximate regional towns or *satellite settlements*, signify the shift of planning focus to the regional scale.[6] Dramatically expanding the outward-oriented growth focus of the previous master plan (almost fourfold from the opening plan's spatial extent of 385 square kilometres to 1959 square kilometres), the plan divides the region into three areas, namely, urban, rural, and ecological zones and proposes the central city, inner suburbs, outer suburbs, and rural settlements as the four tiers of development. Here, plan-makers call for paying special attention towards 'urban nodes', a total of 32 select localities judged suitable for major economic activities, spread across the entire region. However, in contrast with the confident tone of the first master plan, Jaipur's second master plan is decidedly less confident, seeking not only to accommodate the unexpected developments of the past, but also adopting a flexible approach towards future development. For instance, the plan acknowledges the potential role of private real estate developers in the following manner: 'Genuine private developers will be encouraged to undertake development activities of residential and other schemes. Regulations in this regard are [already] being suitably amended' (*Master Development Plan 2011*, Vol. II: preface).

A Contextual Reading

When the preparation of Jaipur's second master plan started in the early 1990s, the ongoing ruptures in the Nehruvian planning model

[6] It is important to note that the shift to the regional focus was then gaining popularity nation-wide, for example, as evident in the development of a plan for the Delhi NCR Region prepared by the National Capital Region Planning Board (NCRPB) in 1988 and the regional plan for Mumbai prepared by the Mumbai Metropolitan Region Development Authority (MMRDA) in 1999.

had become fairly evident in many Indian cities. But the phenomenon was especially prominent in the housing sector that comprises the bulk of city land. Writing in 1982, for example, Madhu Sarin had vividly described how the construction workers overlooked by the Chandigarh plan had turned to building their own informal settlements. Jaipur's first master plan had similarly devoted a measly single paragraph paying lip service to the city's informal settlements. Moreover, the civic agencies and government departments, as described earlier, had failed to coordinate and pursue many of the downstream plans and projects as well.

Thus, Jaipur too experienced a jumble of unanticipated settlements including those of the urban poor and working classes appropriating locations the master plan had put aside for other uses. Organized social networks among government intermediaries, lower-level bureaucracy, and local political functionaries enabled speculators, unscrupulous real estate developers, and subdividers to utilize a loophole in the state's land revenue act allowing 'cooperative societies' to subdivide agricultural land on the urban edge (Gupta 1992). The profiteers used the cooperatives as fronts to build settlements (popularly known by the South Asian euphemism 'colonies') occupying large sections of the urban periphery blocking developments based on the adopted plan (1992). The authors of Jaipur's second master plan acknowledge the massive subversion of the preceding plan in the following words (*Master Development Plan 2011*, Vol. II: 1):

> The proposals of bulk acquisition of land, in many cases, have been unsuccessful and invited legal wrangles. Housing cooperative societies have usurped almost all land in the urbanizable area thus restricting the Jaipur Development Authority (JDA) from taking up urban development programmes envisaged in the master plan.... Rampant illegal construction of buildings took place throughout and Katchi Bastis [informal settlements] have emerged upon large tracts of land.

Taking a forthright stand, Jaipur's second master plan goes on to describe how unauthorized bazaars along the main thoroughfares, and informal settlements and cooperative society subdivisions, many on state-owned land or ecological zones, have sabotaged many of the plan aims and outcomes (*Master Development Plan 2011*, Vol. I). Acknowledging the political purchase of ex post facto legalization of

the built realty for perceived electoral gains, the plan-makers then not only seek to accommodate many of these unanticipated developments but also aim to adopt a flexible stance because, '[i]t is important that the plan should have an in-built dynamism and flexibility to adjust to the socio-economic environment which in present times is ever changing by leaps and bounds' (*Master Development Plan 2011*, Vol. I).

The local planning context, characterized by unforeseen developments contesting the state-centred planning model, shapes the nature and scope of the master plan in other crucial ways as well. On the one hand, the authors justify the master planning exercise by turning to rhetorical generalizations and government support, both explicitly and implicitly, at several places in the plan document. For instance, the 'preface' to Part I articulates the purpose of the master plan in the following words:

> The plan is expected to establish general proposals for the area, to provide [a] framework for detailed policies and proposals for [the] local area, to indicate action areas and priority areas and [*sic*] for intensive action, to provide guidance for Development Controls, to provide [the] basis for coordination decisions between various government departments, committees and boards of the Authorities and local governments etc. (*Master Development Plan 2011*, Vol. I)

The emphasis on the plan's official role, and the underlying hope to tap state power for plan execution, perhaps become clearest in the plan implementation section where the authors propose, rather darkly, 'All lands covered in the Master Development Plan proposal area be frozen. For any transfer of land in the Master Development Plan area, specific permission of JDA be made a pre-requisite' (*Master Development Plan 2011*, Vol. I: 92). But, on the other hand, plan-makers also attempt to adopt a flexible planning approach. For example, they incorporate a diverse range of permitted uses in the land use zoning code allowing for local phenomena such as the residents' continuing preference for mixed-use activities, and not the segregated land uses proposed by the first master plan. Along similar lines, plan-makers call for encouraging private developers in the real estate sector while regulating their activities and accelerating the legalization of cooperative society subdivisions (*Master Development Plan 2011*, Vol. I). This self-evident tension between the authors' invocation of

official support as the source of plan legitimacy and the attention towards local cultural preferences and practical needs to incorporate existing, even if unauthorized, settlements marks the beginning of a small yet crucial shift away from the state's self-professed monopoly over the domain of spatial planning and development.

A Temporal Reading

It is important to note that the time period around the preparation of Jaipur's second master plan during the early to mid-1990s, witnessed multidimensional turmoil while fragile coalition governments ruled at the central and state level. A precarious coalition, led by Prime Minister P.V. Narasimha Rao of the Congress party, replaced an even more precarious coalition led by Prime Minister Chandra Shekhar in June 1991. The new government inherited a grave economic situation, perhaps best exemplified by the International Monetary Fund (IMF) bailout to avert India's balance of payments (BoP) crisis in May 1991. Although barely maintaining a majority in the national parliament, the Rao government initiated economic reforms immediately after coming to power that allowed private sector participation in many walks of national life, including the urban sector (Frankel 2009).

Rajasthan also witnessed political turmoil around the same time. A coalition led by Bharatiya Janata Party (BJP), which was in the opposition at the central level, had formed a government in 1990.[7]

---

[7] In a study of regime differences across Indian states, John Harriss (2000) observes that two features characterize the politics of Rajasthan: persistence of upper caste/class dominance and a stable two-party contest between the right-wing BJP and the ostensibly centrist Congress. The urban politics of Jaipur reflects both the trends even as the BJP tends to dominate the election results. The BJP candidate won the national elections for the city's parliamentary constituency six times in a row between 1989 and 2009, and the BJP has always been the largest party in the Jaipur Municipal Corporation since its formation in 1994 following the 74th Amendment to the Constitution of India. Similarly, the aforementioned member of parliament (MP), an overwhelming majority of the past and present members of the state legislative assembly (MLA) from Jaipur's urban constituencies, and all the mayors thus far belong to the upper Brahman, Bania, or Rajput castes.

The centre dismissed this government, following the infamous Ayodhya incident in which a mob led by Hindu nationalists demolished a highly symbolic but unused mosque in December 1992, but the BJP won the majority of the constituencies in the follow-up elections held during 1993 and came back to power in Rajasthan. In the capital city of Jaipur, meanwhile, the long-standing demands of the residents of cooperative society colonies and informal settlements for regularization had been gathering storm (Gupta 1992). Backed by the local media, these residents demanded extension of basic civic facilities such as water and electricity supply lines, and tenure rights to homeowners that recognized the existence of their settlements and legitimized the ongoing development.

Reading Jaipur's second master plan against the tumultuous backdrop described above uncovers several phenomena. First, facing a rapidly changing polity, plan-makers turn to balancing a range of unforeseen challenges, competing interests, and popular demands. They, for example, invite the participation of private developers, while promoting the regularization of unauthorized settlements and emphasizing the official standing of the master plan at the same time. Observing the inability of the master-plan-based comprehensive planning approach to accommodate the urban dynamic in a timely and efficient manner, they also adopt a flexible approach towards future land uses, for instance, by allowing mixed-use activities in several land use categories. But eventually, authorities failed to follow-up on Jaipur's second master plan on many fronts as well, for instance, by not pursuing downstream actions such as the preparation of zonal development plans. Moreover, unlike the several residential and commercial schemes prepared to implement the first master plan, no such schemes were developed to implement the second master plan; except for a few disjointed residential schemes on JDA land at different locations far away from the urban area. Thus, by this time, it is increasingly clear that the transition from the princely planning to the new kind of master-plan-based comprehensive planning approach has proven to be much more strenuous than the post-Independence planners imagined.

Master Development Plan 2025, Jaipur Region 2011–25 (Jaipur Development Authority)

A Factual Reading

Prepared by the JDA's master plan cell, a new specialized unit set up for master-plan-related matters in 2008, the *Master Development Plan 2025* (MDP 2025) is a voluminous document of encyclopaedic nature. Comprising a total of 830 pages and numerous maps, the MDP 2025 is organized in four volumes and a separate map-book containing a detailed base map of the Jaipur region, existing land use 2009, and land utilization plan 2025 prepared with sophisticated GIS techniques using QuickBird satellite imagery and Cartosat images.[8] The four volumes of the MDP 2025 include Volume I: Introduction and Existing Profile (308 pages), Volume II: Development Plan (181 pages), Volume III: Satellite Towns and Growth Centers (304 pages), and Volume IV: Development Controls and Regulation (48 pages). Hardbound with colourful covers featuring prominent local buildings and explanatory maps, the well-composed document is printed on fine paper and contains many infographics.

Volume I opens with an introduction that describes the adopted planning approach based on an analysis at five different spatial scales (districts, regions, urbanizable areas, zones, and settlements) starting with the Jaipur district. Districts are administrative units, similar to counties in the United States of America (USA), and contain many rural and urban settlements. The next three chapters profile the Jaipur district, the Jaipur urban region, and the Jaipur urbanizable area or what the plan calls U1 area in exhaustive detail. At the broadest level, the plan authors divide the total land area into an ecological zone and the Jaipur city urbanizable area. The former encompasses

---

[8] However, it must be noted many large maps are divided into several A-4-size sheets, making them hard to read. Also, there is little differentiation of land uses, including no sub-classes based on the intensity of land uses. With a simplistic U1 and U2 classification and with no sub-categories of residential and commercial land uses, the master plan has arguably opened up hundreds of square kilometres of area for almost any kind of residential and commercial development activity in a flexible and development-friendly manner.

all the environmentally significant areas such as forests, hills, rivers, and agricultural lands while the latter includes three divisions: U1, which comprises all the existing use zones such as residential and commercial properties in various settlements; U2, which comprises a 3-kilometre buffer along the U3 area; and U3, which includes all the key roads such as national and state highways. Volume 1 concludes with a chapter titled 'Quality of Life' that envisions the region's future through the lens of sustainable development, visualized as the overlap between the environment, economy, and society.

Volume 2 describes the development plan that includes projections for a range of attributes, such as the future population, transportation, recreation, economy, and jobs, and attendant spatial requirements and their locations for the Jaipur region and U1 area. Volume 3 contains detailed development plans for the 11 satellite towns and four growth centres identified for development potential, while Volume 4 includes the development controls and regulation for the entire urban region. Prominent planning ideas include the following: focus on environmental issues such as depleting groundwater and diminishing green cover; attention towards transportation infrastructure and the development of regional settlements; and focus upon (in contrast with the earlier master plans) Jaipur's historical quarters and promotion of the tourism sector.

A Contextual Reading

During the plan-making process in the second half of the first decade of the twenty-first century, the following issues occupied banner headlines in vernacular newspapers that shape the local public discourse in significant ways.[9] First, the population of the urban region had increased fivefold from around 0.6 million at the time of the making of the first master plan in the early 1970s to around 3 million people, while the population of the district had increased from around 2 million to 5.25 million in the same period. Second, reducing groundwater quantity (95 per cent of the irrigation in the Jaipur district depends upon dug and tube wells as per the MDP 2025) and

---

[9] See *Dainik Bhaskar* (2009) and *Rajasthan Patrika* (2009), for instance. For the role of the regional press in shaping the local public discourse, see Jeffrey (2000).

deteriorating quality marked by high levels of salinity, nitrates, and fluorides had created many critical zones in the region. Third, a diverse range of factors such as the paucity of open spaces and parks in many unauthorized settlements, lack of investment in urban infrastructure, and the city's growing tourism industry (the number of visiting tourists had increased from around 0.5 million in 1989 to about 1.75 million in 2007) had combined to catalyse a growing public interest in spatial planning and economic development issues (Vidyarthi 2014).

However, in these respects, Jaipur was not an unusual case and many other Indian cities facing similar issues had begun to pay increased attention to the development of urban infrastructure and civic amenities (Mohanty 2014). Motivated by growing state revenues and the increasing importance of the urban economy, the central government, as described in Chapter 1, had introduced several urban initiatives and development finance mechanisms including the JnNURM launched in 2005. Mandating the preparation of individual city development plans (CDP), the JnNURM had begun to transfer central funds directly into India's 65 largest cities including Jaipur. Along similar lines, the state government had announced several policy measures such as the new township policy for private real estate developers in 2002, and began to experiment with executive actions such as the rehabilitation of informal settlements (City Managers' Association Rajasthan 2003).

When seen against this backdrop, it is clear that the authors of the MDP 2025 responded to the growing interest in civic issues by augmenting the spatial scope and sectoral comprehensiveness of their efforts on the one hand, while stressing on the shift away from the state's self-imposed burden of carrying out comprehensive urban development on the other. For instance, while the authors commissioned detailed studies for plan preparation (like the one carried out by the Geological Survey of India (GSI) analysing land capability of the entire urban region based on various factors such as geology, hydrology, and soil conditions that identified ecologically sensitive land uses) and prepared land use plans for peripheral settlements within the region,[10] they also note (*Master Development Plan 2011,*

---

[10] Here, it is important to note that during personal interviews, several planners pointed out that the land use plans are not detailed, and are frequently prepared in a hurried manner.

Vol. II: 164) the following about the state's role as a developer in the housing sector that constitutes the bulk of city land:

> The residential development has already gone in the hands of [the] private sector and the development agencies have acknowledged it through many policies. Land required for specific activities like industries, circulation and commercial activities should be directly acquired by the responsible agencies matching the land use proposals ... A new beginning is to be made for better implementation [of the master plan].

A Temporal Reading

Table 3.1, comparing and contrasting the three master plans commissioned so far, uncovers the gradual yet significant shifts in Jaipur's post-Independence city planning and development regime. While the plan audience has grown rather marginally to include the educated classes over time, plan supporters and sponsors now include key players such as progressive sections of the state leadership, higher judiciary, and local media. These players recognize that better planning efforts compared to the preceding ones can improve the quality of city life while strengthening the city's economic base. A good case in point is the authorities' growing support for Jaipur's tourist economy with increasing public sector efforts to conserve and promote the city's built heritage that aim to enhance the volume and flow of domestic and international visitors (Vidyarthi 2014).

Here, it is also important to note that a host of urban actors including public activists, real estate developers, emergent entrepreneurs, and elected officials along with the high court now actively influence both the making and implementation of master plans. The latter, for instance, has liberally admitted PILs, often through *suo moto* action based upon newspaper reportage, challenging both the non-implementation of master plan recommendations and the work-arounds state officials have employed to bypass the spatial development activities suggested by the master plan. Originally conceived to allow the state government to amend the rigid and segregated land uses assigned by the statutory master plans in exceptional circumstances, the process of CILU (change in land use) provides a good example of this phenomenon. In 2003, the editor-in-chief of a prominent local

newspaper, the *Rajasthan Patrika*, wrote a letter to the chief justice of the Rajasthan High Court, based on a running campaign in the newspaper about frequent changes in the master plan that, among other issues, have arguably contributed to the degrading quality of the urban environment. In the letter, he argued that state officials were frequently using CILU to permit unforeseen land uses. Converting the letter into a legal case, the court then ordered that changes to the master plan require a gap of five years after the plan notification, and each change has to be justified in the court (Sitapati 2013).

Although Jaipur's current master plan is only a few years old and this temporal reading lacks the benefit of hindsight, the growing interest of emergent planning players in the meaning and purpose of master plans is increasingly clear. In line with Achin Vanaik's (2004) observation that the Indian elites remain votaries of a strong state, there is little doubt that the overall planning approach remains comprehensive with the state machinery playing the most important role. When seen strictly from this perspective, the changes within the master planning approach seem marginal. But when the successive master plans are juxtaposed and examined together, the shifts—both within the documents and in the manner in which their authors understand the existing city and envisage its future—are clearly significant.

Taking Stock

This chapter began by asking: What impact the broader shifts in the country's polity have had on the nature and scope of master development plans for Indian cities? Have the focus and purpose of master plans changed at all or do these continue to offer more of the same? By locating Jaipur's three master plans in the city's historical trajectory of spatial planning and development, we have shown that the transition from the princely mode of planning to comprehensive master plans prepared by civil servant planners turned out to be more onerous than the leaders of independent India imagined. The transition, as envisaged, was never accomplished with the comprehensive master plans remaining only partially implemented. Meanwhile, a combination of diverse factors, such as the degrading quality of the urban environment, spread of unauthorized settlements, growing national and provincial economies, and the emergence of new social groups

and formations, had already begun to transform the Nehruvian planning model through small yet significant changes evident both in the making and implementation of master plans. Among other changes, we have shown that the following three shifts stand out for their salience:

1. In line with the large national/international trends, makers of Jaipur's master plans are now beginning to include other dimensions—such as social and economic—in addition to physical dimensions, the outcomes of which are yet uncertain.
2. Along similar lines, they are also beginning to pay attention to the regional scale. This is especially significant as Jaipur and many other secondary Indian cities are becoming large metropolises.
3. The overall approach has begun to shift away from a government-led planning model to a multi-actor one with additional oversight provided by non-profits and the judiciary.

What do these changes mean for our understanding of the spatial planning practice and literature in contemporary India? As argued in this chapter, the changes in the making and implementation of master plans suggest that the accompanying shifts in the domain of spatial planning and development are both broader and deeper than explained by the existing literature. While the literature on postcolonial planning, which focused upon the cultural resistance to externally imposed political and social projects, and the neoliberal scholarship, which focused upon the convergence of India's urban political economy and spatial changes with the models prevalent in other capitalist societies, explain significant aspects of India's ongoing urbanization, a close reading of Jaipur's three master plans across the factual, contextual, and temporal dimensions reveals small yet significant changes over time. These shifts, as illustrated in this chapter, include state's growing tolerance for regularization and reahibiltation of unauthorized settlements, emergent involvement of non-state actors in the planning and development process, and the shift way from a state-centered comrpehensive approach to spatial planning and development of places. Here, it is important to note that that the courts, some non-profit organizations, and sections of the media are wary that real estate developers and land speculators are exercising

outsized influence and, therefore, frequently serve as watchdogs often using press campaigns and right to information (RTI) mechanisms to provide additional levels of oversight.

On a broader note, the failure of institutional mechanisms to check land speculation remains a nation-wide problem. The 'Conclusion' to this volume, for instance, describes how a large proportion of the land purchased for private special economic zones (SEZs) remains undeveloped—raising concerns of land grab. We are not against private property rights, but the possibility that large-scale purchase of agricultural land by private developers, often in the hope that later, through dubious means, they would get the land regularized, remains worrisome. This kind of speculation often breeds corruption despite a vigilant civil society and activist judiciary. The CILU process, when viewed in this light, could be seen as encouraging land speculation and granting undue favours to real estate developers and land speculators. Planners and decision-makers need to account for these phenomena while making future plans that are equitable and just both in letter and spirit.

A generally similar planning approach and comparable social changes in other Indian cities, however, suggest that Jaipur's planning actors are potentially not the only ones seeking and carrying out changes in the making and implementation of official master plans. The next chapter takes up this story from another angle—explaining how external consultants have played a role in changing the planning regime in the southern city of Bangalore.

4

Learning by Doing

Urban Planning in Bangalore

*Neha Sami**

The question of who plans human settlements is a contentious one and difficult to answer. Several scholars writing on Indian cities have described the prevalence, extent, and efficacy of urban planning in India, especially the role of the government and its agencies.[1] There is also a vibrant body of literature on contemporary Indian cities explaining how non-state players create, support, and shape formal and informal planning processes as well as the politics of these processes. It is not difficult to see that while the overall responsibility for urban planning rests with state and city governments and their agencies, these are far from being the only stakeholders in the

---

* Neha Sami studies the urban politics of development and governance in post-liberalization India. She is part of the faculty at the Indian Institute for Human Settlements at Bangalore, India.

[1] See, for example, Chatterjee (2004); Ghertner (2011); Roy (2009); Sundaresan (2013). This issue is far from a new one. Debates on the role and efficiency of government planning in India have a long history both in academic writing as well as in the policy sphere.

process.[2] Highlighting the complex and intricate governmental machinery responsible for the planning of and in Indian cities, ongoing debates have also illuminated the wide range of actors and institutions involved in this process formally as well as informally, within the government as well as outside.[3]

Indian governments have long created venues and provided support for particular types of formal engagements with non-state actors (Brenner 2004; Sridharan 2008). Planners and policymakers in the Indian national and state governments have frequently invited a variety of advisors, consultants, and institutions to work with them. Examples range from Le Corbusier (in the case of Chandigarh), Otto Königsberger (for Bhubaneswar), and the Ford Foundation (in the case of the master plans for Delhi and Calcutta [now Kolkata]) (Banerjee 2009; Kalia 1985, 2006) to more recent examples of consulting firms such as McKinsey and Company, SCE-Creocean, and Infrastructure Leasing and Finance Services (IL&FS) working with city, state, and national governments (Ghosh 2005; Weinstein 2011).[4] The involvement of external actors—whether in the form of consultants such as McKinsey and Company; or international agencies such as the World Bank; or government officials, agencies, or government-sponsored delegations from other countries—is not unique to the Indian case. Understanding the planning process in Bangalore can help us better examine and raise questions about planning in other cities in the developing world. There are multiple influences that shape policy in cities of the Global South, where 'external input is sought to counter limited local capacity and confidence', and consequently, both the 'international development discourse and national policy imperatives frame local strategy formation' (Parnell and Robinson 2006: 337).

[2] See, for example, Baud and de Wit (2008); Benjamin (2008); Kundu (2011); Sami (2013a); Shatkin (2014); Weinstein (2008, 2011).

[3] In this chapter, the focus is only on the more formal and contractual engagements that non-state actors have had in Indian urban planning and policy. There is a wealth of information on the more informal ways in which a range of stakeholders work to influence policy in Indian cities. See, for example, Kamath and Vijayabaskar (2009); Sami (2013a); Shatkin (2014); Sundaresan (2013).

[4] There have undoubtedly been many colonial and Indian officials, as well as private individuals, who influenced the planning and building of Indian cities before and after Independence. A full discussion of these interventions, however, is beyond the scope of this chapter.

The idea of bringing in external 'consultants' is, therefore, not new or unusual to Indian urban planning. However, the specific nature and type of work that they do has undoubtedly changed over time, as has the process by which these experts are identified and engaged with. Consultants today are much more specialized, and are often brought in by government agencies to work with them on very specific issues that range from providing particular technical expertise to helping with process management. Another change, as Weinstein (2011) shows in the case of Mumbai, is that consultants today are more visible. With a few notable exceptions, while 'consultants on earlier schemes had advised Indian bureaucrats in the background' (Weinstein 2011: 250), today these experts are much more in the public eye, which often serves to legitimize development agendas that states feel both 'obliged and constrained to pursue' (Weinstein 2011: 252). Sood (2015: 5) also highlights the role that multinational real estate developers have played in transferring 'innovations such as township development expertise across national boundaries' as well as the role of multinational consulting firms 'in transferring policy paradigms to cities such as Hyderabad'.

This chapter focuses on the role that external experts or consultants have played in urban planning in Bangalore, and the influence they have had on the planning process itself in the city that has continued to grow rapidly (see Figure 4.1). It also uses the changing roles and varied engagements that Bangalore's government has had with external experts and consultants as the lens with which to understand the transitions in planning practice in the city. From Independence until the late 1990s, most of the planning in Bangalore was carried out by planners within the city government (Sundaresan 2013). This changed in 1999, when a new state government with a focus on urban reform came to power and appointed a consortium of consultants to develop the new master plan for the city (Kamath 2006; Sundaresan 2013). This chapter focuses on two distinct phases in Bangalore's planning history—from 1999 to 2004 (when the 2015 plan for the city was being developed), and from 2010 to the present (when the planning process itself was being rethought with the ongoing process of developing the 2031 plan).

Over time, Bangalore's primary planning agency—the Bangalore Development Authority (BDA)—has consciously moved away from

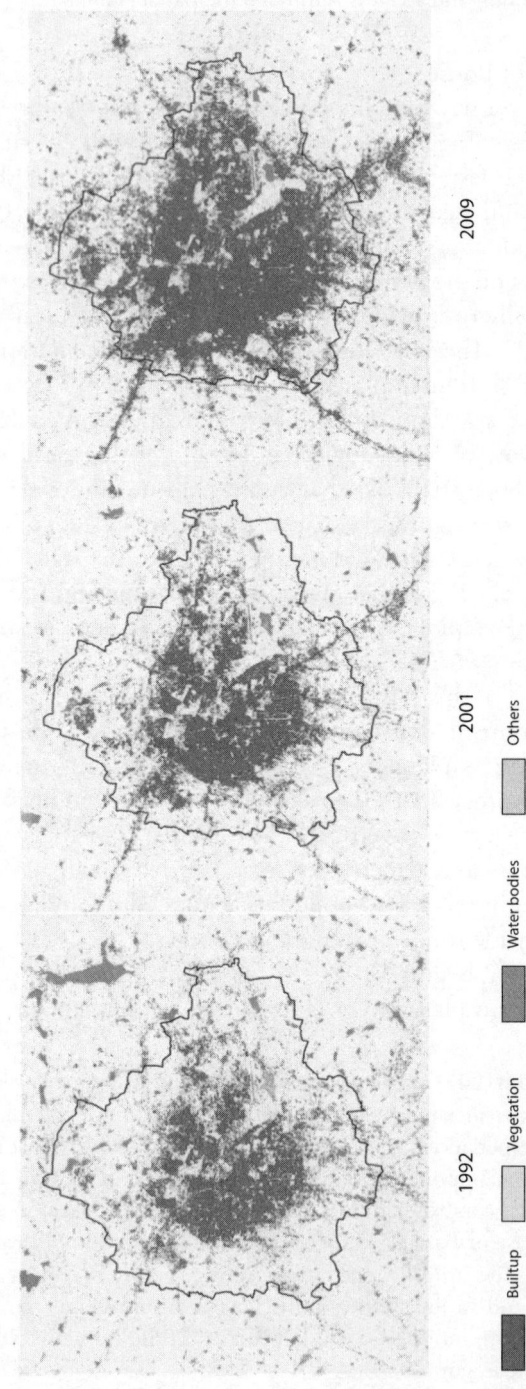

Figure 4.1 Bangalore Built-up Density, 1992–2009

Source: Author's own creation.

1992   2001   2009

Builtup   Vegetation   Water bodies   Others

developing in-house plans, preferring rather to turn to external consultants to carry out this process on the basis of a brief that the BDA provides. Their experiences of working with external consultants over the last two decades have shown, however, that better communication between the BDA (as client) and the consulting firms (as planners) (Friedmann 2011); being specific about the requirements of the assignment; and working closely with consultants, especially to provide local context as necessary, leads to better plan-making.[5] The challenges with plan implementation remain. Further, the shift in Bangalore's plan-making approach has been both slow and strenuous, shaped in part by the regime's dependence on the support of individual civil servants at the head of various urban local bodies (ULBs) that could help or hinder the planning process. It is also rigorously shaped by Karnataka's ongoing political and social dynamic: repeated regime change at the state level, incremental restructuring of the state and city relationship, and a growing demand from a rapidly expanding middle-class clientele for planning in urban and semi-urban areas.[6]

The data for this chapter comes from a range of primary and secondary sources: semi-structured interviews with the key actors involved (such as planners at the BDA, consultants involved with the planning process, other government officials, and knowledgeable observers), reviews of government documents, academic writing such as dissertations and papers, newspaper articles, and reports. Since several of the interview respondents requested anonymity, they are not explicitly identified or quoted in the text.

The chapter begins by briefly describing the role of external experts in urban planning of cities in the post-Independence India.

---

[5] Friedmann (2011) discusses the role of communication between planners and their 'clients' in some detail in his work on transactive planning, building on his own experiences as a consultant to governments in Latin America, highlighting the importance of planners, especially those who come from outside the local context, communicating with local officials or their clients.

[6] In the case of Bangalore specifically, the social and political dynamics between an elite middle class demanding better planning, the state government, and various senior politicians and bureaucrats have been well documented. For more see Ghosh (2005, 2006); Kamath (2006); Sami (2013b); Sundaresan (2013).

A discussion on the planning history of Bangalore, examining the role of both government agencies as well as other non-state actors in the process follows next. The rest of this chapter is devoted to understanding the process by which the 2015 and 2031 plans were developed; the relationship between external consultants, and city and state governments; and how the planning process in Bangalore itself has evolved and changed over this period. It aims to show how city governments in India are trying to be proactive about planning, and the challenges they face in doing so. There are lessons in this not only for other cities in India, but elsewhere as well, especially with governments and international and bilateral agencies turning to consultants for help and advice (Weinstein 2011). This work is also relevant in the context of the current global trend towards decentralization of power and administration to local urban and regional governments.

Working with 'Experts'

External advisors, practitioners, and experts on issues of urbanization, urban planning, and governance have been associated with Indian cities in a variety of ways since Independence. As Kalia (2006) writes, one of the challenges facing the newly formed government of independent India was the building of new cities for a new country: cities which had to house resettled refugees as well as new state capitals for newly formed states, but also needed to exemplify a break from India's colonial past, while representing the future. Faced with a lack of domestic architects and planners with the expertise to take on such a task, the Indian national and state governments turned to architects and urban planners outside the country (Kalia 1999).

The purpose of inviting foreign architects such as Le Corbusier, Albert Mayer, and Otto Königsberger was twofold. The first was to draw on their expertise and experience to define what an Indian city 'unfettered by tradition' (Kalia 2006: 134) as Prime Minister Jawaharlal Nehru demanded, would look like. Second, these initial experiments in city building were also meant to function as a training ground for home-grown urban experts including architects and planners who, in time, would be able to build and manage urban India (Kalia 1985). Neither of these two objectives, however, was

entirely fulfilled. Questions of what makes an Indian city and how to build it are among those that have challenged Indian and international architects and planners over the six decades since Independence, and continue to do so. Although Indian architects are now globally competitive, Indian cities are planned and managed largely by engineers, few of whom have a background in urban planning, architecture, or related fields (Banerjee 2009). There continues to be a shortage of trained urban professionals in Indian cities today and there is a severe lack of urban expertise within city, state, and national government agencies (2009).

Recognizing this constraint, governments and their agencies in India have frequently turned to a range of external 'experts' to help with the planning of their cities. Recent examples include the largest urban renewal programme in India, launched in 2005—the Jawaharlal Nehru National Urban Renewal Mission (JnNURM)— that encouraged greater private sector and civil society participation in the planning and governing of urban spaces. In particular, the JnNURM identified a set of pre-approved consultants that city governments could turn to for help with developing city development plans (CDPs) (Mahadevia 2006). The CDPs were needed to obtain funding under the programme (MoUD 2005, 2006). Additionally, in Bangalore as in other Indian cities, city and state governments have drawn on other non-state actors and organizations, such as the Bangalore Agenda Task Force (BATF) and the Mumbai First (Kamath 2006; Mumbai First 2012; Sami 2013b).

The shortage of trained professionals in ULBs combined with rapid urban spatial and demographic growth and the resulting growing demands placed on governments have meant that consultants continue to play an important role in Indian cities. Bringing in external experts is a means of accessing specialized knowledge that ULBs may not otherwise have access to. Moreover, as interview respondents frequently pointed out, it is often more efficient to hire consultants to do specific tasks rather than hire new staff, given various bureaucratic and regulatory constraints. Further, training government officials is time-consuming and expensive, the quality of the training imparted is rarely monitored, and there is rapid turnover and transfers within government agencies. Therefore, local governments often do not see the value of this capacity building.

Bringing in external advisors has indeed enabled local governments to avail themselves of the expertise that they are lacking. However, there have also been challenges in working with consultants, especially those that come from other geographical, social, and political contexts. This is increasingly true as multinational consulting firms become more involved with various governmental processes. During interviews conducted for this research, several government officials noted that the challenge of working with consultants is that they are often not aware of or grounded in the local environment for which they are planning. They also try to incorporate 'best practices' and processes from other locations, frequently without adapting them to the local context. In such cases, the final output produced is often difficult to use, especially if it does not speak to the ground reality. In the case of Bangalore, local (Bangalore-based) subsidiaries of the consulting firms completed the assignment. However, the staff at the local offices came from all over India as well as from other countries, leaving the question of understanding the local context unresolved. Contextualizing consultants' advice also becomes difficult because often there is little coordination between local government agencies and the consultants, once the contract is assigned.

Bangalore faced a similar situation in the 1990s, when the planning process for the 2005–15 comprehensive development plan was outsourced to a consortium led by a French consulting firm called SCE-Creocean (Ghosh 2005) as part of a larger urban development and reform agenda that came from the then chief minister, S.M. Krishna (Kamath 2006; Sami 2013b; Sundaresan 2013). The 2005–15 plan made an attempt to move beyond just land use planning to make Bangalore's city plan more comprehensive by integrating other concerns, such as transport and economic development, within the same plan document. The consortium also aimed to make it a more participatory process by involving other stakeholders. However, this effort did not succeed. Several concerns with the plan development process, as well as the final plan itself, remained unaddressed, and many recommendations of the plan were eventually not implemented (Kamath 2006; Sundaresan 2013).

Building on this experience, the primary planning agency in the city, the BDA, sought to rework the planning process, first by trying

to build capacity to develop the plan internally, and when that failed, by revising the process by which they invited and chose consultants to assist with spatial planning as well as the planning process itself. One of the primary goals of this revised process was to use it as an opportunity to build internal capacity and enable the urban planners at the BDA to carry out long-range planning and visioning (for at least a 10–15 year period), maintain continuity across plans, and avoid the trap of planning for the immediate future and the constant fire-fighting that comes with such a consideration. This time, however, building on their earlier experience, the BDA reworked the entire process by which they invited bids from consultants, and were also much more specific in laying out the terms of reference (ToR). This revised process continues the attempt made in the 2005–15 comprehensive development plan, to move beyond just land use planning, and aims to make the new 2031 plan more comprehensive and integrative.

At the time of writing this chapter, the BDA had awarded the contract to the Delhi-based arm of the Dutch company, Royal HaskoningDHV (Bhardwaj 2014a; Rohith 2014). However, due to the fragmented governance structure in Bangalore (Sami 2013b), there has been a continuing turf war between city and state agencies as well as various citizen groups about which agency has the responsibility for plan development and implementation (Bhardwaj 2014a, 2014b; Jacob 2008). With the establishment of the Bangalore Metropolitan Planning Committee (BMPC) in January 2014, several community groups and urban experts in Bangalore are now questioning the premise of the BDA's authority to continue with the master planning exercise (Bhardwaj 2014a, 2014b; *The Hindu* 2014b).[7,8]

---

[7] The term 'master plan' is often used with statutory standing in the Indian context to indicate a long-term plan of about 15 to 20 years, typically called a comprehensive plan or a general plan in the United States of America (USA) and elsewhere.

[8] The BMPC was established in January 2014. It is envisaged to be the nodal body for all development and planning in the Bangalore Metropolitan Area. See Government of Karnataka (2014); *The Hindu* (2014a).

Planning Bangalore

Urban planning work in Bangalore is pursued within the larger framework of urban planning in the state of Karnataka that is governed by the provisions of the Karnataka Town and Country Planning (KTCP) Act of 1961. Set up in 1976, the BDA is the local planning and development authority for the city of Bangalore. Planning and development functions were earlier distributed between separate local agencies such as the Bangalore Municipal Corporation, the City Improvement Trust Board, and the Bangalore City Planning Authority. These disparate agencies were combined into a single agency, the BDA (Sundaresan 2013). The BDA, therefore, functions as a public sector developer, a real estate provider, a planning authority, and a service provider.

The BDA is a parastatal body, governed by a Government of Karnataka (GoK) appointed board that comprises representatives from a range of state and local government bodies. Officials of the BDA are appointed from the bureaucracy by the GoK, and are not directly elected. The GoK also appoints a senior bureaucrat as the BDA commissioner, who is the chief executive officer and holds office for a term of three years.[9] In addition, the GoK appoints a secretary to manage the internal administration, and a town planning member (TPM) to act as the head of the BDA's planning division. The TPM is assisted by two deputy directors of planning and five assistant directors of planning (Sundaresan 2013).

The BDA is responsible for developing the master plan for the functional urban region of Bangalore (an area of approximately 1,300 square kilometres or 502 square miles), as well as for providing basic urban infrastructure such as housing layouts, open space, and civic amenities (Sundaresan 2013).[10] As per the requirements of the KTCP Act, the plan for the city is to be revised every 10 years (BDA 2012b). The BDA also regulates all major developments and land use changes within its jurisdiction. It is vested with the power to raise financial resources either independently or through government

[9] In practice, however, there are frequent reshuffles within the bureaucracy that lead to transfers of officers regardless of whether they have completed their term in office or not.

[10] The 'functional urban region' is the area that lies within the administrative jurisdiction of the BDA.

sources. The BDA can also acquire land through eminent domain, the market, or through various forms of leases with private and public institutions and individuals.

While the BDA is responsible for the development of the master plan for Bangalore, and the provision of urban infrastructure, the responsibility for implementing the plan is divided mainly between the BDA and the Bruhat Bengaluru Mahanagara Palike (BBMP) or the Bangalore municipal corporation, which is an elected body. In addition to the BDA and the BBMP, there are several other parastatal and local agencies that share the responsibility for different aspects of plan implementation, as illustrated in Table 4.1.[11]

There have been frequent attempts to transfer the responsibility of planning and development away from the BDA to various other agencies such as the BBMP, the Bangalore Metropolitan Region Development Authority (BMRDA), and the latest in that string— the BMPC. However, these attempts have so far been unsuccessful. Planning in Bangalore is consequently a very fragmented and often contentious process due to overlapping jurisdictions and responsibilities. However, this chapter is concerned mainly with the process of plan development that was carried out under the auspices of the BDA and, therefore, will focus largely on the role of the BDA since this is the main state-sponsored planning effort for the city.

A Brief History

Until the late 1990s, in-house planners employed by the city government—primarily the BDA—planned Bangalore. The BDA prepared its first CDP in 1984.[12] As Sundaresan (2013) writes, the 1984 plan was basic in its approach: the focus was largely on land-use, zoning, and building regulations for the functional urban region of Bangalore. The 1984 plan also officially established the greenbelt around Bangalore. As per the requirements of the KTCP Act, the 1984 plan was revised in 1995. Although it remained focused on

---

[11] For a more detailed description of these and their various functions, see Sudhira, Ramachandra, and Subrahmanya (2007); Sundaresan (2013).

[12] A master plan is called a City Development Plan (CDP) in Bangalore. This CDP is different from the CDP mandated by the JnNURM.

Table 4.1 Functional Distribution between Government Agencies in the Bangalore Metro Area

Agency	BBMP	BDA	BMRDA	BWSSB	BESCOM	BMRCL	BMTC	KSRTC	KUIDFC	KSCB
Jurisdiction	Municipal Limits	Urban Dvpt Area	Metro Area	Metro Area	Metro Area	Metro Area	Metro Area	Statewide	Statewide	Statewide
Water, sewerage, and drainage	Overlapping		Overlapping	Original					Overlapping	
Electricity	Overlapping				Original					
Transport: road	Overlapping	Overlapping	Overlapping				Original	Original	Overlapping	
Transport: rail						Original			Overlapping	
Road infrastructure	Original		Coordinating						Overlapping	
Development control	Overlapping	Original	Coordinating						Coordinating	
Slum clearance and rehabilitation	Coordinating								Overlapping	Original
Urban finance	Overlapping	Original	Coordinating						Original	
Tax collection	Original									

Legend: Original function · Overlapping function · Coordinating function

Source: Author's compilation based on various government documents and Sudhira, Ramachandra, and Subrahmanya (2007).

physical planning, the 1995 revision was a little more detailed in laying out the specifics of land use, zoning, and building regulations.

The elections for the Karnataka state legislature in 1999 changed the manner in which planning was done in Bangalore. For the first time since its inception, plan revision and development did not take place in-house within the BDA. This shift needs to be understood within the context of the larger transformation that was taking place within the state government. A series of ineffective chief ministers prior to 1999, as well as the purportedly growing corruption within the BDA had led to the perception that civic authorities in Bangalore were incapable of managing the city (Kamath 2006; Sundaresan 2013). Bangalore was also facing competition from other cities such as Hyderabad for attracting information technology (IT) and biotechnology firms, and for retaining its position as the preferred location of choice for these firms in India (Sami 2013b). As Kamath (2006: 112) writes, by the end of the 1990s, Bangalore and Karnataka were facing a 'governance deficit between governance needs and governance capacities and a deep-seated legitimacy crisis'. The newly elected Congress government that came to power in 1999 and its chief minister, S.M. Krishna, had a clear reform agenda that emphasized the need to build a 'modern' state using 'modern infrastructure' in an attempt to revitalize a declining state economy (Pani 2006).

'Reforming Urban Planning': Public–Private Partnerships, Planning, and the Bangalore Agenda Task Force

Aiming to break away from the older ways of functioning, the S.M. Krishna government focused on market-based reforms, and planned to tap into the vast pool of knowledge in Bangalore by extensively involving the corporate sector and other non-state actors in governance processes through public–private partnerships (PPPs)—the most prominent of these being the BATF (Kamath 2006; Sami 2013b). The BATF was one of the nine taskforces appointed by the state government to help with its reform agenda.[13] Through the BATF,

---

[13] The remaining task forces addressed health and family welfare, primary and secondary education, IT in higher education, infrastructure, the revival of the Government Flying Training School, women, IT, and biotechnology,

the government aimed to tap into the wide expertise and know-how of its members and their networks to help transform Bangalore into a world class city (Sukumar 2003).[14] This marked a shift in urban-planning-related decision-making in the city. In particular, state government officials and BATF core members took most of the decisions, consciously leaving out local government officials.

The chief minister and several senior bureaucrats felt that ULBs in Bangalore were inefficient and corrupt and needed to be reformed (Kamath 2006). They hoped to pressurize the ULBs, politicians, and lower-level bureaucracy into changing by involving corporate and other non-state actors through the BATF. Although the BATF's stated mandate to make Bangalore 'the best city in India' (Ghosh 2005: 4916) was rather vague, its actual focus was narrower: land and infrastructure development within Bangalore (Sami 2013b). While this narrow focus had wide-ranging impacts on local governance and policy practices in Bangalore, this chapter pays closer attention to the specific impacts it had on Bangalore's urban planning process.

The BATF, together with the BDA, undertook a range of projects that focused on spatial planning and development through the Metropolitan Spatial Data Infrastructure (MSDI) Initiative. However, in most instances, the BDA's role was minimal. With the involvement of the BATF in urban planning, there was an emphasis on the adoption of Western principles of urban design and planning, and the use of technology—especially geospatial techniques—to assist in the planning and development of the city. Some of the anticipated outcomes under the MSDI Initiative included the creation of a digitized land use map of Bangalore based on satellite images, the revision of the CDP, the development of a local server that would store and provide sub-city-level data, and the training and capacity-building of local officials (BDA 2012b; Kamath 2006).

Since the BDA lacked the capacity to implement these proposals, it recommended setting up a consortium of international and

emphasizing the state government's commitment to fostering IT and biotechnology development in Bangalore specifically, and Karnataka more broadly.

[14] For more on the BATF, its functioning, and Bangalore's other task-forces, see Ghosh (2005, 2006); Kamath (2006); Sami (2013b).

domestic consulting organizations. These organizations included four French public and semi-public companies (SCE-Creocean, Groupe Huit, APUR [Atelier Parisien d'Urbanisme], and IAURIF [Institut d'aménagement et d'urbanisme de la région Île-de-France], one university (Paris-Sorbonne University in collaboration with the London School of Economics), and two Indian survey companies (IramConsult and Magnasoft Consulting) (Kamath 2006; Sundaresan 2013).[15] SCE-Creocean led this consortium. The BATF played an important mediating role between the consortium of consultants and the BDA. One of the core members of the BATF acted as the liaison between the two, and conveyed the BDA's expectations to the consultants. Subsequently two BATF staff members were hired by the consortium to coordinate between the BDA and the consultants (Kamath 2006). The planning process, therefore, shifted from being one that was largely managed in-house by the urban planning staff at the BDA, to one where the BDA and its planners had little role to play in the development of the CDP.

One of the key aims for the hiring of consultants for developing the new CDP was to benefit from the knowledge and the technical expertise of a wide range of individuals and institutions that may not have been available to the BDA otherwise. The BATF had also aimed to use this process to build capacity internally within the BDA to enable local officials to carry out long-term visioning and planning, through training and collaboration during the CDP preparation process (Kamath 2006). The consortium for the new CDP for 2005–15 brought together over 100 experts including urban planners, architects, economists, demographers, geographic information system (GIS) and IT specialists, geographers, cartographers, and infrastructure and transport specialists (Sundaresan 2013). The consultants used administrative data from local and state government agencies, and field-based data collected from numerous locations in the city, to develop the database that informed the preparation of the CDP.

---

[15] The involvement of the French consultants and the Paris-Sorbonne University was supported through a loan from the French government for land management under the Indo-French Financial Protocol. The Protocol was signed in 2003 (Kamath 2006).

The new CDP was a much larger document than previous plans, both in its scope and aims. It attempted to integrate spatial planning with social, economic, and infrastructure planning. The entire process took approximately two and a half years.

The BDA undertook the preparation of the CDP (2005–15) with considerable help from the BATF. Although officially, the plan was supposed to be developed in collaboration with the planners at the BDA, there was little actual interaction between the BDA staff and the consultants.[16] Most of this interaction took place through the BATF. The BATF and its members were almost solely in control of all the actual decision-making. They suggested bringing in external consultants to assist with the planning process. Together with state government officials, the BATF oversaw the process of selecting the consultants, and the reform of the planning process as suggested by their proposal. These decisions were implemented without consulting the BDA planning staff (Ghosh 2005; Kamath 2006).[17]

The plan was finally submitted to the GoK for approval in 2005. However, several objections were raised. Most of these focused on the plan development process. There were concerns about the undemocratic nature of the process, especially because of the deep involvement of the BATF and its staff, often by excluding the BDA officials. The lack of public participation was another concern. Although the BDA had committed to a public consultation process, no such consultations were held during the plan preparation process (Kamath 2006; Sundaresan 2013). Further, although the plan was subjected to public review, the objections raised were not taken into consideration.

Given the minimal interaction that the planning staff at the BDA had with the consortium, there was little scope for collaboration between the two, nor was there enough attention given to the training and capacity-building component during the plan revision process. The BDA, therefore, would not have had the capacity to

---

[16] Personal interviews with town planning officials (BDA) in 2014, Bangalore.

[17] Also, personal interviews with town planning officials (BDA) in 2014, Bangalore.

continue with the newly reformed planning process or to maintain the extensive spatial database that had been planned, should the CDP be implemented. Although the GoK eventually approved the 2005–15 CDP in 2007, it was mired in litigation (Jacob 2008), and was not implemented (Khanna 2014).[18]

In addition to the plan being under litigation, there was also political instability at the state level in Karnataka. No political party won clear majority in the 2004 state legislative elections. Consequently, the three leading parties formed a coalition government. However, this arrangement was rendered unstable because of disagreements over power sharing, and Karnataka was finally brought under President's Rule in 2007 until fresh elections were scheduled in 2008. Although the Bharatiya Janata Party (BJP) won the 2008 elections, the state suffered from more political instability during the BJP's tenure. The newly appointed chief minister had to face rebellion within the party and fight allegations of corruption. The political instability at the state level impacted planning and decision-making at the local level with the city governments maintaining the status quo but being unable to implement new plans or modify existing plans. During this time, there was also not much progress made in the litigation against the 2005–15 CDP.

The change in the planning process in Bangalore was brought about largely by an elite middle-class coalition—the BATF—with little reference to the local planning authority. This was a deliberate attempt on the part of the chief minister and senior bureaucrats to supersede local planning agencies, which they felt were corrupt and inefficient (Sami 2013b). The BATF, on its part, insisted on bringing in Western 'experts' who would reform the planning process in Bangalore and help make it a 'world-class city' (Ghosh 2006; Kamath 2006; Sami 2013b). Despite the passage of the 74th Constitutional Amendment that mandated devolution of power to ULBs, most of the key planning-related decisions were taken by an urban coalition made up of the chief minister, senior state-level bureaucrats, and elite middle-class activists. The 2005–15 CDP reflected the priorities of

[18] The petition brought against the GoK and the BDA states that the BDA was 'overreaching its powers' by passing the master plan, which legally comes under the purview of the BMRDA (Jacob 2008).

this coalition. The BDA would, therefore, have had to implement a plan for which they had provided little input.

Learning by Doing: Urban Planning in Bangalore after the Bangalore Agenda Task Force

The S.M. Krishna government failed to win the state elections in 2004. Since the BATF derived its power largely from the backing and support of Krishna and the government, its influence dwindled as well (Kamath 2006; Sami 2013b). However, the impact of the BATF's recommendations was far-reaching. In particular, the BDA began to embrace the use of modern technology and spatial analysis tools to help with the planning process. The use of external consultants also became an increasingly popular method by which the BDA secured expertise that it lacked. Gradually, the BDA also began to outsource to consultants the tasks that were earlier done in-house.

The then-commissioner of the BDA, Bharat Lal Meena was instrumental in making the BDA embrace newer technology to make the plan development and revision process smoother and more transparent. He decided to build on the idea of incorporating modern technology in the planning process that had emerged during the BATF period. In order to do so, he emphasized the need to build internal capacity within the BDA to be able to access and use technology (especially tools such as GIS and satellite imaging) to help generate and manage information that would enable informed planning for Bangalore.[19] There was also a renewed focus on building a spatial database of Bangalore for the BDA through various means including the creation of an in-house GIS cell in partnership with the local academic institutions, and the development of a web-based application called Drushti (which means 'sight' in Kannada, the state language of Karnataka). Using Google Earth as the base, this application allowed users to superimpose the map of the proposed master plan on the existing land use and survey map of Bangalore to assess and understand potential changes that would take place as

---

[19] Personal interviews with academics in 2014, Bangalore; Personal interviews with town planning officials (BDA) in 2014, Bangalore.

the plan was implemented, enabling a wide variety of stakeholders to interact with the master plan (Manjusainath 2013).

However, with the end of Meena's tenure at the BDA, several of these initiatives dwindled.[20] The BDA also faced other challenges especially with internal capacity building. One of the key constraints was the lack of funding within the BDA. Further, planning staff were willing to devote little time to learn new techniques, and they increasingly began to use the in-house GIS cell as consultants to carry out the required spatial analysis rather than learn how to conduct such analyses themselves.[21] This had two side effects: First, the planners at the BDA began to mechanically use the maps and other data generated by the consultants as they were used to doing earlier, and the benefits of actually incorporating the spatial analysis within the planning and visioning process were lost. Second, the consultants that staffed the in-house GIS cell lost interest in the process, since the original purpose of bringing them on board was very different from what they ended up doing. Moreover, given the political instability in the state, there were frequent reshuffles within the bureaucracy, leading to several changes to the BDA's leadership. Realizing that this process was not working, the BDA revisited its approach to planning, and turned once again to consultants to assist with the plan revision and preparation process.

As mentioned earlier, the KTCP Act requires that the BDA update the CDP every 10 years (BDA 2012b). Despite the fact that the last CDP (the 2005–15 plan) had not been implemented and was still in litigation, in 2012, the BDA began the process for developing a new CDP for the horizon year 2031 (BDA 2012a). However, this time, the process was different. Building on the lessons learnt from the earlier experience with the BATF, the BDA issued a call for a Request for Proposals (RfP) from interested consultants to assist with plan preparation. According to interview respondents at the BDA, the process by which the consortium had been built under the BATF and the Krishna government had not been very clear or transparent—the

[20] Personal interviews with town planning officials (BDA) in 2014, Bangalore.
[21] Personal interviews with academics in 2014, Bangalore; Personal interviews with town planning officials (BDA) in 2014, Bangalore.

BDA had not been involved at all in the identification and selection of the consultants, and had very little involvement during the plan preparation stage (Ghosh 2006).[22] This time, however, the process of soliciting consultants was very different—the main distinction being that the BDA was closely involved in all aspects of decision-making.

To start with, the CDP revision process was initiated by the BDA, not by the state government. The BDA's planning staff was closely involved in drafting the new RfP soliciting applications, as well as in creating the new ToR for consultants. The evaluation process, and the shortlisting and final selection of the consultants were also carried out by the BDA. Drawing on the help of a local academic institution, the BDA drafted new ToR that were incorporated into the RfP call (BDA 2012b). The new ToR were based on established international protocols used by multilateral agencies such as the World Bank.[23] The ToR emphasize the need to move away from single-dimensional, land-use-planning-based approaches to urban planning and broaden the scope of the CDP beyond spatial planning and development control (BDA 2012b).

Some of the key changes that the new ToR required include (BDA 2012b):[24]

- Creation of a coordination mechanism between various government stakeholders involved in urban planning, economic development, and service provision to enable the stakeholders to provide input on the plan and to review the output, that is, the draft CDP.
- Integration and reconciliation of key sector plans including transport, infrastructure development, economic development, and environmental plans. These should also be integrated into a geospatial database.
- Sensitivity towards the need to develop a liveable, economically and socially inclusive, environmentally sustainable, and economically

[22] Also, personal interviews with town planning officials (BDA) in 2014, Bangalore.

[23] Personal interviews with academics in 2014, Bangalore.

[24] For more details on the specific ToR, see BDA (2012b).

robust and innovative city; and involvement of all key stakeholders, especially the poor and vulnerable in its visioning, development, and implementation.

- A clearly articulated plan for public participation during the plan development and review process.
- Chosen consultants to assist the BDA with plan implementation and review, and to build internal capacity and establish standard procedures within the organization, especially those related to the use of GIS-based technologies.
- Consultants to ensure that the plan was dynamic and adaptive to change.
- Plan preparation process and the plan itself to be compliant with the Right to Information (RTI) Act (2005).

The BDA's revised process is much more progressive than that of several other cities in India. It includes several features that are not considered in other urban plans, such as, the integration of various sectoral plans, the creation of a coordination mechanism between government agencies, and the establishment of a clear process for public participation. It indicates the desire to move closer to internationally accepted norms to understand urban planning as being much broader than simply spatial or land use planning. In this case too, the BDA drew on the knowledge and understanding of local academics and practitioners to help revise the CDP preparation process, and the RfP. However, building on their earlier experience with the development of the CDP 2005–15, the BDA worked closely with these experts and were able to articulate their requirements clearly.

The entire process of developing the new ToR, and soliciting and evaluating applications took approximately a year and a half. In early 2014, the BDA announced that it had awarded the contract to a Dutch company with an India office based in Delhi—Royal HaskoningDHV (Rohith 2014). However, while the BDA has commissioned the consultants and issued the requisite work orders, the fate of this process and the plan itself remains unclear. There have been objections raised, questioning the premise on which the BDA is taking on the responsibility of developing the new CDP, given the establishment of the new Metropolitan Planning Committee (MPC) in January 2014, although no formal litigation process has been

initiated at the time of writing (Bhardwaj 2014a). While the process of developing the 2031 CDP was an improvement over earlier iterations, it remains to be seen whether these lessons will continue to inform decision-making at the BDA for future plans.

Lessons Learned

The process of revising the CDP for Bangalore has implications not only for planning Indian cities but also cities in other parts of the world. This becomes especially important with the global push for devolution of power to local governments, and the increasing role that non-state actors, especially consultants, are playing in urban planning processes. As Parnell and Robinson (2006) show, this global push towards decentralization comes from particular academic and policy discourses that have emerged largely in the context of the United States of America (USA) where there are much greater levels of municipal autonomy and devolution. Cities in less wealthy countries are encouraged by both international financial institutions as well as donor governments to promote decentralized governance structures and decision-making. However, given the (often) weak capacities of local governments, officials and politicians turn to a wider range of local development agents, whether from civil society, the private sector, international financial institutions, or donor governments.

For Bangalore, and specifically the BDA, the BATF's emphasis on using modern technology and spatial data to develop the 2005–15 CDP made the BDA aware of the advantages of using more modern technology and also made planning staff realize that they lacked these technologies and the know-how to use them. The BDA briefly attempted to build capacity internally, but this did not succeed. The planners at the BDA did not see the value addition of learning these skills and preferred to outsource the data collection and analysis to external consultants. However, it was clear that merely appointing consultants to undertake discrete parts of the plan development process would not be a solution either. To be meaningful, the plan revision and preparation process needed to be conducted in close collaboration with the planning officials at the BDA. The new ToR for the 2031 CDP reflected this realization.

However, the inability of the external consultants to 'anticipate and negotiate the local institutional traditions and ... build broader support among the public and local civil society' (Banerjee 2009: 206) jeopardized the implementation of the 2005–15 CDP. It also limited the extent to which the innovations that these consultants and the BATF brought were absorbed by the BDA and other ULBs. Banerjee's (2009) reflections on why the planning expeditions from the USA to India were not more successful remain relevant—the BATF and its consultants especially, like the American planners, proposed important innovations in the planning process, but were unable to ensure their widespread use because they failed to build Indian capability to engage with these innovations. Nor did they anticipate how the local political and institutional context would impede implementation (Banerjee 2009). The other issue was the lack of communication and coordination between the external consultants, local planning officials, and the larger public. The ability of consultants to absorb and incorporate local 'experience-based' knowledge into the plan itself is critical to develop a dynamic plan document (Friedmann 2011).

However, the struggle that the GoK and the BDA have faced with respect to assigning responsibility for planning for Bangalore needs to be understood within the larger framework of urban governance in India. Despite the devolution of power to ULBs mandated by the 74th Constitutional Amendment Act (1992), implementation has been piecemeal (Sami 2013b). In the case of most Indian states (including Karnataka), 'the local or city government has little autonomy in decision-making and what little there is, is hindered by political and bureaucratic hurdles' (Sami 2013b: 125). Most of this power rests with the state government—the devolution of responsibilities and power is at the discretion of the state government. The powers that ULBs have are not the same across the country because state governments have not uniformly devolved power. Given this situation, it is challenging for ULBs to be proactive about reform, since they lack the authority to take and implement decisions. In addition, governance in Indian cities is extremely fragmented. Consequently, governments and their agencies are currently not capable of meeting the increasing demands placed on them by international capital, inter-city competition, and urban residents. This has led to governments turning to non-state actors for expertise and technical knowledge.

Also as argued earlier (Sami 2012, 2013b), as governments come to rely on non-state actors such as consultants and on task forces such as the BATF, a more hybrid model of urban planning seems to be emerging in Indian cities, where these actors are playing an increasingly important role in policy and planning decision-making. Such trends are evident in Indian cities such as Pune, Delhi, and Mumbai, and in other parts of the developing world where governments are increasingly turning to various non-state actors such as civil society groups and private consultants (Ghertner 2011; Kundu 2011; Parnell and Robinson 2006; Sami 2012; Weinstein 2011).

In part, this evolving approach to urban planning in Bangalore and other Indian cities reflects a growing trend where governments are gradually withdrawing from active service provision and investment, relying increasingly on non-state actors to fill the gap. This is not to indicate that governments are in any way becoming less powerful or relevant, but rather to illustrate their changing role. The involvement of the private sector and other non-state actors continues to take place within a specific framework set by the governments and their agencies.

There are also concerns about how this shift—from government- to non-state-actor- provided services—will impact the manner in which urban residents, especially marginalized groups such as the urban poor, interact with the government (Coelho, Kamath, and Vijaybaskar 2011; Kundu 2011). This was and remains a key issue in the Bangalore CDP preparation process—while the BDA committed to a public participation process during the revision of the CDP 2005–15, it did not deliver on that promise. Consultants and other non-state actors, unlike governments and their agencies, are not required to keep the interests of the wider community in mind, and so may focus only on selected groups. It becomes important, then, to make certain that government agencies and officials work closely with consultants (and other non-state actors) to ensure that the planning and policymaking processes are equitable and speak to a wider range of interests and constituents.

PART III

NEW SETTLEMENT PATTERNS AND EMPIRICAL OUTCOMES

5

Rethinking the Rural (and the Urban)

The dramatic and unexpected increase of census towns[1] (CTs) in India's last census (Census 2011) stimulated discussions about classifying and recognizing areas as 'rural' or 'urban'. Almost every country in the world uses this dichotomous rural and urban typology as the main form of reporting spatial and population distribution. This is done primarily to recognize the differences in the physical, social, and economic characteristics of the geography, albeit very broadly. In many developed countries the use of the rural–urban classification serves to direct development and planning strategy, as well as inform how policy is created and implemented. These classifications are also important because they restrict or permit a region's access to government funding for capital projects, welfare programmes, and services. Ram Bhagat (2005: 61) goes a step further by saying, 'the categorization of rural and urban is the first step for initiating local governance' and this has implications for the political empowerment of marginalized communities, and their potential revenue bases.

---

[1] India's Planning Commission explained 'census' towns as agglomerations that grow in rural and peri-urban areas, with densification of populations, that do not have an urban governance structure or the requisite urban infrastructure of sanitation, roads, and so forth.

In India, however, as throughout the rest of South Asia, with the emergence of new forms of urbanization and evolving patterns of physical development (such as CTs, *desakota* regions,[2] edge cities, and transitional and outgrowth areas), a clear divide between rural and urban does not exist anymore. This has resulted in both government agencies as well as scholars struggling with the question of which frameworks are the most relevant to understand the changing patterns of settlements, and to plan for relevant programmes and services for their residents. Many scholars and government agencies are, however, beginning to acknowledge that the rural–urban dichotomy is outdated and is inadequate for capturing the essence and needs of diverse forms of settlements. It forces us to rethink the nature of 'rurality' in contemporary India and beyond.

This chapter examines India's criteria for rural and urban settlements and their benefits and challenges. It begins with an overview of urban and rural definitions used across various regions of the world. It then dissects India's current use and the efficacy of the rural–urban dichotomy, given the spatial transformations that India is currently going through. Using CTs as an illustration, it elicits real and potential challenges built into the process of reclassification. At the end, it argues for a classification system that respects the continuum of rural and urban, and concludes by putting forward suggestions that might find resonance in the Indian context.

Classifying Rural and Urban

The classification of settlements into rural or urban for statistical purposes has been used by the United Nations (UN) since 1952 (Champion and Hugo 2004). Generally, a minimum threshold of total population and density is required for a settlement to be classified as urban. However, a standard definition of urban does not exist across countries. This diversity is, in fact, supported by the UN so as to recognize the national differences in the characteristics which distinguish urban from rural areas.

---

[2] These are corridors of mixed agricultural and non-agricultural activities connecting large cities of Southeast Asia. This term is explained and discussed in the next chapter.

Virtually all countries have designated and defined urban areas and treat the remainder—the residual territory or 'anything that is not urban'—as rural (Champion and Hugo 2004). The typical set of criteria used to define an area as urban include population size, population density, built-up area, political status, labour force engaged in non-agricultural work, and presence of particular services or activities. Different countries have used these criteria in different ways and combinations to suit their individual context, but the size and density of population still remain the universal indicators of this classification. They are presumed as simple and directly correlate with other economic and spatial variables. 'The size of population as a criterion is dependent on the geographical area, whereas density is not susceptible to the variations of area boundaries' (Qadeer 2000: 1591).

The United States of America (USA) employs a similar criterion list but with different population and density thresholds. Urban areas in the USA are composed of residential, commercial, and non-residential urban land uses that are contiguous agglomerations of 2,500 inhabitants, which generally have population densities of at least 400 persons per square kilometre (or 1,000 persons per square mile). These urban areas are subcategorized into urbanized areas that include central cities, their surrounding fringes (suburbs) that contain populations greater than 50,000 people, and urban clusters that have minimum populations of 2,500 and maximums of 49,999.

The United Kingdom (UK), Sweden, and Brazil, on the other hand, identify urban settlements based on 'built-up areas' (BUAs) (Bhagat 2005). Continuous BUAs in the UK are deemed urban. The UK's Office for National Statistics (2013) defines built-up area as land that is 'irreversibly urban in character', meaning that they are characteristic of a town or city. They include areas of built-up land consisting of a minimum of 20 hectares (200,000 m^2). Any areas with less than 200 metres between them are linked, to become a single built-up area (Office for National Statistics 2013: 4). In Sweden, BUAs must have 200 inhabitants with homes no greater than 200 metres apart. There is no minimum requirement for the land area. In Brazil, on other hand, urban areas are settlements where buildings, streets, and intense forms of human occupations exist;

these areas are classified as 'urbanized' under the legal statutes governing the administrative division of its territory. Interestingly, Brazil defines and classifies rural under multiple categories, based on the distance from an urbanized area.

The above-described criteria are considerably different from the criteria adopted by the South Asian countries of Bangladesh, Sri Lanka, and Pakistan. Here, settlements are classified as urban if they are governed by a municipal corporation, a municipality, an urban council, or a town committee (United Nations [UN] 2015), a criterion that is a colonial legacy. Nepal, on the other hand, uses a single criterion for measuring levels of urbanization—population. Due to the geographical nature of Nepal and its minimal industrialization and development, urban settlements are defined as those with populations of 9,000 inhabitants or greater. Meanwhile, China has taken a differential, privileged approach towards rural–urban classification. It uses a political criterion to determine rural and urban areas—the number of town government seats affiliated with a region (Bhagat 2002).

Unlike South Asian countries, Indonesia uses gradients of 'urban-ness' and 'rural-ness' for delineating urban and rural areas (Champion and Hugo 2003, 2004). It defines urban as meeting the following three criteria:

1. A population density of more than 5,000 persons per square kilometre.
2. Less than 25 per cent of households engaged in agriculture.
3. Availability of urban facilities such as schools, hospitals, banks, and post offices.

Each community is graded between 1 and 10 (where 1 is low and 10 is high) on each of these three criteria, with a maximum overall score of 30. Areas that score 23 or above are classified as urban, and those with 17 or below as rural. The ones in the middle undergo a field assessment to ascertain whether they should be classified as urban or rural. This method is more complex than those of some of the other countries, but still eventually results in all regions being classified as either rural or urban. The key feature to note here is that the process of classification seems to encapsulate the idea of the

'degree of urban-ness', and has the potential to create one or more categories between urban and rural, to reflect the continuum.

In Canada, urban areas or 'population centres' use a multi-criteria approach and are defined as being areas with minimum populations of 1,000, and which have a density of 400 people or more per square kilometre (Statistics Canada 2011). Most recently, the 2011 census attempted to demonstrate the country's dynamic landscape by breaking down population centres into small (1,000–29,999), medium (30,000–99,999), and large urban (100,000+) categories to reflect 'the existence of an urban–rural continuum' (Statistics Canada 2011).

However, the issue that remains is how to measure and classify regions outside of metropolitan areas. For this, Statistics Canada developed and applied the concept of a metropolitan influence zone (MIZ). This concept follows Bourne and Simmons' (2004) approach, which is based on the ideas of interaction and interdependence. This approach argues that individual cities do not exist in isolation; cities grow and change because of their roles in large urban systems. They are affected by growth or decline of their hinterlands and through their interactions with other urban places. In their words, 'the core of the [urban systems] concept rests on the importance of linkages and interaction—the flows of people, goods, capital profits, information and ideas among urban nodes' (Bourne and Simmons 2004: 267).

Essentially, an MIZ is a zone defined by the degree of influence that a larger urban centre exerts outside of its urbanized territory. This influence is largely determined by the percentage of the zone's employed residents who commute to work in a neighbouring census metropolitan area (CMA).[3] Specifically, a rural area can be strongly influenced, moderately influenced, weakly influenced, or not influenced at all by a neighbouring CMA, divided as follows (shown schematically in Figure 5.1):

- Strong MIZ: 30 per cent residents commute.
- Moderate MIZ: 5–29 per cent residents commute.

[3] A CMA is formed by one or more adjacent municipalities centred around a core. A CMA must have a total population of at least 100,000. Of these residents, 50,000 or more must live in the core. A census agglomeration

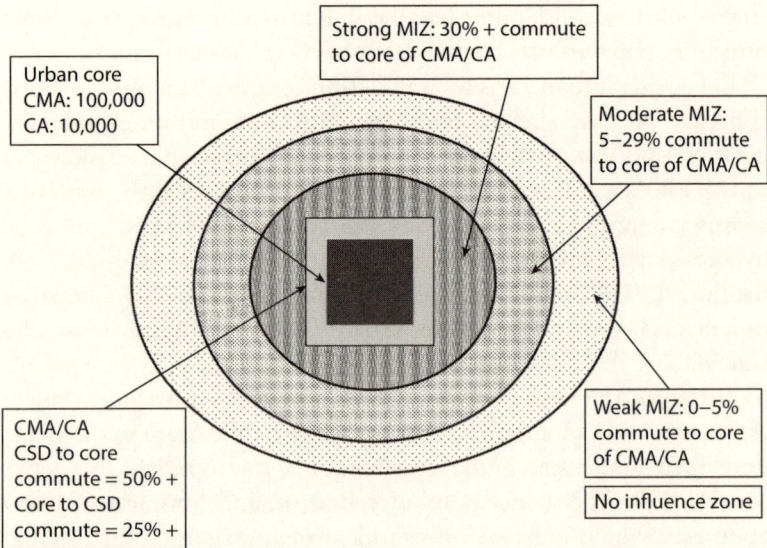

Figure 5.1   Schematic Representation of the Metropolitan Influence Zone (MIZ) Concept
Source: Generated by the authors.

- Weak MIZ: More than 0 per cent but less than 5 per cent residents commute.
- No MIZ: No residents commute.

This classification pays greater attention to the degree of influence of a metropolitan area by measuring physical accessibility and the work commute patterns of people rather than just the place they live in. In doing so, it raises questions about the entire premise of using place as a way of distinguishing rural from urban. It recognizes people's increasing mobility, their changing work places, and the significant time they spend away from their usual residence. Many Canadian

---

(CA) is also formed by one or more adjacent municipalities centred around a core, but the core here must have a population of at least 10,000. A census sub division (CSD) is a general term for municipalities, which are designated by provincial/territorial legislation or areas treated as municipal equivalents, Indian reserves or Indian settlements for statistical purposes.

studies have successfully used this idea to compute the economic health of a rural area.

The Organisation for Economic Co-operation and Development (OECD)[4] has adopted a typology that combines population density, percentage of a population living in rural communities, and the size of the urban centres. For instance, it defines a predominantly rural region as a region that has more than 50 per cent of its population living in rural communities, where a *rural community* has a population density of less than 150 persons per square kilometre. An *intermediate region* has 15 to 50 per cent of its population living in a rural community. A *predominantly urban region* has less than 15 per cent of its population living in a rural community. This typology is based on the regional geography, settlement patterns, and administrative units such as a municipality. The OECD has followed the Canadian model of distinguishing between rural regions that are located close to larger urban centres and those that are not, to provide a regional typology that works beyond Europe and North America. However, it does not adhere to the Canadian idea of commute patterns. Still, this type of classification moves away from the dichotomous category of rural and urban, and employs the notion of the 'degree of rurality', thus acknowledging the urban–rural continuum.

Scholarly attempts, such as those of Cromartie and Swanson (1996) and Butler and Beale (1994), show the urban–rural continuum in the American context by combining these characteristics—distance from a metro core, population size and density, commute patterns, and level of 'urban character'—in concentric bands moving away from the core.

Coombes and Raybould (2001) argue that increasing complexity in settlement patterns and socio-economic conditions means no single measure can represent all the different aspects of settlement structure. They suggest at least three key dimensions to contemporary settlement patterns:

- *Settlement size* is a key indicator of urbanity (Wirth 1938), and relates to the range of facilities and the mix of the economic base.

---

[4] The OECD is a group of 34 countries founded in 1961 to stimulate economic progress and world trade.

- *Concentration* is usually measured in population density, which affects the potential for economic and social interaction, the spread of ideas, the transport network, and the level of local service provision.
- *Accessibility* is about access to basic goods, services, and employment, which shapes demographic and other socio-economic processes.

Distinguishing Rural and Urban in India

In 2011, the absolute increase in India's urban population was—for the first time in history—more than that of the rural. However, an integral part of understanding this growth is the way in which rural and urban settlements are determined and classified. The current classification of urban is based on the following three criteria:

1. Population no less than 5,000.
2. Density of population at 1,000 persons per square mile or 400 per square kilometre.
3. 75 per cent of male workers engaged in non-agricultural sector.

For these areas to become urban in an administrative sense, they must have a municipal corporation, municipality, or notified area committee (also known as a nagar panchayat)[5].

The Indian definition of urban is dualistic in nature as it incorporates an administrative component—as in many South Asian countries—as well as demographic criteria (Bhagat 2002). The latter is of particular significance, as both population size and economic function are key indicators that distinguish rural from urban. During the British colonial era, Indian urban areas or statutory towns (STs) (explained later in the chapter) were classified according to a combination of administrative criteria (municipal corporation, municipality, cantonment board, or a nagar panchayat) and geographic criterion, which stated that urban areas must have a minimum of 5,000 permanent residents. This definition remained in place from 1911 until 1961, when the census criteria for STs were amended and augmented to include

---

[5] A nagar panchayat represents a settlement that is in transition from rural to urban.

requirements of a population density of 1,000 people per square mile (400 per square kilometre) and a minimum of 75 per cent of the population engaged in non-agricultural work.

Further amendments were incorporated a couple of decades later that recognized the following changes: (a) female workers are to be excluded from the 75 per cent of workers engaged in the non-agricultural sector and (b) industrial workers employed in livestock, forestry, fishing, hunting, plantations, orchards, and related activities are considered to be doing agricultural work (previous censuses had defined these industries as non-agricultural) (Bhagat 2005). Even these changes continued the idea of the agricultural–industrial dichotomy, and have been paramount in defining urbanization in the Indian context, not to mention in introducing a serious gender bias.

The presence and density of a population and the percentage employed in non-agricultural work were thought to be indicators of industrial activity. Consequently, they were understood as major drivers of the urbanization process. This is still a key measure of urban and rural designation despite the fact that it falters in the current economic situation, which is much more complex. This measure continues to persist within India's present classification system, which has yet to acknowledge or embrace the new forms of urbanization, the changing economy of the country, and the idea of a continuum of urban and rural. Critics argue that, as a result, urban populations have been underestimated.

Forms of Settlements

Urbanization in India over the last few decades has resulted in a variety of settlement forms, and has been caused by a number of intertwined factors, such as major shifts in the economy and demography, and rural to urban migration. Some forms are identified by the Census of India, while others are not. Some of those that the Census of India recognizes are:

1. *Statutory towns (STs)*: These are areas declared urban by state law, and include all types of urban local bodies (ULBs) such as municipal corporations, notified area committees and nagar panchayats. Criteria for this designation vary from state to state,

but demographic characteristics could play a part or not in the decision. It is determined by concerned state or union territory governments that then notify areas of their status.

2. *Census towns (CTs)*: These are non-statutory settlements deemed by the Census of India to be urban by definition, as they adhere to urban requirements, that is, population size greater than or equal to 5,000; density greater than or equal to 400 people per square kilometre; and 75 per cent of the male workforce employed in non-agricultural sectors. They are not STs and do not become one until they are legally recognized by state law.

3. *Outgrowth areas (OGs)*: These are areas, usually villages contiguous to STs, with some urban infrastructure and amenities such as all-season roads, electricity, a drainage system, tap water, banks, and educational institutions. Railway colonies, university campuses, and port areas contiguous to STs are typically classified as OGs. These areas may or may not be a part of a municipality.

4. *Urban agglomeration (UA)*: This census category encompasses a continuous urban spread consisting of a town and its adjoining outgrowths, or two or more physically contiguous towns together, with or without outgrowths of such towns. A UA must consist of at least a statutory town and its total population, that is, all the constituents put together should not be less than 20,000 as per the 2001 census. In varying local conditions, there have been similar other combinations which have been treated as UAs since they satisfy the basic condition of contiguity. Examples here include Greater Mumbai, and the National Capital Region (NCR), but there are many others. This classification exists in other countries as well, such as Canada.

Table 5.1 sets out the number of UAs, towns, and OGs in 2001 and 2011. Table 5.2 further explains the differences between STs, CTs, and rural settlements. Both the central and state governments further group cities, towns, and UAs by their population size. Class I, for instance, is an urban area with *at least* 100,000 inhabitants. Within Class I, there are cities with a million or more population (referred to as million+ cities) and 'megacities' such as Kolkata, Delhi, and Mumbai with 10 million or more population. Class II–VI cities or towns are classified incrementally but have *less*

Table 5.1 Number of Indian Urban Agglomerations, Towns, and Outgrowth Areas in 2001 and 2011

Type of Towns/UAs/OGs		Number of Towns	
		2011 Census	2001 Census
1	Statutory Towns	4,041	3,799
2	Census Towns	3,894	1,362
3	Urban Agglomerations	475	384
4	Outgrowth Areas	981	962

Source: Census of India (2001, 2011b).

than 100,000 inhabitants. Scholars have argued that the urban size class is intimately related to the level of development, the size of the economy, the level of services and amenities available, and the revenue potential of an urban area (Kundu 2000; Rowland 2001). For instance, Kundu (2000) finds that Class I urban areas tend to have most of the basic infrastructure such as electricity, drinking water, toilet facilities, and other amenities such as hospitals and schools. Given the significant jump in size from the *five* categories below 100,000 to only *one* category above 100,000, clearly, the government does recognize a continuum within the urban category, but mostly among medium and small size cities.

Several other settlement categories exist for identifying areas with unique features, including special economic zones (SEZs), IT townships, export promotion industrial parks, hi-tech townships, and industry-based townships. They are not identified as such in the census and most likely are considered as towns and cities. These new forms continue to develop, solely from an economic point of view, through government incentives and provision of land. These developments have been granted exceptions in the 74th Amendment to the Indian Constitution to form their own elected local bodies or invoke any public participation they prefer in their decision-making processes. For some critics, such developments amount to the public acquisition of private land without due process and compensation. More broadly, such action results in the loss of fertile land and people's livelihoods, all of which arguably add to the growing inequalities in the country. Despite these problems, with the growing number

Table 5.2 Criteria Used by the Census of India to Distinguish Statutory Towns, Census Towns, and Rural Settlements

	Statutory Town (criteria vary from state to state)	Census Town	Rural Settlement
Administrative Units	Municipal corporations, municipalities, notified area committees, nagar panchayats*	Gram panchayats#	Gram panchayats
Population	5,000+ residents	5,000+ residents	Populations less than 5,000 residents
Density	1,000 people per square mile (400 people per square km)	1,000 people per square mile (400 people per square km)	Less than 1,000 people per square mile or 400 people per square km
Labour Force	Primarily employed in the non-agricultural workforce	75% of adult male workers engaged in non-agricultural work	Less than 75% of adult male workers employed in non-agricultural work

Source: Compiled by the authors.

Notes: * A nagar panchayat or nagar parishad is the smallest ULB designated by a state government determined by its population size, density, and economy. The state of Bihar classifies a small urban area with a population between 12,000 and 40,000 as a nagar panchayat. It recognizes as a nagar parishad, a medium-sized urban area, bigger than a nagar panchayat, with a population between 40,000 and 200,000.

Gram panchayat is the rural local body at the village level.

of such settlements, they still must fit within an overall urban and regional development strategy. Otherwise, they may exacerbate the current rural–urban divide.

Yet another form of settlement occurring in India, not recognized in the census or by any level of government, is high-density rural areas termed by Qadeer (2000, 2004) as 'ruralopolises'. This new form is the result of the in-place transformation of rural areas into incipient urban regions through the emergence of high population densities that create expansion pressures. High density lays the foundation for urban spatial organization; therefore, rural areas where population densities reach urban levels turn into ruralopolises.

Qadeer (2000, 2004) argues that high density is a transformative force. That is why it is an almost universal criterion for defining urbanization. It precipitates the need for roads, streets, drains, collective water supply and sanitation, house numbers and street names, municipal governments, planning and environmental by-laws, and more—albeit for urban services and institutions. In other words, it restructures land economy and spatial organization.

In Chapter 6 of this book, we introduce yet another form of settlement: 'urural' areas. We demonstrate that these areas not only exceed the urban density threshold as identified by Qadeer (2000, 2004), but, interestingly, surpass the economic and demographic characteristics that define such areas as rural. Further, these urural areas are subject to increasing pressures on land and public resources, resulting in increased frequency of disputes and conflicts that are mostly related to drainage routes, land ownership, and access to water. Rising unemployment, poverty, and the shift away from traditional agricultural work towards the non-agricultural sector are leading to increased rates of out-migration from the area. As land prices increase, this prompts many rural residents to sell their holdings, which are then converted to non-agricultural uses.

We now turn our attention back to CTs, which initially led our discussion to the issue of the dichotomous classification of urban versus rural.

Census Towns

Following the 2001 census, CTs received limited attention as they accounted for less than 10 per cent of the urban population (7.4 per cent). However, the most recent 2011 census showed a significant increase in the number of CTs (from 1,362 in 2001 to

3,894 in 2011), of which 90 per cent are former villages. These reclassifications of rural areas to CTs account for about 29.5 per cent of urban growth between 2001 and 2011. Meanwhile, STs accounted for 15 per cent of urban growth over the same period; that is, only half of that of the CTs, demonstrating clearly where future growth will lie.

Characterized by their urban-like density, high population, and predominantly non-agricultural workforce, CTs are the quintessence of India's urbanization. Meeting the same population and employment thresholds as STs, CTs are distinguished by the highly urban nature of their demographics, although the governance structure, services, infrastructure, and even spatial characteristics remain rural. This structure has resulted in challenges at the local level, as well as at state and federal levels.

Unfortunately, for a very long time, the government did not acknowledge the changing patterns of urbanization. India's Five Year Plans[6] had not generally recognized the shift from rural to urban and the needs that arise from this until recently in the Twelfth Five Year Plan[7] (2012–17). The plan acknowledged that there is a 'synergistic relationship between rural prosperity and the continuum of urban development from small towns through larger cities to metros' (Planning Commission 2011: 108). It recognized the increasing trend of CTs between 2001 and 2011, saying: 'As more Indians will inevitably live within urbanized conglomerations, with densification of villages, sprouting of peri-urban centres around large towns, and also migration of people into towns, the quality of their lives and

[6] Based on soviet-style centralized planning, India's Five Year Plans were developed by the National Planning Commission until it was dissolved and subsequently replaced by a new entity—the NITI Aayog (National Institution for Transforming India)—in 2015. The Commission used to set the long-term vision and priorities for the entire nation, and allocated funds to realize that vision. The plans outlined and evaluated the challenges of the times, and established goals to address national economic and social growth. These Five Year Plans always, almost exclusively, addressed the issue of rural development.

[7] At the time of writing this chapter, the government decided that the Twelfth Five Year Plan would continue and come to end in 2017 as originally planned. After the completion of the Plan, these Five Year Plans would be replaced by a new 15-year plan.

livelihoods will be affected by the infrastructure of India's urban conglomerations' (Planning Commission 2011: 108).

Challenges

The binary lens through which rural and urban settlements in India are looked at, presents challenges at the most basic levels of governance. Census Towns are a good illustration to elicit such challenges. The primary ones identified are tax revenues, infrastructure and services, and the politics of governance.

Tax Revenue

In India, 'Non-municipal towns [CTs] governed by Gram Panchayats qualify for rural development funds from the central government, which sometimes provides state governments a strong incentive to keep their [legal] status unchanged' (Bhagat 2005: 65). At the same time, the state governments might hesitate to grant these towns municipal status as this could lead to the draining of their resources in the form of grants to municipalities. However, because of their urban growth levels and corresponding service needs, CTs often outgrow the funding provided to rural areas. This has resulted in funding shortfalls—when CTs fail to be *legally recognized* as towns, they are unable to apply for the funding that is available to STs. These funding shortfalls further result in CTs retaining many rural characteristics such as infrastructure and services that are far below the standards required of urban areas, especially for that population size and density.

The failure to recognize CTs as urban settlements results in the loss of tax revenue not just to the community but also to the state. For example, towns lose out on revenue that could be created through service charges and taxes, such as those on vehicles and property. Their residents often have strong motivations to forego a state-granted municipal status since they would be often taxed at higher rates by the various levels of the government than a non-municipal town such as a CT would. Avoiding ST status means they avoid these costs. Furthermore, state subsidies allow rural towns to pay reduced electricity rates and virtually nothing for services such as education and healthcare (Bhagat 2005). While panchayats on average generate

15 per cent of their own revenues from taxes and service charges, municipal local bodies must generate about 70 per cent revenue for the upkeep of infrastructure and provision of services (Bhagat 2005). Therefore, there are few incentives for rural towns to become STs, since this would result in the loss of rural status and the development grants that the state governments provide to these localities. This is unlike other countries around the world where the classification of settlements as rural or urban allows these areas to apply for additional grants and funding from higher levels of government. Additionally, many areas reclassified from rural to urban gain further taxation powers.

A good illustration of the above situation is the reclassification of hundreds of nagar panchayats into village panchayats by the Government of Tamil Nadu in 2004. Even though many panchayats chose to revert to town panchayat status in 2006 due to 'practical difficulties' (Order no. 55 dated 14 July 2006), it is still interesting to note the reasons behind the original reclassification in the government's order (Order no. 270 dated 11 June 2004). It read as follows:

> Since most of the town panchayats are financially weak, and rural in character, the Government considered that the town panchayats having a population of not less than 30,000 may be reclassified as village panchayats so as to enable them to receive more funds from the Government of India and State Government under various grants and assistance. It is found that out of 611 town panchayats in the State, 568 town panchayats are having [sic] a population of not less than 30,000.

One other obstacle to generating revenue is the size of urban settlements. Even large Indian cities are ill-equipped, not to mention lax, in collecting taxes or developing additional tax bases so as to become self-sufficient. This issue was one of the reform agendas of the Jawaharlal Nehru National Urban Renewal Mission (JnNURM). Nevertheless, urban size is intimately related to the level of development and revenue potential (Rowland 2001). Kundu (2000) and Bhagat (2005) show that smaller-sized urban centres are disadvantaged as their economic bases are generally weak due to less diversified tax bases. They also rely heavily on agricultural tax income, which brings in less revenue compared to other uses. So, they argue that

smaller STs are simply not well positioned to be self-sufficient and thus lean on federal and state government grants, which are fewer for urban centres. The point here is that even if CTs gain ST status, their smaller population size is a disadvantage to them because it makes it hard for them to generate enough revenue to meet their infrastructure and service needs. A single federal or state funding formula intended to fit all sizes of urban areas is thus clearly inadequate to fulfil the needs of the many regions' residents: seeking or retaining their municipal status may not be in their best interest. Amalgamating or grouping contiguous small urban centres to increase the size and diversify the economy for efficient governance may be a way forward.

In addition to these concerns, the allocation of funds between rural and urban development is vastly inequitable. In the 2016–17 budget, the Government of India allocated INR 87,765 crore (or USD 12 billion) worth of grants for panchayats in rural areas to improve their education programmes, health services, road and water development, employment programmes, and poverty alleviation schemes. Meanwhile, the Ministry of Urban Development's (MoUD) budget allocation was only INR 20,466 crore (or USD 3 billion), a quarter of the allocation for rural development, under the assumption that urban bodies have the ability to generate their own revenues. This is another reason for states to keep small- and medium-sized (urban) settlements classified as rural to ensure their access to such funds.

Infrastructure and Services

As noted before, compared to STs, CTs lack basic infrastructure and services that are commonplace in urban areas, largely due to shortfalls in financing their construction and maintenance. These shortfalls mean that access to basic services such as toilets and potable water is restricted or non-existent. The panchayats that manage these settlements often cannot afford to connect households to water supplies, so private wells and public pipelines are often the only sources of water in CTs (Samanta 2014). These water resources are often combined with one another, as towns lack the ability to provide adequate quantities of household water to their residents. Additionally, many CTs have poor and underfunded drainage and

sewerage infrastructure. These systems can become overwhelmed, especially during the rainy season when rainwater mixed with household wastewater leads to sewer blockage and causes sewage to flood the streets.

Compared to STs, which often prioritize the construction and maintenance of roads, CTs often neglect to allocate funds or have difficulty accessing funds for road construction and maintenance, just as with the water and sewerage infrastructure noted above (Samanta 2014). Thus, in many CTs, roads often remain rural in character—narrow, unsurfaced, and poorly maintained. However, because of the intense development pressure in these urban areas, development often occurs regardless of poor infrastructure, such as insufficiently wide and surfaced roads, or lack of appropriate safety mechanisms (such as streetlights) (Samanta 2014). Low quality roads ultimately result in poor circulation of traffic and goods.

Politics and Governance

Given the administrative component of India's binary classification system, politics has played a major role in whether areas are classified and recognized as rural or urban, since each state government has the discretionary power to make such decisions (Samanta 2014). In addition, Bhagat (2002) points out that state governments may more easily control panchayats than municipal bodies. He further suggests political strategies at the state level may also account for the number of CTs because politicians may be reluctant to overextend limited state funds for municipalities, when rural development grants are so readily available.

However, Sivaramakrishnan (2013) takes a different approach when he argues that CTs would be better off remaining as panchayats since there are more avenues for panchayats to pursue government funding and various other concessions. Also, the monies available are often larger amounts. Panchayats, which are intended to govern smaller, rural populations, however, often lack the teeth and administrative capacity necessary to urbanize rural areas. For example, they lack the strict building regulations required of municipal towns. The dichotomous rural–urban classification results in CT residents falling victim to problems ranging from 'land speculation to utter neglect

of basic services and infrastructure' (Samanta 2014). Table 5.3 summarizes the potential benefits and challenges of CTs and STs.

Discussion

As this chapter has shown, India has yet to adopt a classification system that formally recognizes human settlements beyond a basic rural and urban divide. This classification system has been further complicated by the divisive views held by residents, business owners, local governments, and state governments, which act to either support or resist the transition of their respective settlements between the rural and urban divide.

Table 5.3   Potential Benefits and Challenges of Census and Statutory Towns

BENEFITS	CHALLENGES
Of Rural Status (Including Census Towns)	Of Rural Status (Including Census Towns)
• No property or municipal taxes • Lower electricity costs and tariffs • Free water, primary education, basic healthcare, employment, and poverty alleviation programmes • Access to a significant amount of funding and programmes from the Ministry of Rural Development • No planning regulations (good for business and factories)	• Inadequate infrastructure, including roads, electrification, sewerage, etc. • Lack of soft infrastructure such as social services, hospitals, and schools • Uninhibited growth of buildings and homes (issues of land encroachment)
Of Being a Statutory Town	Of Being a Statutory Town
• Increased tax base and revenue for the town administration • Access to better infrastructure and increased services/amenities • Access to government urban development initiatives	• Residences and businesses subjected to taxation • Stricter planning regulations • Businesses subjected to more rules and regulations

Source: Compiled by the authors.

The case of CTs and urural regions, described in Chapter 6, calls attention to the dichotomous nature of categorizing human settlements in this way. While these rural and urban labels may in no way reflect a settlement's true characteristics (which is the case with many CTs), this categorization nevertheless dictates the type of government, services, amenities, infrastructure, and revenue sources it may access. According to Samanta (2014) and Pradhan (2013), nearly 70 per cent of CTs identified in 2011 had already met the criteria of STs articulated in the 2001 census. While it is premature to assume these towns should be granted ST recognition simply because they meet the criteria, it does highlight the need to clearly lay out a transitional category or multiple classifications within it, as also enabled by the 74th Amendment (Bhagat 2002).

The 74th Constitutional Amendment identified three types of urban administrative bodies. One of these three is applicable to rural areas transitioning into urban areas, namely nagar panchayats. However, while the Amendment clearly addresses rural areas, the definition of what constitutes an urban area still remains ambiguous and unquantifiable, leaving this classification open to political influences (Sivaramakrishnan 2011). States have also failed to uniformly identify transitional areas in India, with virtually no states even attempting to define what constitutes transitional areas between STs and rural villages. As such, the Amendment's failure to use criteria that quantifiably recognizes this threefold classification (rural, urban, and transitioning areas) means that politics will continue to play a role in the designation of municipal towns.

We find that Indian government policy seriously lacks the conceptual and empirical innovation to address its contemporary forms of urbanization. It could benefit from adopting a system similar to that in Canada or Indonesia, or a combination of both. Regardless of which model it adopts, India's classification strategy must evolve with time, account for new, hybrid forms of urbanization, and recognize the continuum that currently exists between the urban and the rural. Although Canada's system still takes a dichotomous approach, its subcategories recognize the diversity of its settlements and the existence of a rural–urban continuum. The concept of a MIZ could be of benefit as this influence is getting more pervasive in India due to increased road connectivity and the melding of rural and

urban economies. Commute patterns along with the labour force characteristics of both full- and part-time workers, along with others, could be powerful attributes of the metropolitan influence.

We may have to look beyond the idea of metropolitan influence, as Pradhan's (2013) research shows that a dual urbanization process is in play in India. For instance, the CTs are growing not just within proximity to megacities and large towns but also in the countryside. These areas are remote and far from the commute zone and metropolitan influence of Delhi, Kolkata, Chennai, or Mumbai. Pradhan's research also shows that many of these CTs are not stand-alone settlements but part of a larger cluster of settlements that are in relative proximity to each other. Perhaps Indonesia's consideration of the availability (or lack thereof) of urban infrastructure and amenities is a way to tackle the issue of the urban–rural divide. After all, it is about providing relevant services, necessitated by population size, density, economies of scale, and other related factors.

In 1971, the Census of India introduced a concept—standard urban areas (SUAs)—as a potential method to tackle the emerging challenges with classifying urban areas. The criteria for a SUA are the following:

- A core town with a minimum population of 50,000
- Contiguous areas consisting of both urban and rural administrative units that have close, mutual socio-economic links with the core town
- A meaningful probability that the entire area will fully urbanize over the next two to three decades

The idea bears similarities with the Canadian MIZ as it relies on the intensity of interaction with the urban core, reflected in commuting for work and/or education, and the sale and purchase of commodities. It also creates possibilities to provide comparable data continuously for three decades for a definite area of urbanization, which would generate a meaningful picture of the transition from rural to urban. It is not clear whether any further work or data has been collected to advance this idea.

In India, the incentive for urban areas to retain their rural status is largely the availability of federal funds for rural areas. However, this appears to be contrary to the situation found in many countries

around the world, where urban bodies often receive more funding due to their population size and designation as cities and have the ability to generate their own resources through the power of taxation. With a few exceptions, this, in fact, provides strong incentives for settlements to become legally recognized as urban. Therefore, in India, along with a new classification system, what is needed is a rationalization of rural and urban ministries' budgets derived from on–the-ground realities and needs.

* * *

The discussion on dichotomy goes beyond just rural versus urban. Especially in the case of India, little distinction has been made in the hierarchy *within* these rural and urban categories, even as spatial planning for settlements occupies a prominent position in the national discourse. Under the current system, rural has been dealt with as a residual category, taking in whatever is not 'urban'. We need to move away from this thinking and see rural instead as an integral part of settlement systems. Although the 74th Constitutional Amendment does not fully define it, 'urban' does provide room to recognize the transitional status of rural regions. Within the Indian federal system, it is the state governments that are responsible for municipal governance. Unfortunately, even though it is about 25 years since the constitutional amendment was passed, most state governments have not attempted to develop a clear set of criteria for identifying different categories of urban (or rural) areas for municipal governance. This has resulted in policy planners subjectively classifying rural and urban areas, and the panchayats' inability to use funds for their infrastructure and service needs, regardless of how these areas are classified.

Within the urban context, there has been limited discussion on the varying levels of urbanization. Small- and medium-sized STs surely cannot be compared to a large megacity with the same basic urban categorization. The diversity within this category is important not only for policy and revenue purposes, but also because of the consequences for people's quality of life and social issues more broadly.

If the state is to provide appropriate levels of infrastructure and services, as well as to develop effective policy for a holistic, inclusive

approach to spatial development, it needs to reject its traditional approaches to conceptualizing settlements. The scale and rapidity of socio-demographic and economic change in the last few decades have surpassed the concepts that underlie them. Indian policymakers need to rethink their current approach and seek out strategies that are imaginative and inclusive, but above all more appropriate to the new realities of the urban and economic development processes and their variations across regions—which are, in turn, rooted in larger urban and rural systems. The new approach must be tailored to take into account history, politics, and the varied geography of India, while remaining flexible to meet unexpected developments. This change in approach would lead to clearly defined and classified rural and urban areas, and respect for the nuances among them; it could provide a funding formula that would equitably allocate funds and enable areas to raise their own funds. This would be the first step towards eradicating subjective designations and unsettling anomalies in India's urban landscape. Such an approach would support equal, fair, and proper allocation and distribution of scarce state resources. A sense of predictability would prevail, which would then allow localities and regions to appropriately plan for and control the ways in which they wish to grow.

6

High-density Rural Regions

A Tale of Three Villages in India

How does an agrarian rural area in contemporary India change—physically, economically, and socially—when its population density reaches urban levels? Who plans spatial and social infrastructure in such areas and how? This chapter attempts to answer these questions.

High population density is seen as a crucial attribute of urbanity (Castells 1977; Harvey 1985; Qadeer 2000, 2004; Rex and Moore 1967; Wirth 1938). Thus, one might expect that high density and population pressure would transform the spatial organization, land market, and housing and community needs of a rural area, endowing it with urban characteristics. Vast regions that are economically and socially rural but whose population densities qualify them as urban—what Qadeer (2004) identifies as *ruralopolitan* densities (described in detail later in this chapter)—have emerged in India, neighbouring countries in South Asia, and many parts of the Third World.[1] As

---

[1] 'Third World' is a political economic term that emerged during the cold war. Many third world countries are former colonies. Another popular term is 'developing countries', although the main criticism of this term is that *all* countries are developing; not one has come to the end of its economic journey. The World Bank uses gross national income per capita to classify countries (low-, middle-, and high-income countries).

Qadeer (2000: 1583) points out: 'Among such areas are parts of rural Java, most of Bangladesh, central Punjab and the Peshawar valley in Pakistan, the South Yangtze River valley in China, the Mekong Delta in Vietnam, the lower Nile valley in Egypt, the islands of Barbados, Jamaica and Cape Verde, north-east Nigeria, Burundi and Rwanda.'

Along the Ganges River in India, on the route from Delhi to Kolkata, in Kerala, and along the coast of Odisha, rural population densities frequently range from 400 persons per square kilometre to 1,500 to 2,000 persons per square kilometre. As noted in Chapter 5, India has adopted the United Nations (UN) guidelines on urban–rural designations, and defines a rural area as having a maximum density of 400 persons per square kilometre. This density criterion, along with two other requirements (a population of less than 5,000 and at least one-quarter of the adult male population employed in the agriculture sector) form the definition of a rural area in the Census of India. The rural area designation is not simply an 'academic' classification. It carries significant policy imperatives influencing the level of government funding and service provision these areas could potentially receive.

This chapter identifies socio-economic characteristics and community infrastructure in high-density rural areas, from the village to the district level, and describes evolving settlement patterns within these areas. The assumption is that as the population density and the population reach the urban thresholds, they prompt the creation of various urban facilities, services, and local government institutions, such as roads, streets, drains, collective water supply and sanitation, house numbers and street names, municipal governments and planning, and environmental by-laws—without which the quality of life for local residents is severely impaired. In other words, the restructuring of the land economy and spatial organization is accompanied by the development of basic urban infrastructure and civic amenities.

In order to address an issue that remains largely unrecognized and thus unexplored, this chapter tests these propositions through a detailed empirical analysis of the living conditions in high-density rural districts in the state of Bihar. Bihar forms a part of the mega region of 2,500 by 400 square kilometres in the fertile Ganges valley. It has high densities without the presence of large cities.

Using a multiple case-study approach, this chapter compares the physical, social, and economic conditions of three villages in Bihar that have high densities. It also assesses the economic changes these villages have experienced, to determine whether these changes are consistent with the third criterion of rural designation, namely, the employment of residents in the agriculture sector. The chapter concludes by making a case for the provision of urban infrastructure in these villages and across other such high-density areas, currently designated as rural.

Literature Review: Classifying High-density Rural Regions

High-density rural settlements within the context of contemporary urban India are relatively unexplored. Moreover, a high-density rural region is both a little-understood phenomenon and a distinct type of human settlement. In the Western world, the urbanization of the countryside is a topic that has been examined in the context of suburbanization and urban sprawl. Some scholars, however, such as Afshar (1994), Ginsburg (1991), McGee (1991), Qadeer (2000, 2004), and Zhu (2004), offer valuable perspectives and interpretations of changing land and density patterns, particularly in Asia.

Using experiences and observations from several Asian counties, Ginsburg (1991) talks about the idea of 'extended metropolis' regions such as the corridor between Bangkok and its airport, or Mumbai and Pune, which Ginsburg (1991) has described as 'dispersed metropolises'. He describes them as zones that appear be taking on a new form of socio-economic organization, which is neither urban nor rural but preserves essential ingredients of both. In his words 'this is a complex and compound regional system that consists of central cities, fringe areas, exurbs [described a little later in this chapter], satellite towns and extensive intervening areas of dense population and intensive traditional agricultural land uses' (1991: xiii). The physical landscapes in these extended metropolitan zones have not changed much. Most people live in villages and almost all of the land is under cultivation. However, most of their income comes from non-agricultural sources such as employment in village and small-town industries, remittances from those who have moved to central cities, or commute to the central cities on a daily basis. He attributes this largely to ever-increasing improvements in the transportation system.

In the context of the Third World, the phenomenon of non-agricultural activities infiltrating rural areas has also spawned McGee's (1991) concept of *desakota* (in the Bahasa Indonesian language, *desa* means village and *kota* means city), meaning corridors of mixed agricultural and non-agricultural activities connecting large cities of Southeast Asia (see Figure 6.1). Within these linear corridors, which connect urban centres, are rural villages that have experienced substantial increases in population growth and have been transformed with a mix of agrarian and urban land uses. McGee (1991: 16–17) identifies six characteristics of a desakota region:

1. A large population engaged in smallholder cultivation.
2. An increase in non-agricultural activities.
3. An extremely fluid and mobile population.
4. A mixture of land uses: agriculture, cottage industries, and sub-urban development.
5. Increased participation of the female labour force in industrial and service sectors.
6. 'Grey zones', where informal and illegal activities cluster.

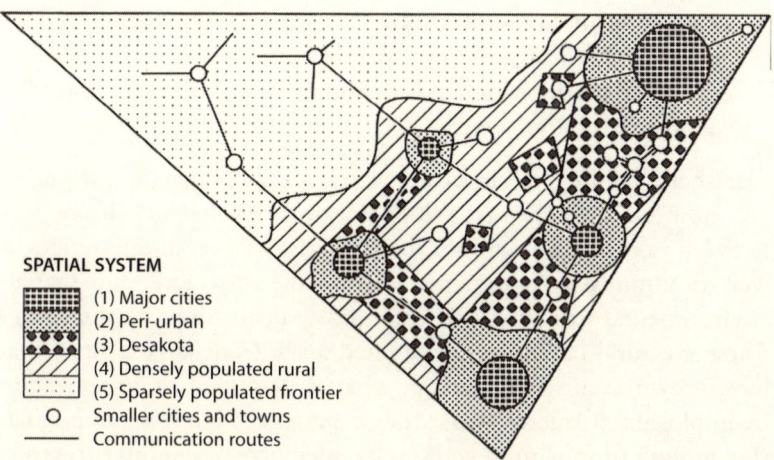

SPATIAL SYSTEM
(1) Major cities
(2) Peri-urban
(3) Desakota
(4) Densely populated rural
(5) Sparsely populated frontier
O   Smaller cities and towns
——— Communication routes

Figure 6.1   McGee's Spatial Configuration of a Hypothetical Asian Country
Source: McGee (1991).

Dupont's (2004) description of the peri-urban regions around the Indian capital aligns with McGee's and Ginsburg's concepts. He describes a hodgepodge of urban forms at the periphery of Delhi, alongside rural villages. Some of these urban forms are 'planned' by public and private sectors while others are not. He attributes most of the planned development to the Delhi Development Authority (DDA), since this body created satellite townships and large-scale housing projects. He also credits the neighbouring state government —Uttar Pradesh—for the development of industrial towns such as Noida. Informal urbanization of the periphery mostly consists of unauthorized residential colonies on agricultural land, squatter settlements on vacant land, upscale farm houses, and privately developed large-scale housing projects. Many of the inhabitants of these places work in the Delhi core region.

Qadeer (2000) identifies the urban potential of high population density in rural areas. As noted before, he labelled such regions *ruralo-polises*. According to Qadeer (2000), a ruralopolis is a hybrid settlement system that is spatially urban but economically, institutionally, and socially agrarian and rural. He characterizes a ruralopolis as an area with the following features:

1. High population density
2. An agricultural economic base
3. Small landholdings and pressure on land
4. Extended corridors or bands of homesteads and villages sprawled amidst farms and woods

Elsewhere (2004: 9), Qadeer explains a ruralopolis as a 'form of urbanization that emerges with large institutional deficits or lags between needs and provisions for facilities, services and resources as well as administrative organizations on the one hand, and spatial-environmental structures and community institutions on the other'. These are rural communities situated away from large centres that have grown exclusively through what is described as 'urbanization by implosion' (Qadeer 2004). They experience high levels of population growth from within, without parallel increases in infrastructure, institutional capacity, or public services.

Rural parts of an urban area have long been called *rurban* (Afshar 1994), but for Qadeer (2000) the focus is on the transformation

rather than a settlement type or zone. For him, new rurban forms arise from the process of altering rural forms, which are situated at the periphery of large metropolitan areas and cities, through pre-existing urban patterns and lifestyles. Examples of these rurban forms are rooftop or backyard chicken farms or keeping large animals such as cows, goats, sheep, or pigs in cities, and rural industries making items such as gunny bags, shopping bags, handicrafts, and carpets. Conversely, computer cafés in the countryside would also qualify. Investigations into these alteration processes inform us of the changing nature of rural areas, but also identify the changes driven by urban activities that encroach on the countryside.

The concept of *in situ urbanization*, coined by Zhu (2004), focuses primarily on the dramatic growth in rural villages as a direct result of government intervention. Zhu examined urbanization in the rural areas of the Quanzhou municipality in China, where growth has been largely instigated by government investment schemes. These schemes have been aimed at developing township and village enterprises in the rural areas in a bid to stop the flow of rural-to-urban migration. Such activities have led to the rise of rural industries in China, which has called into question the definitions that distinguish rural and urban areas (Zhu 2004). It is noteworthy that in situ urbanization has been experienced in rural regions of both China and India. However, unlike in China, where it is fuelled by government intervention, the Indian experience is mostly a natural one, with little or no government involvement.

Other familiar terms, used mostly in the West, are exurbia and peri-urban regions. Exurbia refers to areas of small and diffused residential communities found on the peripheries of metropolitan areas. They are territorial zones around a city where acreages, country homes, housing estates, and industrial plants are scattered among farms, agricultural fields, and woodlots. Peri-urban does not have a consistent definition, but it is largely a mix of urban and rural activities, leading to forms similar to rurban areas. The area retains rural characteristics, but is subject to changes in its physical configuration, economic activities, social relationships, and so forth.

Unlike extended metropolises, desakota regions, rurban forms, exurbia, or peri-urban zones, the rural areas discussed in this chapter are remote, far from zones of urban influence. Further, their density (a key criterion) as well as their economy (a criterion not considered

in Qadeer's ruralopolis) have evolved past the current definition of rural due to this in situ transformation that occurred *without* government intervention or support. We refer to these rural areas as *urural*. The 2011 Census of India considers them rural and not census towns (CTs). Census towns are those settlements that continue to be administered as rural areas but have crossed the thresholds of urban characteristics with respect to size, density, and nature of workforce. We hypothesize that urural may be more rural in their physical characteristics. Further, when compared to CTs, these areas have fewer or no institutions such as banks and schools or infrastructure such as sewerage, drainage, and water supply systems.

Methodology

Using a multiple case-study approach, we studied two higher-density villages and one lower-density village in the eastern part of Bihar. A lower-density village is included in the case study in an effort to control for density effects. While attempts were made during data collection to isolate the effects of density, the situation on the ground is complex and it is not always possible to control for all variables. We study the changing nature of these settlements but not the complex political and social processes shaping local conditions, effects, and institutional practices (procedures, regulations, and decisions) such as caste effects, class issues, state and local politics, the efficacy of government schemes, corruption in local governance, and the impact of natural calamities and environmental degradation.

Bihar is a classic case of a ruralopolis. It is one of the poorest states of India, predominantly agricultural, heavily rural (89 per cent), but intensely populated with an average density of 880 persons per square kilometre (Census of India 2011). Bihar's rural growth pattern and high-density village settlements present an ideal setting to explore the phenomenon of high density in rural areas.

Based on prior fieldwork in the area, the villages of Mahisan in the district of Madhubani, and Diwan Parsa in the district of Gopalganj were identified as higher-density villages appropriate for this investigation. The population densities within the districts of Madhubani and Gopalganj in 2011 were 1,279 and 1,258 persons per square kilometre, respectively. Samhauti Buzurg, a lower-density village in

the southwest district of Rohtas, was chosen as a 'control' case study; the population density of Rohtas is 763 persons per square kilometre.

It is noteworthy that densities of all three villages exceed India's urban density threshold of 400 persons per square kilometre. However, two of them have not yet *individually* reached the population size of 5,000 persons, although they are in close proximity to other villages. In fact, each village is surrounded by scores of other villages of varying population size within a radius of about a couple of kilometres. Even if a single village does not muster a population of 5,000, two or more villages located within less than a kilometre of each other can easily reach this number.

Data sources included the following:

1. Satellite images from the Indian Space Research Organisation.[2]
2. Census data from 1991, 2001, and 2011.
3. Village- and household-level data from the Institute for Human Development (IHD), collected in 2009 and 2011. These data include the following socio-economic indicators:
   (i) Literacy
   (ii) Wages
   (iii) Migration
   (iv) Land use
   (v) Land value
   (vi) Physical and social infrastructure
   (vii) Government schemes
   (viii) Disputes over land
   (ix) Access to amenities

This quantitative data was complemented by interviews with key informants, including local government officials such as block development officers (BDOs),[3] and local community leaders such as the

---

[2] IRS-1D PAN 2008, IRSP6 L4MX of 13 February 2008, 21 December 2009, and 14 January 2009, IRS-1C PAND and PANB of 8 January 2001 and 1 February 2002.

[3] A block development officer is the official in charge of a block, an administrative unit in a rural area earmarked for administration and development in India. S/he monitors the implementation of all the programmes related to the planning and development of the block, which usually covers several gram panchayats.

panchayat mukhiya and gram mukhiya,[4] as well as first-hand observations across multiple site visits. Wherever village-level data is missing for a particular variable, pertinent district-level data is employed as a proxy to understand the situation at the village level.

In 2011, for the first time since Independence in 1947, the absolute increase in population in India was higher in urban areas than in rural areas. While this trend varies from state to state and from region to region, India remains a predominantly rural country, with 69 per cent of the population in 2011 living in rural areas (Census of India 2011). At the national level, India's population density has increased from 325 persons per square kilometre in 2001, to 382 persons per square kilometre in 2011. Thus, it seems safe to assume that, given the proportion of the population still living in rural areas, this increase in density is due to growth not only in urban centres but also in rural regions.

Bihar (see Figure 6.2) is the second most densely populated state in the country (surpassed only by West Bengal), and the second most rural state at about 89 per cent rural population (behind Himachal Pradesh).[5] While the urban population in Bihar has grown steadily at 35.4 per cent between 2001 and 2011, the rural population has also kept pace, growing at about 24 per cent between 2001 and 2011 (Table 6.1). Despite higher population growth, urban areas accounted for only about 11 per cent of Bihar's population in 2011. Agriculture contributes only about 20 per cent of the state's total GDP, while it employs more than 62 per cent of the total workers in the state (IHD 2012a).

[4] Panchayati raj is a system of governance with a 3-tier structure of panchayats: gram panchayat (village level); mandal parishad, block samiti, or panchayat samiti (block level); and zila parishad (district level). *Gram panchayat* or the village council is the basic unit of administration comprising the lowest tier of the panchayati raj. It is governed by a council of elected members who take decisions on key issues affecting a village's social, cultural, and economic life, with jurisdiction over a group of villages. The council also has responsibilities for civic administration, and has the authority to tax members of the community. The head of the gram panchayat is known as the panchayat mukhiya and the head of a village (gram) is the gram mukhiya.

[5] West Bengal is more urban, while Himachal Pradesh is much less dense than Bihar. Hence, the two states were excluded from the study.

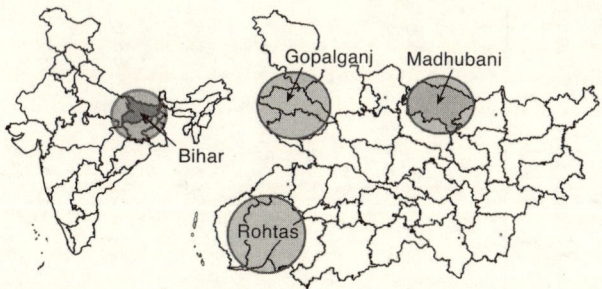

Figure 6.2 Location of Bihar within India [Left] and Location of the Three Study Districts within Bihar [Right]
Source: Generated by authors based on Census of India.

As noted, the three case studies are located in the Madhubani, Gopalganj, and Rohtas districts of the state (see Figure 6.2). Madhubani and Gopalganj are among the top six densest rural districts in the state. Rohtas, conversely, is one of the least dense, but is also slightly more urban (14.4 per cent) than the other two. In keeping with the national and state trends, the urban population growth in all three districts is higher than the rural population growth. Madhubani is one of the least urban districts; only 3.6 per cent of the district population resides in urban areas. The area is famous for its distinctive spinning, weaving, and handicraft and art works, especially the well-known Madhubani paintings.

Many districts in Bihar—such as Vaishali, Siwan, Sheohar, and Samastipur—have higher population (see Table 6.2). We have not included them in our case studies for various reasons. Vaishali and Siwan have shown higher rural growth between 2001 and 2011, but

Table 6.1 Demographic Data for Bihar, 2001 and 2011

Year	Total Population (in crores)	Urban (in crores)	Urban (in %)	Rural (in crores)	Rural (in %)	Literacy Rate in Rural
2001	8.3	0.9	10.8%	7.4	89.2%	43.9%
2011	10.4	1.2	11.5%	9.2	88.5%	59.8%

Source: Generated by authors based on Census of India.

Table 6.2 Demographic Information on Selected Districts in Bihar, 2001 and 2011

District	Decal Growth Rate (2001–11)	2011 Population: Rural (Urban)	2001 Population: Rural (Urban)	% Urban (2011)	% Rural (2011)	Rural Growth Rate (2001–11)	Urban Growth Rate (2001–11)	Literacy Rate 2011
Madhubani	25.2	4,325,884 (161,495)	3,450,736 (124,545)	3.6	96.4	25.4	29.7	69.9
Samastipur	25.3	4,113,769 (147,797)	3,271,338 (123,455)	3.5	96.5	25.8	19.7	63.8
Gopalganj	18.8	2,399,207 (162,805)	2,022,048 (130,590)	6.4	93.6	18.7	24.7	67.0
Sheohar	29.0	628,130 (28,116)	494,699 (21,262)	4.3	95.7	27.0	32.2	56.0
Siwan	22.2	3,147,551 (182,913)	2,564,860 (149,489)	5.5	94.5	22.7	22.4	71.6
Vaishali	28.6	3,261,942 (233,079)	2,531,766 (186,655)	6.7	93.3	28.8	24.9	68.6
Rohtas	20.8	25,32,153 (4,27,765)	2,103,116 (347,632)	14.4	85.6	20.4	23.5	73.4

Source: Generated by authors based on Census of India.

at the same time, they are slightly more urbanized. Another issue was the limited availability of data pertaining to these areas, beyond the census. Further, Sheohar was carved out of Sitamarhi district in 1994, making it challenging to compare and contrast the data temporally. Finally, although Samastipur exhibits similar characteristics to those of Madhubani, the latter was chosen to ensure that the study areas were geographically far apart from each other, to avoid any 'interactive influences' among the case studies.

The Three Villages in Bihar

We analysed the three villages—Mahisan, Diwan Parsa, and Samhauti Buzurg—based on the density and economic criteria that distinguish a place as rural or urban. Along with these demographic characteristics, we also looked at literacy, wages, migration, land use, power and water supply, facilities inside or in the vicinity of the village, and government social and economic development programmes. The data on the type and seriousness of disputes in the villages gave us a glimpse into the challenges facing the area. Table 6.3 describes some of the salient characteristics of the three villages.

Mahisan, Madhubani

Mahisan, located in the northern district of Madhubani and bordered by Nepal on the north, is the most heavily populated of the three villages, with a population of 6,293 persons in 2011. Mahisan has experienced nearly a tripling of its population during the past few decades. Between 2001 and 2011, specifically, Mahisan's population density increased by 44 per cent, resulting in a village population density of 1,683 persons per square kilometre—almost double the average density across Bihar, which is 881 persons per square kilometre.

Mahisan is located about 3 kilometres from the block centre of Madhepur, which lies across a river, but is connected via an all-weather road. The Madhepur block consists of about 83 villages with varying population sizes: some are smaller than Mahisan, while others are bigger. About 25 per cent of the villages in the block have a population of 5,000 or more. Of these, 18 have a population

Table 6.3 Comparison of the Three Studied Villages: Mahisan, Diwan Parsa, Samhauti Buzurg

	Mahisan	Diwan Parsa	Samhauti Buzurg
Dominant group (% may not add up to 100% because of rounding; SC/ST/OBC = Schedule caste/ Schedule tribe/ other backward class)	General (20%); Muslims (34%); SC/ST/ OBC (47%) [Dominant castes: Brahmin (20%), Musahar (21%)]	SC/ST/OBC (58%); Muslims (13%); General (30%) [Dominant castes: Brahmin (23%); Gond (17%)]	SC (41%); ST (14%); OBC (14%); Muslims (9%); General (22%) [Dominant castes: Paswan (27%); Brahmin (17%); Kharwar (6.9%)]
Household with migrants	84.4%	67.1%	37.5%
Average yield of paddy	9 quintal/acre	14 quintal/acre	22 quintal/acre
Agricultural labour households	23.5%	13%	40.5%
Farming households	40.5%	34.6%	70.8%
Men aged 15–59 whose principal occupation is agriculture and allied activities (census 2011)	81.5%	21.8%	40%
APL/BPL households	36/64	54/46	38/62

Source: IHD Survey.

between 5,000 and 9,999 and three have a population of over 10,000. Madhepur itself is a small town (although administratively still a village) of over 25,000 residents. Being the block headquarters, it has a block office, a government hospital, a police station, a degree college, two banks, a few places of worship, and a large market. It serves Mahisan residents' immediate medical, educational, and commercial needs. The district centre and a nagar panchayat[6] city called Madhubani is located about 50 kilometres from the village. The nearest railway station is in Jhanjharpur, also a nagar panchayat[7] city, about 22 kilometres away.

The village of Mahisan is spread over six *tolas*,[8] of which several are so isolated that they cannot be reached by a motor vehicle. During the rainy season, many tolas are susceptible to flooding and frequently get cut off from the rest of the village. Muslims, the largest religious group in the settlement, constitute one-third of the total households. They are followed by Hindus of various castes, starting with Musahars,[9] a scheduled caste group,[10] who constitute about one-fifth of the total number of households. Brahmins, constituting another one-fifth of the total households, are the dominant caste in the village by virtue of their historical control over land and tradi-tional political supremacy. The village continues to be dominated by large landowners who belong mostly to the upper caste Brahmin, along with a few Muslim families. Scheduled castes, predominantly

---

[6] The Bihar government has a three-tier system of Urban Local Bodies (ULBs), namely Municipal Corporations (Nagar Nigam), Nagar Parishad, and Nagar Panchayats. This is based on the population and the level of urbanization achieved in an area. According to the Bihar Municipal Act, a Nagar Parishad is a medium-sized urban area, bigger than a Nagar Panchayat, with a population between 40,000 and 200,000.

[7] Bihar classifies a small urban area as a Nagar Panchayat, where the population is between 12,000 and 40,000.

[8] A tola generally refers to a neighbourhood or a part of a settlement inhabited by people of one caste or occupation.

[9] Musahars are the lowest and poorest untouchable caste.

[10] The scheduled caste is a designation recognized in the schedule of castes in the Constitution of India and given to a group of historically disad-vantaged people in India. The designation allows the group to access various government welfare programmes.

Musahars, as well as poor Muslims usually do not own land and work mainly as wage labour in the village. They can be frequently seen living along roadsides and on other public lands in makeshift tents.

Just over a third (36 per cent) of Mahisan's households are classified as above poverty line (APL), while the remainder are deemed as below poverty line (BPL). 'Below Poverty Line' is an economic benchmark and poverty threshold used by the Government of India to indicate economic disadvantage and identify individuals and households in need of government assistance.

Lying in the catchment area of three major rivers—Kosi, Kamla Balan, and Bhutahi Balan—the village and the entire district are prone to severe floods during the monsoon. As recently as 2008, a breach in the Kosi embankment caused disastrous flooding in the area that resulted in hundreds of deaths. This constant threat of floods severely affects the lives of the people, their assets, and the local agricultural activities.

Diwan Parsa, Gopalganj

The village of Diwan Parsa, located in the northwest region of Bihar in the Gopalganj district, is a high-density rural settlement. Although much smaller in population size than Mahisan, it has a growing population of 2,068 persons and a density of 1,720 people per square kilometre. During the last few decades, the village population has more than doubled. Despite its smaller population, Diwan Parsa's population density is much higher. Diwan Parsa has nevertheless experienced similar socio-economic changes as Mahisan as its density has increased by 30 per cent since 2001.

Diwan Parsa is located about 6 kilometres from the block centre of Phulwaria, linked with a semi-pucca[11] road, and is about 35 kilometres from the main town of Gopalganj. A number of other much smaller villages, such as Dubaulia, Kapur Chak, Dhana Chak, Chaube Parsa, and Panre Parsa are among the 99 villages in the block, all of which are situated in close proximity. Almost 20 per cent of all villages in the block have a population between 2,000 and 4,999, while only one has a population exceeding the 5,000 mark.

---

[11] Pucca is a Hindi word that means solid or permanent.

The village of Phulwaria has a slightly larger population than Diwan Parsa. Being the block headquarters, it has banks, schools, a hospital, a police station, a power substation, and other facilities. Many of these facilities are available in this village, partly because it is home to a highly powerful state-level politician. Of late, Phulwaria has become a sort of tourist place where foreigners and media persons come to see what a politician's village looks like.

Compared to Mahisan, Diwan Parsa has a higher proportion of villagers belonging to scheduled castes, scheduled tribes,[12] and other backward classes, as well as upper caste Hindus but much fewer Muslims. Diwan Parsa is also residentially segregated along caste lines, but the lines are not as rigid as those observed in Mahisan. Brahmins and Bhumihars[13] continue to be cultivators—almost all are either peasants who own large estates or the descendants of erstwhile landlords. Members of scheduled castes remain mostly agricultural labourers, while those belonging to the lowest caste households are mostly casual labourers.

Diwan Parsa is slightly better off economically than Mahisan. This may be due to a higher agricultural yield in comparison to Mahisan, and fewer natural calamities. In terms of household poverty rates, Diwan Parsa has an almost equal distribution of BPL and APL households (Census of India 2001; IHD Survey 2009).

Samhauti Buzurg, Rohtas

Samhauti Buzurg had a population of 2,088 in 2011, which is almost the same size as that of Diwan Parsa, but much lower than that of Mahisan. It also has comparatively lower density (1,013 persons per square kilometre). Between 2001 and 2011, its density increased by 11.3 per cent, remaining significantly lower than in Mahisan and Diwan Parsa. This increase is roughly half of the previous decade's increase, which was about 20 per cent.

---

[12] Scheduled tribes refer to indigenous groups whose status has been formally acknowledged in the schedule of tribes in the Constitution of India.

[13] Bhumihars are Brahmins, most of whom own land, or *bhumi*.

Samhauti Buzurg is situated about 3 kilometres away from the block headquarters of Dinara. The village is still not linked by a pucca road. However, it is accessible by vehicle except during the monsoon season. Dinara is a much larger village with a population of about 12,000. The Dinara block is made up of 181 villages that surround Samhauti Buzurg. Eighty per cent of these villages have a population size of less than 2,000 with two exceptions: one village with above 5,000 and one with above 10,000. Only a handful of villages have slightly larger population sizes than that of Samhauti Buzurg, the rest have smaller populations. Scheduled castes and tribes make up the majority in Samhauti Buzurg. However, Brahmins continue to remain the economically dominant caste. They own most of the land and enjoy important social and political connections.

Samhauti Buzurg remains a primarily agricultural village, with more than 70 per cent of households involved in farming and 40.5 per cent of households employed in agriculture-related activities (Census of India 2001; IHD Survey 2011). Compared to the two higher-density villages described previously, only 14 per cent of Samhauti Buzurg's population is engaged in the non-agriculture sector. The village is in an area known for its high-quality soil and reliable access to water; as a result, it has among the best crop yields in the state of Bihar, if not in the entire country. Interestingly, despite being relatively well off, nearly two-thirds of the households in the village hold a BPL card (Census of India 2001; IHD Survey 2011). This is perhaps because of widespread corruption, or political clout in the distribution of these cards.

Findings

This section discusses shifting socio-economic characteristics, land use changes, hard and soft physical infrastructure, and conflict and encroachment of land potentially arising out of density and population pressures.

Labour Force and Employment

A detailed analysis of the three districts from 1991 to 2011 reveals a substantial decrease in the percentage of workers employed in the

agriculture sector. According to the Indian census, the percentage of the overall population engaged in agriculture as cultivators and labourers in the district of Madhubani remained around 89 per cent between 1981 and 1991. However, it dropped precipitously since then—66 per cent in 2001, and then 53 per cent in 2011. A village-level breakdown reveals that in Mahisan village in this district, the number of workers employed in this sector dropped from 97.8 per cent to 66.6 per cent between 1991 and 2001. In Census 2011, this proportion stands at 74 per cent. It is important to note though, that 18 per cent were marginally employed in the agriculture sector; that is, they worked six months or less in this sector. A slightly higher proportion, 25.6 per cent, were similarly employed in 2001.

In the district of Gopalganj, the proportion of agricultural workers decreased from 89 per cent in 1991 to 56.7 per cent in 2001, and 35 per cent in 2011. In the village of Diwan Parsa specifically, the percentage fell rapidly—from 88.7 per cent in 1991 to 53.6 per cent in 2001, to a mere 18 per cent in 2011; however, 46.5 per cent were reported to be marginally employed in agriculture during 2011. In the district of Rohtas, the percentage of agricultural workers decreased from 83.2 per cent in 1991 to 51 per cent in 2001, and then down to 40 per cent in 2011, a smaller drop compared with the other two higher-density districts. Compared to the other two villages, Samhauti Buzurg witnessed a much steeper fall in agricultural workers between 1991 and 2001, from 88.8 per cent to 33 per cent. In 2011, this proportion was 31.6 per cent with almost double, 62 per cent, employed marginally in the sector.

In Diwan Parsa and Samhauti Buzurg, the proportion of marginal workers in the agriculture sector increased significantly between 1991 and 2001. Many of these are casual labourers who work in the agriculture sector when work is available. The rest of the time they are engaged in non-agricultural enterprises such as construction, brick-making, or repairing or producing and selling goods such as carpets, shoes, or agricultural machinery in their own villages or nearby settlements.

Our analysis of IHD Survey data shows that in 2011, a substantial proportion of villagers—almost 45 per cent in Mahisan and 36 per cent in Diwan Parsa—were engaged in non-agricultural enterprises. The majority of the non-agricultural work performed in these

villages was construction-related.[14] In Samhauti Buzurg, however, only 14 per cent of villagers were employed in non-agricultural work (IHD 2011). This is partly because a substantial portion (62 per cent) as mentioned before, are marginal workers, which is the highest among the three villages.

A sufficient proportion of adult males[15] employed in the agriculture sector is one of three criteria a community must meet to be classified as rural under the census definition. For a rural designation, at least one-quarter of the male population must work in the agriculture sector.[16] In Mahisan, in 2011, 81.5 per cent of working-age men engaged in farming and agriculture-related activities as a primary source of income (Census of India 2011). These proportions were 83.42 per cent and 97.6 per cent in 2001 and 1991, respectively. Clearly, over the years, a gradual movement away from agriculture as a primary activity has occurred.

Of the working males in Diwan Parsa, only 21.8 per cent were employed in the agriculture sector as their main source of employment, a steep drop from 64.8 per cent in 2001 and 87.8 per cent in 1991 (Census of India 1991, 2001, 2011). A similar pattern emerges in Samhauti Buzurg where the recent proportion of male workers in agriculture is 40 per cent, less than the 48.6 per cent in 2001, and significantly lower than the 93.8 per cent in 1991.

As noted above in the village-level analysis of the labour force, although Diwan Parsa and Samhauti Buzurg are smaller in population compared to Mahisan, these two villages' economies have shifted away from agriculture towards non-agricultural activities. While the trend indicates an overall decrease in those involved in the agriculture

[14] The analysis of IHD's 2009 and 2011 data shows that in Mahisan, only 64 per cent of households were engaged in agriculture and 45 per cent in the non-agriculture sector. The total is more than 100 per cent, perhaps because the two activities are not mutually exclusive. Some residents carry out both agricultural and non-agricultural activities.

[15] As discussed in the previous chapter, the census definition excludes women workers, which introduces a serious gender bias in the definition.

[16] A strict definition of a non-agricultural workforce in an urban (or rural) category reflects the archaic agricultural–industrial dichotomy of the 1950s and the 1960s.

sector, especially men, there has been a rise in the number of female farmers as men migrate to cities or towns to find jobs or engage in non-agricultural work. For example, in Mahisan in 2001, only 45 women were engaged in farming, but by 2011 this figure rose to 259. This is still a small number, but it shows a sixfold increase in just over a decade. Also, although a substantial majority of male workers in Mahisan claim to be employed in the agriculture sector, it is possible that many are not fully employed in this sector. They may still consider themselves to be farmers or peasants by occupation, but our analysis of the IHD Survey indicates that their livelihoods are most likely a mix of earnings from both agricultural and non-agricultural activities.

Although the overall picture is not absolutely clear, the trend certainly suggests that farming is no longer the primary occupation of villagers. Many villagers, especially men—arguably half, if not almost three-quarters, of them if we include marginal agricultural workers—rely on non-agricultural activities to supplement their household incomes. Lack of local employment, small landholdings, and low wages in the agriculture sector may comprise a few of the many interacting factors responsible for this trend. Some of these factors are explored below.

Migration

The limited availability of employment in agriculture within the village, as well as natural calamities such as floods or drought, force villagers to seek work elsewhere—either in a neighbouring village, in a town or a major metropolitan city, or outside the country. As shown in Table 6.3, both higher-density villages have households in which at least one member has migrated out of the village: 84.4 per cent of the households in Mahisan and 67.1 per cent in Diwan Parsa. Samhauti Buzurg meanwhile, has experienced a much smaller incidence of migration, affecting only 37.5 per cent of the households in 2011 (Datta and Mishra 2011).

Many migrants travel to nearby towns or villages for construction work. In Diwan Parsa, this number grew to nearly 40 per cent of the total migrant workers by 2011; in Mahisan, the proportion was 36 per cent. Many from Diwan Parsa have also found jobs in the

Middle Eastern countries. This reflects in the remittances sent back to the village (INR 38,909 on average annually, equivalent to about USD 575), which are more than double the amounts remitted in the other two villages. However, most of the migrants work within the country, and move temporarily from one rural area to another.

In higher-density villages such as Mahisan and Diwan Parsa, the local agricultural economy cannot support the employment needs of a growing population, which is demonstrated by the high rates of outmigration. The village of Samhauti Buzurg, which does not suffer from the same population density pressures, has lower outmigration rates, suggesting higher levels of local employment in the agriculture or non-agriculture sector.

Wages

Wages in the agriculture sector have remained low, although they vary from village to village, depending on the type of labour, the season, and whether meals are provided by the employer. There has been a small increase in wages in recent years, but that is perhaps partly due to the effects of increasing remittances, the government employment scheme (Mahatma Gandhi National Rural Employment Guarantee Act, or MGNREGA),[17] and the pull of the construction industry, which pays higher wages.

For example, the average daily wage of a male worker in agricultural labour work in Mahisan was about INR 50 (less than USD 1) in 2009. If a worker worked every day of the year, he would earn INR 18,250 annually. Meanwhile, the average annual remittance to the village was INR 19,788 in 2009. Government employment paid about INR 92 daily, while the construction industry paid about INR 100 for an unskilled labourer. Clearly, there is little incentive to work in agriculture when other options with higher and more secure earnings are available (see Table 6.4).

[17] MGNREGA refers to the Mahatma Gandhi National Rural Employment Guarantee Act of 2005. The act aims to enhance the economic security of people in rural areas by guaranteeing 100 days of wage employment in a financial year to rural households whose adult members volunteer to do unskilled manual work.

Table 6.4 Comparison of Average Wages (in INR) in 2009 in the Three Villages

Work	Mahisan		Diwan Parsa		Samhauti Buzurg	
	Men	Women	Men	Women	Men	Women
Agricultural Labour Work (2009/2006)	50/ 40	–	100/ 50	90	80/ 50	80
Non-agricultural Labour Work (2009/2006)	70/ 50	–	100/ 60	–	80/ 50	–
MGNREGA	92	92	102	–	89	89
Construction (Skilled/ Unskilled)	200/ 100	–	200/ 100	–	200/ 100	–
Carpenter	250	–	220	–	225	–
Remittance from Migration (Annual)	19,788		38,909		19,308	

Source: IHD Survey (2009, 2011).

It may be noted that the shortage of labour in places such as Samhauti Buzurg has led to higher wages in the agriculture sector and the emergence of new forms of arrangements such as contract labour (IHD 2012b). Agricultural labourers are readily available in the village of Mahisan, so the village can rely on using labour drawn from its own community members, unlike the other two villages. Perhaps this is what accounts for low wages in agriculture in Mahisan. A temporary shortage of labour does occur during the rice plantation season (the months of July and August), since a large number of agricultural labourers migrate to rural parts of other states such as Punjab during that time (IHD 2012b).

Literacy

The literacy rate across the inhabitants of Diwan Parsa in 2011 was 79.4 per cent, notably higher than that in the other two villages (57.4 per cent in Mahisan and 68.9 per cent in Samhauti Buzurg). Diwan Parsa experienced a dramatic increase in literacy rate in 2011,

Table 6.5   Comparison of Literacy Rate in the Three Villages

Village	% of literate population			
	1981	1991	2001	2011
Mahisan	23.2	23.8	30.8	57.4
Diwan Parsa	11.7	23.0	36.3	79.4
Samhauti Buzurg	42.3	27.8	52.2	68.9

Source: Census of India (1991, 2001, 2011).

surpassing Samhauti Buzurg, which had much higher literacy (52.2 per cent vis-à-vis 36.3 per cent in Diwan Parsa) in 2001 (Table 6.5). The across-the-board rise in literacy can be attributed to the state as well as the national government's attention to providing access to education in rural areas. In interviews, we noticed that farmers, irrespective of whether they were literate or not, were eager to get their children educated because they did not see much future in farming. A few mentioned sending their children to private schools in nearby towns and villages where education and training facilities were available. They saw a better future for their children in the emerging service-based economy, where education is key for upward economic mobility.

Land Use

The conversion of agricultural land into non-agricultural land is a characteristic of an area experiencing population, density, and economic pressures. These pressures also produce parallel effects in the housing market. As residential densities increase, facilities such as streets, drains, waste disposal, and piped water supply become necessary. A market for house lots emerges where none may have existed before. A growing population also demands amenities and services, such as schools and hospitals, which require the conversion of agricultural land to non-agricultural uses.

Mahisan has experienced a significant conversion of agricultural land to non-agricultural uses from 6.7 per cent of the land used for non-agricultural purposes in 1991 to 24 per cent in 2009 (see Tables 6.6a and 6.6b). Across the district of Madhubani, however, the rate of conversion was only about 5 per cent between 1991

Table 6.6a Land Use Changes in the Three Districts, 1991–2010

Villlage	Non-agricultural Land	Net Sown Area	Orchard Area
Madhubani	4.97%	7.41%	70.6%
Gopalganj	13%	7.4%	5.03%
Rohtas	1.5%	2.6%	250%

Source: Directorate of Statistics Evaluation, Government of Bihar.

Table 6.6b Percentage of Non-agricultural Land

Village	1991 (Census)	2009 (IHD)
Mahisan	6.7	24.0
Diwan Parsa	8.4	10.4
Samhauti Buzurg	13.7	N/A

Source: Census of India 1991; IHD Survey 2009.

and 2010. Diwan Parsa has also seen an increase, albeit at a much slower rate, from 8.4 per cent non-agricultural use in 1991 to 10.4 per cent in 2009 (Census of India 1991; IHD Survey 2009). However, Diwan Parsa is part of a large agglomeration of villages, which may have undergone a higher rate of conversion. When we look at the Gopalganj district, where the village is located, the conversion rate between 1991 and 2010 was fairly high, at about 13 per cent. In comparison, the conversion rate in the Rohtas district, where Samhauti Buzurg is located, is just 1.5 per cent over the same period. Our preliminary analysis of remote-sensing data obtained from various Indian satellites between 2001 and 2009 suggests the increasing conversion of land for non-agricultural purposes in both high-density Madhubani and Gopalganj districts.

The rising number of orchards growing cash crops, replacing rice and wheat, is indicative of the changing land use and economy (see Table 6.6a). The main crops continue to be rice, wheat, maize, and lentils of various kinds. However, the prices of these traditional crops are so low that they do not provide enough for villagers to survive on, leading to an increasing shift towards cash crops such as fruits. Both Mahisan (70.5 per cent) and Diwan Parsa (5.03 per cent) are undergoing this

change, but the shift is more evident in the former, as the higher percentage demonstrates. In Samhauti Buzurg, while the percentage of land converted into orchards may seem high (250 per cent), the absolute number is almost negligible. Rice and wheat remain the two major crops in the area, and the average yield of both these crops is almost double that of the other two villages, partly because of better irrigation through a system of canals. Production of crops such as khesari pulse, gram, potatoes, lentils, and vegetables has begun to replace historical sugar cane cultivation in the area (IHD 2012b).

Land Value

Between 2009 and 2011, land prices rose considerably in the villages (see Table 6.7). Diwan Parsa in particular has seen much larger increases than the other two villages. Villagers attribute this rise to remittances from migrant workers and investment in house construction.

We think that a number of intertwined factors, including increasing land value, low earning from crops, and outmigration, are leading to further consolidation of ownership of land among key parties. This might be responsible for increasing landlessness among the villagers and a growing marginal labour workforce, since the agriculture sector fails to provide year-round employment for the locals.

Physical Infrastructure

Availability of and access to physical infrastructure and amenities within these districts and rural villages reflect the varying effects of density pressures on rural villages. Both Madhubani and Diwan Parsa are classified as rural villages, but, as already observed, their

Table 6.7 Percentage Increase in Land Values in the Three Villages, 2009–11

Village	Irrigated Land	Unirrigated Land
Mahisan	51.2	60
Diwan Parsa	150	N/A
Samhauti Buzurg	42.5	N/A

Source: IHD Survey (2009, 2011).

population density and economies have surpassed the rural definitional criteria. Their rural classification presupposes a level of infrastructure development which, according to the evidence, is no longer adequate to sustain the population growth these areas are experiencing. We describe the status of the physical infrastructure in the next few paragraphs.

Toilets

All three villages fall well below the national average for residents' access to a toilet. Almost 76 per cent of households in the state of Bihar do not have access to a toilet, compared to 53 per cent nationally. A district-level analysis reveals that about 80 per cent of households in Madhubani and Gopalganj lack access to toilets, higher than the state average. In Rohtas, however, a district with a lower population density, 71.8 per cent of households lack these facilities. In all the three villages, 85–92 per cent of households defecate in open fields or along the roads. This has its own sets of issues—both social and health—sometimes leading to serious disputes among villagers, as well as deviant behaviours. Lack of a toilet at home is much more of a problem for women. For them, it is not only a health and sanitation issue but also a safety and security issue[18] as they mostly go out in the night time, for privacy reasons, to relieve themselves.

Water

Access to water is a major issue, especially in higher-density villages (see Tables 6.8 and 6.9), and could become worse as the demand for this basic human need increases in the future. None of these three villages had a running or piped water supply except for a couple of connections each in Mahisan and Diwan Parsa, which are most likely in houses of upper-caste wealthy farmers. Groundwater and rain are the only two sources of water available for irrigation or for drinking.

---

[18] Of note here is a 2014 case of two girls who were allegedly raped and murdered in a village in Northern India when they went out in the night to relieve themselves. See Anand (2014); *Hindustan Times* (2014).

Table 6.8 Access to Pumps and Piped Water in the Three Villages

Village	Public Handpump (working/existing)	Private Handpump (working/existing)	Piped Water in House (working/existing)	Net Sown Area	Irrigated by Tube Well	Unirrigated
Mahisan	37/47	387/387	2/2	701.0	500 (71%)	90.6
Diwan Parsa	14/14	90/90	2/2	232.5	232.5 (100%)	N/A
Samhauti Buzurg	12/14	285/285	–	508	476 (93.7%)	N/A

Source: IHD Survey (2009).

Table 6.9 Irrigated Land (in Acres) in the Three Villages

Villages	Net Sown Area	Irrigated by Tube Well	Unirrigated
Mahisan	701.0	500 (71%)	90.6
Diwan Parsa	232.5	232.5 (100%)	N/A
Samhauti Buzurg	508.0	476 (93.7%)	N/A

Source: IHD Survey (2009).

Groundwater is accessed through tube wells and handpumps, a vast majority of which are bored privately. At the same time, some households resort to alternative sources of water, such as wells and ponds. Mahisan has had a serious scarcity of drinking water in the past; however, this situation has eased a bit recently through publicly and (mostly) privately installed handpumps. Canals are generally rare or absent and where they do exist, as in Mahisan, their engineering and construction are usually so flawed that they cannot carry or retain enough water for irrigation purposes.

Drainage

An analysis of households without home drainage systems shows Bihar at 57.7 per cent, worse off than the 2011 national average of 48.9 per cent. Between 2001 and 2011, Bihar experienced only a meagre 4.3 per cent improvement in households that had access to drainage infrastructure. Madhubani is the worst among the three districts – per cent of its households have no drainage system. In the district of Rohtas, conversely, only 19.6 per cent of the households were without drainage systems. The figures from Rohtas may be attributed to the higher level of urbanization.

Electricity

According to the Census of India (2011), household electrification in the state of Bihar is only 16.4 per cent, well below the national average of 67.2 per cent. While some improvements were made in the three districts between 2001 and 2011, only 12.6 per cent and 16.5 per cent of the households in Madhubani and Gopalganj, respectively, have electricity in their homes. In Rohtas, 25.5 per cent

of residents have access to electricity. Clearly, availability of electricity does not correspond with increases in population density and size. Among the three villages, only Mahisan and Diwan Parsa have a supply of electricity; however, between 1991 and 2011, the number of domestic connections has increased little. The existing connections are limited to a few households among Muslims and Brahmins in Mahisan, and Brahmins and Bhumihars in Diwan Parsa.

Roads, Buses, and Railways

Road and rail connectivity has increased over the last few years. Government schemes such as the Pradhan Mantri Gram Sadak Yojana (PMGSY),[19] Mukhya Mantri Gram Sadak Yojana,[20] and MGNREGA have contributed to bringing paved roads to a great many villages in Bihar. Table 6.10 contains information about road connectivity and access to an intra- or inter-state bus stop or railway station.

Table 6.10   Access to Transportation in the Three Villages

Village	Connectivity by Paved Road	Distance to Bus Stop	Distance to Railway Station
Mahisan	Yes	2 km	5 km
Diwan Parsa	Yes	3 km	16 km
Samhauti Buzurg	3 km away	3 km	40 km

Source: IHD Survey (2009).

[19] Pradhan Mantri Gram Sadak Yojana means the prime minister's village road project. It is a central-government-sponsored nation-wide plan run by the Ministry of Rural Development. Its aim is to provide good all-weather road connectivity to unconnected villages.

[20] Mukhya Mantri Gram Sadak Yojana means state chief minister's village road project. Each state has launched its own road project to provide road connectivity to smaller villages that are usually not covered under the PMGSY.

Social Infrastructure

The following sub-sections examine the status and quality of social infrastructure such as schools, primary healthcare facilities, and government programmes related to social and economic improvements in the three villages under study.

Education and Healthcare

A notable change in the education infrastructure has been the rise in the number of primary schools (see Table 6.11). For instance, in 2001, Mahisan had only one primary school. In 2009, there were three government primary schools, one government middle school, and one madrasa.[21] Similarly, Diwan Parsa had only one primary school in 2001; by 2009, it had one government primary school, one religious or private primary school, and one new government middle school. Samhauti Buzurg has one government primary school and one government middle school. The proliferation of madarsas has been a result of special government welfare schemes to support and educate Muslim children in rural areas.

Table 6.11 Educational Facilities in the Three Villages, 2001 and 2009

Village	Total Educational Facilities		Primary Schools Including Government, Religious, and Private Schools		Middle Schools Including Government and Private		Colleges
	2009	2001	2009	2001	2009	2001	2009
Mahisan	5	1	4	1	1	<5 km	<5 km
Diwan Parsa	3	1	2	1	1	<5 km	>10 km
Samhauti Buzurg	2	1	1	1	1	<5 km	<5 km

Source: Census of India (2001) and IHD Survey (2009).

---

[21] A madrasa is an educational institution, particularly for Islamic religious instruction.

Education has played a role in opening up employment opportunities and creating occupational diversification. It may also be responsible for the higher incidence of migration from rural to urban areas. Overall, it appears educational facilities have more or less kept pace with the increase in population density and the ensuing need for such an infrastructure.

Little has changed in terms of healthcare infrastructure, however. This is the case across many rural areas in India. New government health programmes have placed Accredited Social Health Activist (or ASHA)[22] workers in many villages; these workers connect the community to the public health system. However, Mahisan, the densest and largest village by population size among the three villages under study, does not have a single ASHA worker (see Table 6.12). None of the three villages has a doctor. Public compounders,[23] nurses, and midwives sometimes visit these villages, but their visits are irregular. The rural areas are heavily dependent on the private healthcare system, which imposes a financial burden, especially on the poor (IHD 2012a).

Government Social and Economic Welfare Programmes

Access to social welfare programmes such as Anganwadi centres,[24] and the Mid Day Meal (MDM) Scheme[25] seems to be available in

---

[22] An ASHA is a health activist in the community who works to increase awareness on health issues, to mobilize the community towards local health planning, and to increase the use of and accountability for the available health services.

[23] A compounder is a pharmacist. In India, however, a compounder has traditionally acted as a primary care provider.

[24] The anganwadi means 'courtyard shelter' in Hindi. As a part of the Integrated Child Development Services programme to combat hunger and malnutrition, a typical Anganwadi centre provides basic healthcare in Indian villages. Recently, they have been restructured to act as early childhood development centres, catering to preschool children from 3 to 6 years of age.

[25] The MDM Scheme is a programme of the Government of India, designed to improve the nutritional status of school-age children nation-wide.

all three villages (see Table 6.12). The three villages were serviced by Anganwadi centres (there are five centres in Mahisan and one in each of the other two villages). The Public Distribution System (PDS)[26] shop is available in two of the three villages and is about a kilometre outside the third village.

Diwan Parsa and Samhauti Buzurg have a MDM programme that offers adequate quality food, but the programme ranked poorly in terms of regularity and reliability. While there are variations in the availability of services among the villages, the evidence suggests that service provision is not increasing proportionately with the increases in population and density. Our analysis of the IHD Survey shows us that between 2004 and 2009, 33 per cent of households in Mahisan benefited from the Indira Awas Yojana,[27] while in Diwan Parsa 37.5 per cent of households benefited from the scheme between 2006 and 2011.

Under MGNREGA, more villagers in Mahisan and Diwan Parsa were employed, compared with Samhauti Buzurg. In Mahisan, approximately 21.7 per cent of households were employed in 2009 (IHD Survey 2009). This figure was higher in Diwan Parsa in 2011, with 28.4 per cent of households employed in the MGNREGA scheme. In 2011, only 8 per cent of households in Samhauti Buzurg were employed under this scheme (IHD Survey 2011).

The higher employment rate under MGNREGA in the higher-density villages indicates the lack of job availability in these communities. In theory, MGNREGA jobs pay a standard minimum wage; however, this wage is often much lower than prevailing wages or almost as much as wages in agricultural labour work, which pays the least (see Table 6.4). Samhauti Buzurg seems to offer more job

[26] The Public Distribution System (PDS) is an Indian food security system. Established by the Government of India under the Ministry of Consumer Affairs, Food, and Public Distribution and managed jointly with state governments in India, it distributes subsidized food and non-food items to India's poor.

[27] The Indira Awas Yojana is a flagship rural housing scheme to financially help with the construction or upgrade of dwelling units of members of Scheduled Castes/Scheduled Tribes and other BPL non-Scheduled Caste/non-Scheduled Tribe households.

Table 6.12 Access to Social Programmes in the Three Villages

Village	Midday Meal	Anganwadi	ASHA Worker	Visits of Health Professional	Public Distribution System	Subsidy for Toilet (HH; toilets installed)
Mahisan	Good quality but very poor in regularity	Yes, present (5)	Not present	Doctor (never); Compounder & Nurse mid wife (weekly)	Generally good	0; 0
Diwan Parsa	Adequate quality but poor in regularity	Yes, present (1)	Yes, present	Doctor (never); compounder (never); Nurse mid wife (monthly)	Grain not available	0; 0
Samhauti Buzurg	Adequate quality and adequate regularity	Yes, present (1)	Yes, present	Doctor (Never); Compounder (Never)	No PDS point in the village	0; 0

Source: IHD Survey (2009).
Note: HH refers to households.

opportunities as well as competitive wages. As a result, its residents do not use this government scheme as much as the residents of the other two villages.

Conflicts and Encroachment

Lack of basic human needs such as drinking water or a shortage of employment can lead to serious social conflicts due to an increase in competition for limited precious resources. There has been a dramatic rise in the frequency as well as the seriousness of disputes related to common property resources such as village ponds, roads, grazing land, drinking water, and drainage. The absence of civic infrastructure seems to be contributing to these disputes (see Table 6.13).

Among the three villages, numerically, Mahisan has witnessed more water- and drainage-related conflicts. However, on a per capita basis, Diwan Parsa is the most conflict-ridden.

Table 6.13   Frequency of Water- and Drainage-related Conflicts and Most Serious Disputes over Five Years* in the Three Villages

Village	Water-related Conflict	Drainage-related Conflict	2009	2011
Mahisan	7	2	Land Crop grazing Drinking water	Common property resources Land
Diwan Parsa	4	0	Land Criminal	Common property resources Land
Samhauti Buzurg	2	1	Benefit from community/ government scheme Drainage	Other land

Source: IHD Survey (2009, 2011).

Note: * In both 2009 and 2011 surveys, the following question that was asked to the respondent: 'What were the most serious disputes in the village during last 5 years?'.

In Samhauti Buzurg, there were at least two instances in which lower castes were excluded from using the village pond. It was alleged that at times, the upper castes illegally claimed possession of the pond and prevented others from accessing it. Our interviews with residents in the two villages revealed that many members of the lower castes engaged in indentured labour just to have access to water. This is a modern form of slavery, controlled through access to water.

Land pressures in Mahisan and Diwan Parsa have resulted in encroachments on public land (with some instances of encroachments on to private land). This problem is particularly rampant in Mahisan. It is mostly the poor who tend to encroach because they cannot afford to rent or own land. Government land, community buildings, and village roads are the most likely areas to be encroached upon, although disputes over trespass on private land for animal grazing have also been recorded.

Our analysis suggests that rising population density could be one of the reasons for the rise in the number of conflicts. An increase in density is exerting pressure on these villages' resources, including drinking water, land, housing, and employment opportunities. If these services are not developed or increased to accommodate density increases, conflicts could grow further.

Tables 6.14, 6.15, and 6.16 summarize the issues in the three villages as expressed by the inhabitants of these places. The views were sorted between respondents who were below or above the poverty line (BPL; APL). While a few overlaps were present, noticeable differences exist between the two sets of views. The views also vary from village to village. Across the three villages, the BPL households reported a serious lack of some very basic human needs—jobs, drinking water, and health services—while the APL households were more concerned about the lack of government welfare programmes, a public irrigation system, electricity, and educational facilities, among others. Both groups across all the villages agreed that there have been improvements in accessing roads and jobs, but mainly outside their own village.

In sum, higher-density villages seem to be characterized by the following:

1. High unemployment and increasing employment in the non-agriculture sector
2. Increase in outmigration and dependence on remittances

Table 6.14 Problems in Mahisan

	APL	BPL
Better off	Social condition	Outside jobs
	Access to education	Health facilities
	Agricultural productivity	Social condition
Things that have worsened	Access to electricity	Drinking water
	Benefit from government programmes	Political situation
		Work availability in the village
	Political situation	
Difficulty faced by people	Water logging/flood	Wrong selection of BPL HH
	Bribes by govt. officials	Inefficient PDS
	Low wage rate	No employment
	Seeds/fertilizers	Electricity
	Wrong selection of BPL HH	Water logging/flood
Important thing the village lacks	Public irrigation system	Community centre
	Water	Electricity
	Electricity	Job opportunities
	Drinking water	Proper PDS
	Health facility	MNREGA job cards

Source: IHD Survey (2009).
Note: HH refers to households.

3. Shifting land uses from agricultural to non-agricultural purposes
4. Little or no water for agriculture or drinking
5. Lack of electricity, toilets, and drainage facilities
6. Poor health facilities
7. Higher frequency of land-, water-, and drainage-related conflicts

* * *

Our analysis suggests that the urural villages of Mahisan, Diwan Parsa, and Samhauti Buzurg have transformed gradually into 'urban' communities, both demographically and economically, but seriously lack urban infrastructure and amenities. From the

Table 6.15   Problems in Diwan Parsa

	APL	BPL
Better off	Access to roads Benefits from government programmes Access to education facilities	Wage rates Outside jobs Access to roads
Things that have worsened	–	Benefits from government programmes Access to electricity
Difficulty faced by people	No toilets made under Total Sanitation Campaign (TSC), Fields washed away by flood Increasing input cost in cultivation, Labour problem, No/irregular electricity supply (village or specified tolas)	No employment at local level; No industry; No agro-based industries.
Important thing the village lacks	Lack of community centre, Panchayat Bhawan (Village council building), Kisan Kendra (Centre for farmers) Lack of educational facilities (Infrastructure as well as teachers) Lack of Anganwadi centres. Lack of public irrigation system canal, tube wells. Lack of connectivity (Pucca road, Bridge), brick soling.	

Source: IHD Survey (2009).

definitional perspective, Mahisan surpasses all the three criteria—population size, density, and economy—of being rural. Diwan Parsa, though smaller in size, is part of a larger conurbation of villages mustering 5,000 or more population, and is also well past

Table 6.16   Problems in Samhauti Buzurg

	APL	BPL
Better off	Agricultural productivity	Access to electricity
	Others	Access to roads
Things that have worsened	Others	Social conditions
		Others
Difficulty faced by people	Road connectivity	Road connectivity
	Drainage-related problems	Electricity
		Lack of health services
	Community centre/Gram Panchayat building	Drainage
	PDS system	
Important thing the village lacks	Electricity	Community centre/ Panchayat building
	Public irrigation system	Road connectivity
	Community centre/ Panchayat building	Public irrigation system
	Education facilities	Job opportunities

Source: IHD Survey (2009).

the density and economy thresholds.[28] Even Samhauti Buzurg, which is economically well-off and is about the same population as Diwan Parsa but less dense than both Diwan Parsa and Mahisan, shows a dramatic shift away in its residents' reliance on agriculture as their primary occupation.

Such rural areas are the new frontier in rural and regional planning in India. Barring some progress in educational facilities and improvements in road connectivity, other forms of physical and social infrastructure and services are not commensurate with the urban characteristics of these villages—especially their population density and the economy. The spatial and socio-economic characteristics

[28] Denis and Marius-Gnanou (2011) show that many of the new CTs are not stand-alone settlements either. They are a part of a cluster of settlements.

of these areas are close to those described in Ginsburg's 'extended metropolis' or even McGee's desakota concept, especially with respect to these features: the rural nature of these landscapes which also reveal shifting land uses, the non-agricultural economy, the improving connectivity, and the dense but also migratory population. However, as noted earlier, urural areas are remote and far from any metropolitan zone of influence.

There could be two possible explanations for similarities in the spatial and socio-economic characters of urural areas and those of either extended metropolises or desakota regions. Either the metropolitan influence transcends far beyond what we have traditionally understood or these characteristics appear despite the absence of a metropolitan area in the vicinity. Such appearance may perhaps arise because of rapidly diversifying and interconnected rural–urban economies and an ever-improving transportation system beyond a metropolitan area, one that allows people to traverse much longer distances in short amounts of time.

Dupont (2004) helps somewhat with this quandary, using Delhi as an illustration. He says that Delhi has had a continuous and considerable flow of immigrants from rural areas. These immigrants to Delhi, who mostly live in peri-urban parts of the metropolitan area, maintain diverse relationships—economic, social, and emotional—with their native rural places. Their life and work space transcends urban–rural borders, extending beyond the limits of the metropolitan area or any urban area to include their home villages, which may be physically distant from the Delhi metropolitan area, any other metropolitan area, or urban area. Perhaps this circular movement of migrants between the metropolis and the diverse places with which they have relations extends the metropolitan or other urban influence.

Interestingly, many places in Bihar—such as Chanari and Bhardua in Rohtas district, Bahadurpur in Darbhanga district, and Paharpur in Gaya district—are smaller or of similar size to Mahisan, but have been considered CTs in the Census of 2011. In the continuum of urban–rural settlements, urural areas seem more rural in their physical characteristics than their CT counterparts. But, by definition, urural areas are urban and thus ought to qualify for urban governance and amenities, just like the transitional areas and the nagar panchayats do, and the CTs can. A urural zone should be considered

a transitional area. The Constitution lets the state government decide how to define and treat these areas. The state should consider creating multiple categories within transitional areas which are ripe for urban amenities and services. The urural category would be one such critical category. Also, according to Chawla (1995), the Constitution does not limit the state government from designating municipal districts. These could include multiple villages, even if individually they may not surpass a population mark of 5,000.

The findings of this study further suggest that urural areas need urban amenities (water, drainage, sanitation, and healthcare in particular), irrespective of the population size of individual villages in view of the fact that they may face unprecedented population density pressures. An increase in disputes and public encroachments might be a result of population density pressures on land, and a lack of public resources.

Increasing unemployment and poverty; and the shift away from traditional agricultural work towards the non-agriculture sector have prompted changes in the migratory patterns of rural residents. Migration is increasingly becoming a necessity for a large percentage of the rural population. Migrant remittances are now a major form of subsistence in high-density regions. Increasing land prices have prompted many rural residents to sell their holdings, which are usually converted to non-agricultural uses such as houses and shops.

Despite major advances in enrolment in primary education, the quality of education remains a concern. It requires attention on several fronts—recruiting qualified teachers; checking teacher absenteeism; and providing secondary, and higher and technical education. Also, the public health system in rural areas is almost non-existent. Despite some success of the ASHA programme, no other public health facilities are available. Some government schemes have been more successful than others. Providing bicycles and uniforms to girl students, old age pensions, child development schemes such as Anganwadi, and many road development projects are some strategies that have been more effective than other approaches.

The trends identified in this research highlight the necessity for both national and state governments to revise the outdated definitions distinguishing rural villages from urban areas, to recognize multiple forms of rural and transition areas in between, and to update their current agricultural policies. The government needs to recognize the

reality of these zones of intense urban–rural interaction and direct investment to these underserved areas.

In 2004, the central government launched a scheme called Provision of Urban Amenities in Rural Areas (PURA) under a public–private partnership (PPP) framework between gram panchayats and private sector partners. The approach is intended to bridge the urban–rural divide by involving the private sector in introducing badly needed physical and social infrastructure such as roads, electricity, transit, internet and information technology services, and market connectivity. Since its inception, scheme has been revised several times. In the most recent re-configuration in 2012, the then Minister of Rural Development argued that a rework was necessary because the earlier versions of the scheme failed (*Economic Times*, 2012). He attributed the failure to inadequate focus on physical infrastructure and the areas which are neither rural and nor urban.

At the time of writing this chapter (February 2016), the Government of India launched a scheme called the Shyama Prasad Mukherji Rurban Mission, with the stated goal of stimulating local economic development (for example, through agro-processing units), and enhancing basic urban services such as piped supply of water, sanitation, drainage, and solid waste management in rurban clusters.[29] The mission is in line with what this research espouses, but it is too soon to comment on whether this initiative will be successful. Overall, it is clear that urban amenities in high-density rural areas are becoming a necessity and cannot be treated as luxuries. The consequences of inaction are increasing poverty, further rural-to-urban migration, and possibly large-scale social unrest.

Density alone cannot be identified as the single contributing factor for the changes in the studied settlements; we find that other complex and intertwined factors—including population size,

[29] A 'rurban cluster' is a cluster of geographically contiguous villages with a population of about 25,000–50,000 in the plains and coastal areas, and a population of 5,000–15,000 in desert, hilly, or tribal areas. Some of the parameters the Ministry of Rural Development and state governments could use to monitor or address concerns include the following: population growth, rise in land values, non-farm workforce participation, and girls' enrolment in school.

economy, and geographic location—are causing major shifts in these settlements. We also noticed that caste differences, state and local politics, and local leadership impact the use and implementation of several government welfare schemes, and thus affect people's quality of life. Committed local panchayats and BDOs in particular can make a significant difference in rural people's lives. Because of the scope of the research, and resource and time constraints, these factors could not be explored fully. As is evident, a lot more work is needed to comprehend this highly under-researched area of study in India.

7

Spatiality, Governance, and Development Imaginations of SEZs in India

*Sudeshna Mitra**

Special Economic Zones (SEZs) emerged as a prominent and controversial policy tool in the post-liberalization India. The enclaving concept behind SEZs is not new, as spatially separated townships and zones with autonomous governance and infrastructure regimes to facilitate economic activities have been common in India through the twentieth century. For example, the industrial township of Jamshedpur was set up in 1907 and planned incrementally (Sinha and Singh 2011) and the Kandla Export Processing Zone (EPZ) was developed in 1965 as one of the first export zones in the global South (Tantri 2013). However, recent SEZ policies have attracted attention

* Sudeshna Mitra is a faculty member at the Indian Institute for Human Settlements, Bangalore, India. She works on urban and regional economic development issues, focusing on public–private negotiations over land and real estate.

because they are perceived as facilitating extensive land acquisition for large-format projects, exacerbated by prolific SEZ approvals, especially between 2006 and 2008. As of January 2015, 491 SEZs were formally approved and 32 SEZs had in-principle approvals (Ministry of Commerce and Industry [MoCI] 2015a). However, research highlights that small format SEZs are more common and, despite rapid approvals, operationalizing SEZs has been slow and difficult. More than half the land (52 per cent) designated for SEZs remains unutilized (Comptroller and Auditor General of India [CAG] 2014). Most successful SEZs are located in already industrialized and urbanized locations, raising questions about the policies' effectiveness in promoting new centres of economic activities, their role in displacing comprehensive local-level economic planning and in absorbing public investments into economic infrastructure at locations with growth potential.

Despite the apparent lack of success, SEZs are a significant component of India's post-liberalization story. They have generated public debates regarding priorities driving land utilization policies, legitimacy of state-sanctioned land aggregation, and usefulness of enclaving to pursue investments. These debates have encouraged redrafting of the national legislation on land acquisition, with reference to definitions of 'public purpose', public and private roles in 'public' projects, and compensation and rehabilitation criteria based on land rights beyond ownership. Despite SEZs being de-prioritized, these debates continue to be relevant. Spatial segregation and enclaving dominate economic planning practice, and in current initiatives such as special investment regions, freight corridors, and infrastructure corridors, economic enclaves are assuming regional and interstate dimensions. Enclaving as a mainstream economic strategy is significant, as India's urban areas already highlight the complexities of coterminous and persistent spatial and economic inequality.

The significance of SEZs in India goes beyond their stated economic role and operationalization success, and extends to imaginations of spatial exclusion, autonomous governance, and the development they have helped prioritize. Four SEZ characteristics are addressed here: (a) as a typology of economic enclaving, in the global South in the post-War period; (b) as a governance model within the context of rescaled state power and competitive regional governments;

(c) as a spatial development model of exclusive spaces, through state-sanctioned land aggregation; and (d) as an economic model based on spatial and legal exceptions, to target external investments.

The chapter has three main sections. The first section traces enclaves as a part of national economic policies and global business strategies in the second half of the twentieth century. The next section examines the transformation of economic enclaves in India. The third section highlights concerns that SEZs have elicited in India, including spatial and legal exceptionalism, within the context of urban and economic planning in the country.

Information Technology (IT) SEZs are examined separately, as interventions to promote high-tech sectors of the 'future'. IT SEZs offer a link between economic liberalization and aspirational discourses of urbanized hypermodernity (Mitra 2015). Although IT SEZs are of a small format, many metros have developed IT suburbs, for example, Cyberabad in Hyderabad, Rajarhat in Kolkata, Whitefield in Bangalore, among others (Chacko 2007; Kamat 2011; Ramachandraiah 2003). These developments have anchored a returning diaspora (Saxenian 2002, 2006), after the global IT sector bust in 2000. This diaspora, mainly from the United States of America (USA), has been instrumental in transplanting spatial and lifestyle imaginations linked to American-style technoburbs, onto peri-urban areas of large Indian cities. Those associated with the sector have played a significant role in urban governance in cities such as Bangalore. Proposals made by NASSCOM (National Association of Software and Services Companies) and McKinsey to the national government go beyond SEZs and demand IT 'townships' at the scale of Gurgaon and Pune, new airports, and new captive infrastructure, among others. IT SEZs highlight concerns regarding India's urban transitions linked to high-end service sectors and claims of hypermodernity, rife with social and spatial dichotomies, even as absolute poverty levels have fallen.

Broader Significance of India's SEZ Experience

Two conversations dominate research on contemporary economic enclaves: (a) what enclaves reveal about the relationship between 'place' and global capital, as the first becomes substitutable with efforts

to decrease territorial 'frictions', and the second becomes increasingly footloose and tied into financialized logics and flows across nation state borders, and (b) what enclaves reveal about the exigencies of nation states within a dynamic global economic order and uneven terrain of sovereignty and citizenship that emerges with nation states negotiating between territorial and economic logics of power.

In both conversations, the focus is on the modern state as the 'site' for territorial power, adapting as logics of global capital evolve. The experience of SEZs in India, however, shifts the focus. Much of the Indian SEZ story has been about the challenges of developing SEZs, rather than the dynamics of their subsequent operations, which raise their own questions regarding the making of territoriality and relationships between 'place', capital, and governance. In India, SEZs have been associated with state governments (and to a lesser extent, the national government) laying claim to powers of territorial sovereignty at the local level, within a fractured milieu of regional identity politics, often exercising and negotiating territorial claims with local governments and actors, including community groups, landowners, and developers, exacerbated by the lack of 'place'-specific economic planning. This has created graduated sovereignty and citizenship and called into question the fundamental land–state–society terrain of rights and powers. Negotiating these fundamental relationships has been instrumental in halting many SEZ projects. Further, domestic capital has been more prominent than global capital, in the form of corporates, such as Reliance Industries and the Adani Group, and developers, such as DLF and Shapoorji Pallonji. The SEZ experience reveals an expansion of the private sector's role in planning, land aggregation, and project implementation; and changing norms of planning practice with increasing privatization of its content and processes. Market sentiments and business best practices have been significant in mediating relationships between 'place' and capital. However, market-led optimism, which translated into SEZ projects being approved rapidly and in significant numbers, was not justified by new economic growth that SEZs were able to attract. Most SEZs remain undeveloped or exhibit productivity levels at par with the overall economy, despite being located frequently and selectively near existing growth hubs.

Global Perspectives on Enclaves

Economic Enclaves: A Definition

'Economic enclaves' refer to 'free zones', with special policy environments to host foreign investments and export-focused economic activities. They are physically, legally, politically, and often socially separated from the hinterland; and exchanges between the zone and its region are strictly legislated. The legal forms of zones and economic activities permissible within them have transformed over time. Custom-bonded warehouses allow storage, repacking, and transportation to facilitate international transshipment. More complex enclaves include EPZs, which allow export-oriented production. Complex legislative environments and a wider range of permitted economic activities, including higher order service functions, such as financial services, are available at 'free ports' such as Singapore and Hong Kong, city-scale SEZs such as Shenzhen, cross-border zones such as the Indonesia–Malaysia–Thailand 'Growth Triangle', and Offshore Financial Centres, such as Mauritius, Montserrat, and the Bahamas (IMF 2000).

Export enclaves proliferated across the global South, from the 1950s, as the import substitution approach towards industrialization gave away to an export-oriented approach (Amado 1989). SEZs were made mainstream by China's experiments with liberalization in the 1980's. Located within a state-controlled economy, Chinese SEZs were more than production sites. They hosted parallel and self-sufficient economies, more tolerant of capital mobility, with a stable regulatory environment, and access to labour, land, and capital that mitigated investment risks.

Economic Enclaves in the Post-World War II Period

Post the War, the global economy underwent significant restructuring. Global production premised on mass industrial production in the global North and a 'classic' division of labour, faced a crisis of 'overaccumulation' (Harvey 1981, 2001) in the 1960s and the 1970s. The crisis was characterized by production overcapacities, falling returns on domestic investments, and mass redundancies. As production moved to the global South to allay crisis conditions (Frobel, Heinrichs, and Kreye 1980), the New International Division of

Labour (NIDL) emerged. The crisis conditions, in part, were shaped by post-War European reconstruction efforts, funded by the Marshall Plan and new Bretton Woods institutions. European nations received significant funding for reconstruction,[1] and deployed these nationally, for social and economic development projects, including basic infrastructure, housing, and new industrial facilities, among others, based on Keynesian principles. The cycle of investments and returns remained virtuous, as long as Europe was an expanding market, with increasing propensity and capacity to consume. However, as European products began competing with American products for the limited Euro-American consumer base, markets saturated. This led to production overcapacities and eventually, falling returns on investments.

With NIDL, vertically integrated Fordist production[2] systems, located in the Global North were replaced by complex buyer-led commodity networks, across nation-state borders, mediated by new business protocols, such as short-term contracts, third-party buyers, and retailer–manufacturer relationships. Efficiencies were enhanced through Information and Communications Technologies (ICTs) and standardized manufacturing processes. Management control was often retained in the Global North (Gereffi 2001) by retailers and buyers. Buyers were able to choose products from multiple locations and hedge against risks such as product defects and manufacturing delays (Gereffi and Korzeniewicz 1994). Cross-border investment patterns also changed. Countries hosting low-cost production often received project-specific investments and created specialized enclaves, in response. More than 100 EPZs were developed across 50 countries of the global South over the 1970s and 1980s, across Taiwan, the Philippines, the Dominican Republic, Mexico, Panama, and Brazil, among others (Amado 1989).

Low-cost production locations sought to reduce place-based 'frictions' (Harvey 2001), such as differences in quality and cost of infrastructure, labour costs, access to credit, regulatory environment,

[1] The World Bank's loan (then the International Bank for Reconstruction and Development) to France after the War continues to be the single largest loan ever given out by the Bank.

[2] Refers to assembly line production, from raw materials to final product at a single location. Developed by Henry Ford, it was the hallmark of post-War (1940s to 1960s) mass production across the USA and Europe.

among others, to be more competitive, often engendering a 'race to the bottom', with 'soft' costs underwritten by the host nation state to reduce investment risks and demonstrate state guarantee. The literature on first-generation enclaves, such as 'maquiladoras' and mining extraction zones, highlights the impacts of underwriting externalities (Beneria 2001, Campbell 2002; Frey 2003; Pyle 2001). However, reducing 'frictions' made space 'slippery' (Markusen 1996), as locations became substitutable. Economic enclaving, locational competitiveness, and 'best practices' need to be understood within this context of global production and trade, where investors were able to focus on advantages rather than limitations of a 'place', and be separated from a place's development needs. This is distinctly different from the objectives that fuelled post-War investments into Europe. Enclave-based investments predominantly prioritize competencies to participate in global networks (Alfaro and Iyer 2012). Their relevance to a development agenda, abetted by trickle-down theories, hypothesize that benefits would transfer to the region. However, empirical studies highlight that enclaves often create parallel economies and a social division of labour, which privileges global, rather than local, connections. Research also highlights that zone-based growth has regional impacts through planned linkages, rather than an automatic 'trickle down' (Massey, Quintas, and Wield 1992).

Despite limitations, enclaves have become common across the global South, with countries using them to fulfil economic and political agendas strategically. India and China have used them to contain liberalization and maintain barriers between domestic and foreign industries. Taiwan and South Korea have used enclaves to incrementally liberalize their national economies. Enclaves have been used to build core competencies in sectors, such as high-end ICTs, manufacturing, and the knowledge economy sector, where entry barriers of cost and quality of infrastructure have traditionally restricted production to developed economies.

India's Experiences with Economic Enclaves

Economic Planning in Post-Independence India

Economic planning and spatial planning in India have historically not been integrated well. Economic planning has been sectoral, undertaken through national and state-level five-year and annual

plans, with a rural, rather than an urban focus. Spatial planning has been restricted to urban areas, particularly metropolitan cities. State governments have more agency[3] than municipal governments in city-level spatial planning, through town and country planning departments and urban development authorities. State-level industrial authorities undertake industrial planning and development of industrial estates, parallel to urban authorities. City development authorities enjoy financial leverage as land development agencies, often subsuming the political leverage of elected municipal governments. Despite land being central to urban growth and politics, instruments such as master plans, have no explicit economic planning element and primarily focus on land use and development controls. Post-liberalization, state governments' involvement at the city level has also meant that state capitals have become default sites for the urban economic agenda of the state governments,[4] especially in destination branding for external investors. With non-spatial economic planning focused on rural areas, and spatial planning in urban areas without clear economic objectives, autonomous economic zones and industrial townships reveal a governance gap, and a lack of integrated economic planning for secondary and tertiary sectors in the country.

India was one of the first countries in the Global South[5] to experiment with economic enclaving.[6] Though the Industrial Policy Resolution (1948) prioritized the import-substitution approach for India (PAR-FORE 2007), the Mudaliar Committee (1964) recommendations were accepted and the Kandla EPZ was established in 1965,[7] followed by the Santacruz EPZ in 1972. Each EPZ in India was based on the recommendation of a committee (Tantri 2013).

---

[3] Land is a state subject, which gives legislative and executive mandate to state governments.

[4] Examples: Hyderabad during the Chandrababu Naidu (TDP) government, Kolkata during the Buddhadeb Bhatacharjee (CPI(M)) government and the Mamata Bannerjee (Trinamool Congress) government.

[5] Legally enacted free trade zones existed in the USA since the 1930s, as customs-free transshipment zones (Amado 1989).

[6] Before Kandla only Shannon, an airport-based zone in Ireland (1959) and Mayaguez in Puerto Rico (1962) were operational.

[7] Kandla was developed to promote exports, aid regional industrial development, and substitute Karachi port, post partition (Tantri 2013).

Performance of the first-generation economic enclaves in India was poor (Kundra 2000; Tantri 2013).[8]

In 2000, after a decade of liberalization, EPZs were replaced by SEZs. In China, SEZs were designed as self-contained economies. In India too, SEZs broadened the EPZ palette, in terms of 'comprehensiveness' of economic activities. Although SEZs were imagined as self-sufficient, with retail, housing, hospitals, schools, infrastructure, incentives, and investment-friendly regulatory micro-climate, more than 55 per cent of the 196 operational SEZs in India are small-format IT SEZs. There are 20 large-format multipurpose SEZs (MoCI 2015b), typically 1,000 hectares, the minimum limit for a multipurpose SEZ (Government of India 2005).[9] Despite scale differences, SEZs in India, like in China, have allowed the pace and spaces of liberalization to be rolled out, without concurrent structural economic, social, and infrastructure reforms; and have created spaces with autonomous governance, separated from local rural and urban administrative bodies.

Rise of Political Regionalism and Interstate Competitiveness

Rapid SEZ approvals by state governments highlight the model's significance to competitive local place-making efforts, including the rebranding of cities as investment destinations and creating enclaves to anchor investors, which increased after liberalization.[10] The imperative for local place-making emerged from economic and political regionalism, which ran concurrent to liberalization. Starting

---

[8] Poor performance of zones and poor trade performance in general, were noted by the Alexander Committee on Import and Export Policies (1978), Review Committee on Electronics (1979), Dagli Committee on Controls and Subsidies (1979), Tandon Committee (1980), Committee on FTZs and 100 per cent EOUs (1982), and Abid Hussain Committee (1984). See Tantri (2013).

[9] SEZs in India typically range between 10 hectares and 5,000 hectares.

[10] Undivided Andhra Pradesh under Chandrababu Naidu was the forerunner of interstate competition. In promoting Hyderabad, Naidu often emulated/competed directly with Bangalore, which enjoyed international recall as an IT destination; for example, the Shamshabad international airport was operationalized to compete with Bangalore's international airport. Naidu was included in the 'dream cabinet' of world leaders by the World Economic

with the 1989 national elections, no single party was able to secure a clear majority, leading to historically unique political alliances, in which regional parties became significant (Sinha 2004). Political motivations spurred devolution of power to the state level, supported by market-oriented reforms, instituted through legislation and regulations,[11] emphasizing fiscal conservatism and financial responsibilities of state governments. State-level agendas gave a uniquely political flavour to interregional competition and local place-making efforts.[12]

Political Economy of Instituting SEZs in India

SEZs, as policy instruments, traversed various political regimes. They were advocated by the Congress (I) as a part of liberalization. The SEZ policy was foreshadowed by 164 circulars on EPZs and export oriented units (EOUs) in the 1990s, justifying enclaves (Aggarwal 2004; Tantri 2013). The Bharatiya Janata Party (BJP)-led National Democratic Alliance (NDA) created SEZ regulations[13] in April 2000, after Murasoli Maran's (the then commerce minister) visit to China. The SEZ Act was passed by the Congress (I)-led United Progressive Alliance (UPA) government in 2005, and SEZ Rules were ratified in 2006 (MoCI 2015c). The history of how SEZs were instituted

---

Forum (see Ghosh 1999; India Environment Portal 1999; and *World Heritage Encyclopedia* n.d.) magazine (1998), named South Asian of the Year (1999) by *Time* Asia magazine, and Business Person of the Year (1998) by *The Economic Times*. (see In Naidu's time, Hyderabad hosted Bill Clinton, G.W. Bush, Tony Blair, and Bill Gates. Hyderabad was Microsoft's first main offshoring destination.

[11] This included divestment in public enterprises, delicensing, deregulation in investment protocols, opening up to foreign investors across sectors, and liberalization of the banking and financial sectors (Joshi and Little 1996).

[12] An emblematic example of inter-state competition, overlaid with personality politics, was the text 'Suswagatam' sent by Narendra Modi, then Gujarat chief minister, now prime minister, to welcome Ratan Tata to Gujarat to set up the Nano car project, when the Singur plant (West Bengal) was shut down due to protests.

[13] Available at MoCI's website on SEZs, http://www.sezindia.nic.in/.

belies elite versus pro-poor policy binaries set up between the BJP's 'Shining India' campaign and the UPA's grassroots agenda (Brosius 2009; Jenkins, Kennedy, and Mukhopadhyay 2014) and refocuses attention on how SEZs were eventually operationalized.

Before the SEZ Act was passed, there were seven central government SEZs and 11 SEZs promoted by state governments and public–private ventures. The numbers shot up dramatically between 2006, when the SEZ Rules were notified, and 2008, when the global economy reached crisis conditions. By March 2008, 453 SEZs had formal approvals and 136 SEZs had in-principle approvals (Alfaro and Iyer 2012).

The rapid approvals were short-lived. In January 2015, 491 SEZs had formal approvals, that is, 38 new approvals over seven years, since 2008 (MoCI 2015a). One hundred and forty-five SEZs were notified in the period (MoCI 2015a), highlighting long project gestation. As of September 2014, INR 380,284 crore (USD 63.4 billion),[14] had been invested in SEZs (MoCI 2015a). The slowdown in approvals reflected deflated market sentiments following the crisis. Moreover, over 200 SEZ projects were involved in land disputes by August 2008 (Alfaro and Iyer 2012). Following several violent land-related conflicts[15] and public mobilizations, the model was de-prioritized. The CAG (2014) audit report highlights a significant lag between the number of approvals and actual operationalization. Only 39 per cent of notified SEZs have been operationalized (CAG 2014). Frequently, SEZ developers were unable to deliver, and the CAG (2014) assessed that 52 per cent of land aggregated for SEZs remains vacant, and manufacturing in SEZs has declined. As of January 2015, 67 SEZs were officially cancelled or de-notified. The rapid rate of approvals highlight a radical change, with government decisions based on market-led optimism rather than economic review. The seven EPZs established before the SEZ era, subsequently converted to SEZs, were all based on recommendations of committees. Although these zones did not perform well before liberalization, they account for

[14] Assuming exchange rate of USD 1 = INR 60.
[15] For example, Nandigram in West Bengal, Pollepally in undivided Andhra Pradesh, and POSCO in Odisha.

73 per cent of SEZ exports (as of 2006–7), after liberalization (Palit and Bhattacharjee 2008).

The post-liberalization period witnessed increasing fractures in national politics and the rise of regional parties with regional agendas, which were often premised on identity politics (Kohli 1989). These factors made SEZs attractive to state governments and policymakers. They imagined SEZs would be efficient instruments, which, not-withstanding broader political economy exigencies, would facilitate a foreign investment agenda through private sector participation and autonomous governance. This sentiment is reflected in the prolific rate of SEZ approvals.

The planning and operationalization of SEZs occurred without participation of locally elected bodies and local communities, strengthening the perception of SEZs as state- and national-level government economic interventions, driven by greenfield and standardized imaginations. These visions were challenged at the time of land aggregation, and state governments were implicated in their role of facilitating such aggregation. The ground-level politics of land aggregation, especially in large-scale multipurpose SEZs[16] (some located on fertile multi-crop lands) (Rawat, Bhushan, and Surepally 2011) became flashpoints for anti-SEZ protests. Area under SEZs approximates 50 times the size of urban Delhi (Kumar 2006). The significance of this is amplified, as most SEZ projects are concentrated around major urban centres (CAG 2014).

Central- and State-government-level SEZ Legislation

Between 2000 and 2006, SEZs functioned under the Foreign Trade Policy (MoCI 2015c). New SEZ rules were notified as a part of the Export–Import, or EXIM, policy, converting EPZs to SEZs. The SEZ Act broadened the palette,[17] by allowing 100 per cent foreign direct investment (FDI) through the automatic route and single window

---

[16] For example, the first (and largest) multipurpose SEZ in Mundra (Adani Group), Maha Mumbai SEZ (Reliance Industries), Nandigram Chemical SEZ (Salim Group), seven SEZs proposed in Goa, and POSCO SEZ in Odisha.

[17] EPZs were basically incentivized industrial estates, for export-oriented production.

clearance. It allowed SEZs to self-certify exports and imports and act as foreign territories. It allowed development by public, private and/or joint sector entities, and extended fiscal and non-fiscal incentives to both developers and units. It expanded the definition of 'units' to include the service sector. It eased regulatory requirements for offshore banking units within SEZs, allowed sub-contracting and export/import based transfers between SEZs and domestic tariff areas (DTA), and offered tax benefits to DTA suppliers (Government of India 2005).

State governments were to follow with state-level legislation. However, only a few states such as Gujarat, West Bengal, Madhya Pradesh, Haryana, Punjab, Uttar Pradesh, Rajasthan, and Tamil Nadu enacted SEZ legislation (Mody 2010). A handful of other states—Karnataka, Jharkhand, Odisha, and Goa—have only SEZ policies. Seventeen states have neither state-level legislation nor regulations (CAG 2014). Only some states, such as Rajasthan and Odisha, have sectoral/industrial focus in their SEZ acts. In most states, similar to the central SEZ legislation, the focus is on guarantees; incentives and exemptions, including subsidies for power and water charges and infrastructure development; exemption from levies such as stamp duties and registration fees; and easing of regulations, including environmental conditionalities. State-level SEZ legislation highlights the focus on lowering costs for SEZ developers and units, echoing a logic of a 'race to the bottom'.

Key Concerns with SEZs in India

Economic Path Dependence of SEZs in India

The SEZ Act highlights its objectives as economic growth, in terms of employment and export-oriented production, by leveraging foreign investments, new technologies, and creation of new infrastructure (Government of India 2005). In part, the model was meant to break the path dependence from existing economic growth patterns (Jenkins, Kennedy, and Mukhopadhyay 2014), limited to 3–4 per cent per annum until the late 1970's, and increasing to 5–7 per cent per annum after the 1980s (Basu and Maertens 2007). However, SEZ performances mirror general patterns, both spatially, as well as in production and employment levels (Prasad and Ray 2010). As per

the CAG (2014) '[T]rends of national databases on economic growth of the country, trade, infrastructure, investment, employment, etc. do not indicate any significant impact of the functioning of SEZs on the [*sic*] economic growth.' Also the original seven central SEZs contribute 73 per cent (INR 428.96 billion) of the total exports from all SEZs (2006–7).[18]

The spatial distribution of SEZs reveals a concentration in already (and comparatively) industrialized states (Table 7.1), in proximity to large urban centres, and in districts with higher levels of development, highlighting the leveraging of existing locational advantages[19] by developers (CAG 2014; Mody 2010; Mukhopadhyay 2009). This belies the significant infrastructure expenditures and losses underwritten by public agencies to create exceptional environments. The CAG (2014) estimates that SEZs have availed tax benefits of INR 83,105 crore (USD 13.85 billion) between 2006–7 and 2012–13.[20] Without comparable incentives, EOUs contributed 21 per cent of the national trade during 2008–9 (Tantri 2013). Meanwhile, SEZ exports were 6.4 per cent of total merchandise exports in 2006–7. IT SEZs contributed 2.1 per cent of total software services exports in 2006–7 (Palit and Bhattacharjee 2008). Further, as Sengupta, Kannan, and Srivastava (2007) highlight, 63 SEZs notified between April 2006 and January 2007 accommodated occupiers such as Reliance Infrastructure, Flextronics, Wipro, Tata Consultancy Services, Ansal, and Satyam Computers, among others, each an established entity that did not require nascent industry treatment. Zone incentives may have arguably diverted and deterred general investments and underwritten losses (Bussolo and Nicita 2005), thereby impacting social welfare spending.

[18] Calculated using 2006–7 MoCI data in Palit and Bhattacharjee (2008).

[19] SEZs near urban areas: Maharashtra: 79 of 110 SEZs; Andhra Pradesh: 64 of 103 SEZs, Tamil Nadu: 36 of 68 SEZs, Karnataka: 35 of 52 SEZs, Gujarat: 36 of 50 SEZs, Haryana: 41 of 46 SEZs (Mody 2010: 4, based on MoCI data till June 2009).

[20] There are multiple estimates of potential tax revenue losses: Ministry of Finance and NIPFP: INR 175,000 crore (between 2005–10), Ministry of Commerce: INR 33,065 crore, ICRIER: INR 19,429 crore–INR 24,261 crore (PAR-FORE 2007).

Table 7.1   State-wise Distribution of Approved SEZs (as of 21 January 2015)

States/UTs	Formal Approvals	In-principle Approvals	Notified SEZs	Exporting SEZs (Central Govt + State Govt/Pvt. SEZs + Notified SEZs under the SEZ Act, 2005)
Andhra Pradesh	40	4	30	18
Chandigarh	2	0	2	2
Chhattisgarh	2	1	1	1
Delhi	3	0	0	0
Goa	7	0	3	0
Gujarat	35	4	28	18
Haryana	34	3	25	6
Jharkhand	1	0	1	0
Karnataka	59	0	39	25
Kerala	32	0	25	14
Madhya Pradesh	19	1	9	2
Maharashtra	69	9	52	25
Manipur	1	0	1	0
Nagaland	2	0	2	0
Odisha	8	1	4	2
Puducherry	1	1	0	0
Punjab	8	0	2	2
Rajasthan	9	1	8	4
Tamil Nadu	55	4	51	36
Telangana	60	0	42	24
Uttar Pradesh	31	1	22	10
Uttarakhand	1	0	0	0
West Bengal	12	2	5	7
GRAND TOTAL	**491**	**32**	**352**	**196**

Source: MoCI (2015a), available at http://www.sezindia.nic.in/.

Stand-alone Economic Interventions

Frequently, SEZs have been deployed as standalone interventions without supporting policies and programmes required to link them to

the local economy. Rawat, Bhushan, and Surepally (2011), using the example of Pollepally SEZ (located 96 kilometres from Hyderabad), highlight that the state government used the SEZ model in lieu of a broader industrialization agenda. The SEZ model hypothesizes economic transitions from agricultural to manufacturing and service sector jobs. However, without local-level economic planning and employment schemes (Aggarwal 2006), such transitions are rarely manifested, especially when SEZs anchor specialized sectors, such as IT, electronics, biotechnology, and pharmaceuticals. In Pollepally, there was a loss of agricultural employment with compulsory land acquisition, but the rehabilitation and resettlement programme did not envisage job training for the affected population to help them transition to skilled and unskilled jobs in the pharmaceuticals-based SEZ. These concerns are exacerbated with job loss amongst landless populations that do not receive monetary compensation (ADB 2007). Tantri (2013) highlights that lack of policy and programmatic details regarding SEZ labour sourcing opens up possibilities for exploitation via intermediaries. Rawat, Bhushan, and Surepally (2011) also highlight that loss of farmland and agricultural livelihoods impacted local groundwater management systems and food systems, and affected marginalized and vulnerable social groups disproportionately.

The economic impact of SEZs has also been compromised by the blurring of lines between economic and real estate investments, especially as land aggregated for many SEZs has remained undeveloped. After de-notification, SEZ land has been diverted for commercial purposes (CAG 2014). With volatile politics emerging around land transfer, such blurring has become significant. In 2006, the Reserve Bank of India cautioned banks to treat loans given to SEZs at par with real estate loans (Dhoot 2006). The CAG (2014) assesses that in four states, 11 developers/units have raised INR 6,309.53 crore (USD 1 billion) by mortgaging lands within SEZs. About 35 per cent of this loan has been diverted to other purposes, since no development in the SEZs has been undertaken.

Government-sanctioned Land Aggregation

Many anti-SEZ mobilizations coalesced around land aggregation. SEZ approvals were perceived as state sanction for large-scale land

transfers to developers and new users, within a highly contentious situation of unequal landholdings, vulnerable land tenures, and poorly legislated provisions for resettlement and rehabilitation for the landless (Mody 2010). In facilitating land aggregation, governments played a key role in determining uses that deserved development priority, reviving fundamental questions around land–society relations and land rights in a postcolonial society.[21] In the violent aftermath of forcible land acquisition, for example, the Nandigram chemical SEZ, where 14 villagers were shot dead, state governments stepped back from direct land acquisition. In April 2007, an Empowered Group of Ministers (EGoM) advised against state governments acquiring land for developers and recommended that developers aggregate barren/wastelands directly (Mody 2010; PAR-FORE 2007). However, this neither addressed nor resolved questions of development priorities, land and livelihood loss, and formal versus informal land rights, underlying SEZ protests.

The aggregation of wastelands has exacerbated unequal landholding patterns, since poor quality lands often support marginalized socio-economic groups. Rawat, Bhushan, and Surepally (2011) highlight that in the Pollepally SEZ (Andhra Pradesh), land acquisition focused on 'assigned lands', poor quality lands, allotted by the government to marginalized social groups[22] (Asher 2008), rather than fertile land, owned by upper castes. In Mundra SEZ (Gujarat) acquired land was labelled 'wasteland',[23] which impacted its value and compensation

[21] These questions were the basis of land reforms, after Independence, but welfare agendas shifted from rationalizing land relations to programmatic interventions.

[22] Acquisition of assigned lands in undivided Andhra Pradesh was made possible by an amendment in the Andhra Pradesh Assigned Lands (Prohibition of Transfers) Act, 1977, allowing acquisition of 'alienated' lands. However, the case research highlights that the acquired assigned land was not alienated.

[23] Land classification is derived from revenue land records held by functionaries, such as Patwaris. These records, that are open to manipulation even under normal circumstances, become further suspect in politically charged situations, such as land aggregation.

amounts. Both Pollepally and Mundra highlight use and value propositions embedded in land transfers. Land valuations for compensation, based on 'market' rates, reflect the transaction value of land under different uses, and do not monetize livelihood loss and cost of economic transitions for affected populations[24] (Rawat, Bhushan, and Surepally 2011). Such valuations privilege land as a commodity rather than a production resource.

Certain protests became emblematic, including Nandigram, which gave the Trinamool Congress a platform to win the West Bengal elections, after 34 years of Communist Party of India (Marxist) (CPI(M)) rule; the first referendum of farmers organized in Raigad, Maharashtra, which summarily rejected the Maha Mumbai SEZ; the successful grassroots mobilization in Goa (Sampat 2013), which led to the rollback of seven SEZs and denotification of three operational SEZs; and the successful pre-election mobilization by a section of landed elites in Punjab, which led to a rollback of SEZs in the state. Research highlights that across multiple SEZs, land aggregation and acquisition were associated with lack of information, misinformation, intimidation, unequal financial incentives, and in some cases interventions into local elections (Jenkins, Kennedy, and Mukhopadhyay 2014; Rawat, Bhushan, and Surepally 2011). Even in states where SEZs did not face outright protests, for example, Gujarat and Tamil Nadu, land negotiations were premised on unequal power relations, unequal financial imperatives, and implicit coercion to accept compensation to avoid compulsory acquisition at low prices, among others (Jenkins, Kennedy, and Mukhopadhyay 2014).

SEZs opened up debates about 'public purpose' and propositions of land value associated with compensation and rehabilitation (Alfaro and Iyer 2012; Grasset and Landy 2007; Morris and Pandey 2007). In successive reports, the CAG has questioned the 'public purpose' of acquiring land for SEZs, especially with reference to de-notified projects, where land has been diverted to commercial purposes (CAG 2013, 2014). These debates have been instrumental

---

[24] Various authors have highlighted underreported values during transactions to avoid registration fees, which results in 'market'-based compensations being low (Gill 2007; Kasturi 2008).

in the repeal of the 1894 Land Acquisition Act and enactment of the Right to Fair Compensation and Transparency in Land Acquisition, Rehabilitation and Resettlement Act, 2013, (LARR Act) by the UPA government after considerable debate and multiple amendments. The LARR Act expanded compensation and rehabilitation terms, made it difficult for multi-crop lands to be acquired, and required a social impact assessment process before land acquisition. At the time of writing this chapter, the issue is ongoing with the BJP-led government seeking to amend the LARR Act, and resorting to the ordinance route in the face of opposition. The proposed amendments would expand the types of projects that do not require a social impact assessment. The ordinance route, as well as the proposed amendments, have evoked sharp protests and put the BJP-led NDA government on the defensive, despite its overwhelming political mandate in the 2014 general elections.

Within a milieu of multi-stakeholder politics, the rapid approvals given to SEZs highlight state governments laying claim to territorial sovereignty to operationalize an economic vision, rather than giving away territorial sovereignty, as highlighted by Ong (2000), in her argument about economic enclaves being spaces of graduated sovereignty, where states compromise their territorial power. However, SEZs in India reveal that the success of such territorial claims has ultimately been determined by the quality of political relationships the state government had in place with the electorate, local landed elites, and local business owners. In certain states, local political and economic relationships made protests less intense. In highly urbanized Tamil Nadu, certain economic transition pathways from the rural to the urban economy were in place, and SEZ protests were more contained.[25] In undivided Andhra Pradesh and in Karnataka, landed elites shared the state governments' vision regarding the proposed economic transition and were able to participate in it, which allowed some SEZs to operate smoothly, despite significant rural distress in both states. In Haryana, the economic vision of landed elites, primarily from the agricultural sector, differed from the state government's urbanization agenda, which led to the state's land

[25] Tamil Nadu also had a large land bank that SEZ projects have drawn upon.

acquisition laws being made more pro-farmer and stringent (higher compensation rates and land reverting to the state in case the SEZs were not implemented). SEZs were rolled back entirely in Punjab, again because a section of landed elites did not share the particular vision of economic development, highlighting that historically formed relationships determined the relative success of operationalizing SEZs. Thus, despite greenfield and post-history imaginations of operational efficiency, SEZs have ultimately been products of their time and place.

Remaking Public–Private Relationships

SEZs highlight how the post-Independence, state-led developmentalist agenda broadened to include the private sector more substantively in the post-liberalization economic agenda. Land and infrastructure developers, corporates, business lobbies, and private consulting firms have become involved with planning, development, and governance of SEZs and helped normalize development narratives about economic zones facilitating foreign investments. Private consultants and business lobbies frequently assumed the position of 'experts', and developed protocols for SEZs, based on global 'best practices'. Jenkins, Kennedy, and Mukhopadhyay (2014) highlight that the Planning Commission report (prepared under the UPA government), used to formulate SEZ regulations under the NDA government, drew heavily from management consulting firms' reports. In 2004, Gujarat was the first state to pass a state-level SEZ act, which is considered a model act to be emulated (Mody 2010). Gujarat's approach towards SEZs was shaped significantly by the Adani Group's Mundra SEZ experiences, one of the first multipurpose SEZs in the country and still one of the largest. The private sector's role in planning and implementing SEZs is reflective of the broader trend towards privatization of planning, historically associated with the allocation and provision of public goods (Goldman 2010). Greater involvement of the private sector has allowed state industrial bodies to step away from land development, as for example, in the case of the State Industries Promotion Council of Tamil Nadu (SIPCOT).

The SEZ Act requires state governments to facilitate SEZs (including private sector SEZs) from the approval stage. Before forwarding

a proposal to the central board of approvals, the state government has to guarantee that the proposal adheres to the SEZ Act and Rules and that necessary infrastructure would be made available to the developer.[26] In discourses of good governance, the role of the state government as facilitator of investments and infrastructure as well as the guarantor of the investment risks associated with these projects (Wallerstein 1991) has been normalized.

Most negotiations between the government and the private sector have become focused on land and concessions. Broader concerns, including the creation of sustainable and quality jobs, transfer of fiscal and non-fiscal benefits to the region, and economic and environmental impacts on surrounding areas, among others, are left to developers, who mention these concerns in initial proposals. However, as the CAG (2014) highlights, the subsequent audit of these claims is poor, without independent systems or metrics to hold developers responsible.[27] Economic, social, and environmental concerns are aggregated within the purview of government permissions, often outweighed by business-led discourses regarding 'ease of doing business'.

Local Economic Impacts of Autonomous Governance and Planning

SEZs are examples of enclaved governance, exceptional both in their relation to local administrative bodies and in the constitution and autonomy of their internal administration. The SEZ Act gave the SEZ governing body more autonomy, as compared to EPZs. As per the act, SEZs are to be governed by appointees of the central government, including members of the central board of approval, the SEZ administration authority, and the approval committee (providing single window clearance to SEZ units). The approval committee comprises of nine members, of which six are central government

---

[26] This applies even when developers approach the Board of Approvals first, and secure state government permissions subsequently.

[27] The CAG (2014) notes that poor auditing has allowed developers to misrepresent facts, and about INR 1,150 crore (USD 191.7 million) remains undetected.

nominees, two are state government nominees, and one is a representative of the SEZ developer (Government of India 2005). The SEZ governing body has powers to self-certify exports (Jenkins, Kennedy, and Mukhopadhyay 2014), resolve labour issues,[28] and determine industrial profile within the zone (Government of India 2005). The scale of certain SEZs and their concentration near urban areas has drawn attention to the separation between the powers available to local governments to govern urban economies and resources, and the autonomy granted to parallel governance structures of co-located urban SEZs. For example, in 2007, of the 61 SEZs approved in undivided Andhra Pradesh, 35 were located in the metropolitan region of Hyderabad[29] (Palit and Bhattacharjee 2008).

Enclaved economic zones have also been instrumental in limiting access to market reforms to certain businesses (Bhagwati 2007). It has valorized imaginations of deregulation and business facilitation based on needs of external investors, rather than barriers and challenges within local economies with economic potential. Chandrababu Naidu, a role model for good governance and market-oriented reforms, used SEZs extensively in undivided Andhra Pradesh as a part of his strategy to attract high-profile corporates and investors. Much of the state-level urban economic agenda was concentrated in Hyderabad, highlighting an external-investor-led economic identity occupying the imagination of good governance.

SEZs reflect some continuities in economic planning practice in India, since economic enclaves and industrial townships have been

---

[28] The act gives the Development Commissioner power over labour issues. In certain SEZs this practice holds, for example, Kandla (Gujarat), Santacruz (Maharashtra), Noida (Uttar Pradesh), and Vishakhapatnam (Andhra Pradesh). In other cases, the State Labour Commissioner is involved to different extents, for example, Falta (West Bengal), Chennai (Tamil Nadu), and Kochi (Kerala) (Tantri 2013).

[29] In Karnataka, 31 out of 47 approved SEZs are in Bangalore. In Maharashtra, 24 SEZs are in Pune, and 23 are in Mumbai and Thane district, out of a total of 93 approved SEZs. In Tamil Nadu, 19 out of 46 SEZs are in the Chennai metropolitan region. Eleven of UP's 22 SEZs are near Delhi, in Noida and Greater Noida. Thirty-seven of Haryana's 47 SEZs are in Gurgaon (now Gurugram), near Delhi (Palit and Bhattacharjee 2008).

common through the twentieth century. However, earlier enclaves were often developed within agendas of balanced regional development and located in places with undeveloped potential rather than existing economic hubs. SEZs are predominately located in areas where economic potential has already developed, leveraging existing agglomeration benefits, rather than catalysing new growth. The SEZ Act highlights that state governments have to provide power infrastructure and environmental clearances, among others, to SEZs. A proliferation of SEZs, in places with existing advantages thus requires additional infrastructure investments, not compensated through local taxes and levies. Moreover, these zones preferentially divert investments in areas of economic potential (Mukhopadhyay and Pradhan 2009). SEZs also continue the trend of local governments remaining separate from planning and governing high value economic zones. Separation from local politics has counter-intuitively been used to build a counter-narrative, in the face of popular mobilizations, that SEZs are apolitical spaces of development.[30]

Certain state governments deployed SEZs to fast-track a business-friendly image, circumventing structural institutional, legislative, and infrastructure reforms, amidst election time-cycles and multi-stakeholder politics. Desai (2007) highlights that 'SEZs are business-friendly but not market-friendly'. The spatial and legal separations, between urban SEZs and urban economies, represent a binary approach, privileging global connections and local exclusions, accentuating patterns, where absolute poverty levels have dropped, but inequality has increased and greenfield imaginations predominate. Comprehensive local economic planning remains nascent, with premium spaces, such as SEZs, airport-based special zones, and IT townships being prioritized (Bhattacharya and Sanyal 2011; Graham and Marvin 2001). The government's role in mediating

---

[30] The Singur Nano plant (West Bengal) was not an SEZ. However, Ratan Tata's open letter to the 'youth of West Bengal' highlights apolitical development claims. In his letter after the Singur incident, Tata asked the youth if they 'want to stay as they are' and exhorted them to abandon a 'destructive political environment', and get behind a 'modern infrastructure and industrial growth' agenda.

disputes and alternative claims over land has become manifestly more important and insufficiently developed.

Information Technology SEZs in India

While public protests emerged around some of the largest, most land-intensive SEZ projects, more than 55 per cent of SEZs target the IT sector. IT SEZs reveal a confluence of spatially-focused economic strategies, with the aspiration to increase India's global economic relevance, in sectors of the 'future', such as the knowledge economy sector.

India's global competencies as an offshoring destination, even at the low-skill end of the IT industry chain (Carmel and Tjia 2005), questioned dominant narratives about economic possibilities in the global South, which had focused on low-cost production (Gereffi and Korzeniewicz 1994). New theories emerged envisioning agrarian economies 'leap-frogging' over the manufacturing stage, and becoming service-led economies (Amsden 1989), countervailing Euro-American development trajectories. Books such as Friedman's *The World is Flat* (2005), based on India's IT experiences, created elite visions of a hypermodern future in the global South (and India) that were part of a new global mythology of convergence. Yet the spatiality that has emerged around IT SEZs emphasizes that these claims of hypermodernity are being made in the face of increasing spatial and social dichotomies.

The Indian IT sector as a global phenomenon and its role as an economic driver in India, are claims easily questioned. The global Software and IT services market offshores only 5 per cent of its total expenditure (Carmel and Tjia 2005), and the Indian IT sector contributes 7.5 per cent towards the national GDP (NASSCOM 2012). In 2008, the majority of IT EPZs and EOUs in the country transitioned to the SEZ category, as the 20-year tax incentives associated with EPZs were to lapse.[31] With the transition, they gained another

---

[31] The end of IT sector incentives was recommended by the Kelkar and Shome committees (Palit and Bhattacharjee 2008; Tantri 2013). The 2002–3 budget proposed an end to incentives by 31 March 2009.

20 years of tax incentives. Narayana Murthy of Infosys, critiqued this move within the industry,[32] but later retracted his statement. The IT sector's demands for tax incentives, despite its global success, re-engages with the effectiveness of incentives in promoting economic growth, which is relevant in the case of other SEZs as well.

The attention and support that the IT sector has received, has encouraged 'blind-spots'. Manufacturing enclaves attracted extensive critical research on environmental issues and labour issues (Beneria 2001; Frey 2003; Pyle 2001). However, IT enclaves, perceived as 'white-collar' and non-polluting, have evaded similar scrutiny, especially in their role of normalizing urban spatial and social fragmentation. IT SEZs, in the range of 10 hectares, have been nodes around which new spatial imaginations of hypermodern urban development have become manifest (Ramachandraiah 2008). Peri-urban townships, designed to be self-sufficient and self-contained 'sub-cities', targeting external investors, not just from the IT sector, but also developers and investors for high-end residential, commercial, and hospitality projects (Chacko 2007; Kamat 2011; Ramachandraiah 2003) have emerged around large cities (Chacko 2007; Chakravorty 2000; Dupont and Sridharan 2007; Kennedy 2007; Ramachandraiah 2003; Shaw and Satish 2007).

The Microsoft website states the following about its Hyderabad campus, 'Our 54-acre green campus in Hyderabad has been designed to match Redmond standards.' Such statements, which have seeped into policy discourse, highlight industry-led benchmarking of an enclave's internal planning rather than its relationship to the city region. Transportation concerns that plague the relationship between Redmond and Seattle are also relevant in the peripheries of Hyderabad, where the Microsoft campus is located. Hyderabad's Outer Ring Road (ORR) developed as the main transport linkage in the city's periphery has been instrumental in branding Hyderabad as a destination for external investors. It is a 159-kilometre-long, eight-lane, high-speed, limited-access road, encircling the main city, connecting Cyberabad to the west, the new airport at Shamshabad

---

[32] See http://www.moneycontrol.com/video/business/it-industry-does-not-need-tax-exemption-narayana-murthy_449125.html.

to the south, the Biotechnology hub to the northwest (Genome Valley), the secondary IT hub to the east (Raheja Mindspace), the International School of Business to the south (250 acres), as well as several SEZs, golf courses, and high-end real estate projects, such as Singapore Township and Malaysian Township.

The ORR has opened an area 2.5 times the size of the main city on the urban periphery to external investors. Much of this land has become part of a speculative market with frequent transactions and aggregated holdings awaiting an economic and real estate boom (based on interviews with local real estate brokers and field observations). There is no public transportation on the ORR, although it has point connections to the city's public rail and bus systems. People working in these peripheral enclaves, especially in low-paying service capacities, are transported in from the main city, through chartered vehicles, effectively controlling the movement of a service population. Free movement on the ORR is possible only with private transportation. The ORR is designed to allow entry and exit into the city without interactions with the main city becoming necessary. Budgeted at INR 3,000 crore (USD 600 million),[33] the ORR is a significant public infrastructure investment, ultimately meant for privatized transportation. As the case of Hyderabad highlights, high-end, enclave-based developments, with higher levels of infrastructure in the urban peripheries constitute a significant departure from the dominant pattern of peri-urban development, which Roy (2009: 826) describes thus: 'rapid periurbanization ... unfolding at the edges of the world's largest cities is an informalized process, often in violation of master plans and state norms but often informally sanctioned by the state'. These patterns are visible in the peri-urban interstices between Delhi and other towns in the national capital region (NCR), as well as metros such as Kolkata, Bangalore, and Hyderabad. In Hyderabad, areas opened up by the ORR, which are not enclaved, are developing piecemeal, with rural settlements mirroring urban areas in consumption patterns and development profiles.

Émigrés who returned to India after the global IT bubble burst in 2000 in a process called the 'reverse brain drain' (Chacko 2007;

---

[33] See Deccan Chronicle (2010).

Saxenian 2002), are economically and politically powerful, giving voice to desires to manifest American-style IT suburbs in India's cities. NASSCOM, the business association for IT corporates and private consultancies such as McKinsey have facilitated the translation of such desires into policy. For instance, NASSCOM exhorted the national government not only for tax breaks and IT Parks, but also 'at least five new "Gurgaon-plus" and five to seven new "Pune-plus" integrated townships ... immediately develop a master-plan for 10–12 integrated townships with associated urban infrastructure including international airports, roads and land development ... facilitate large scale land acquisition (>1000 acres) and land development (e.g. sanitation system, power supply) for each integrated township ... expedite modernization of existing international airports' (NASSCOM– McKinsey 2005).

IT SEZs, more than any other type of SEZs, are linked to new hypermodern urban imaginations, premised on transitions to the service economy, with a focus on high-value service sector jobs, rather than the service sector jobs of cleaners, drivers, and guards also linked to such zones. The sector's global cost advantages leverage informality in work contracts with low wages, making it possible to maintain a high-quality lifestyle at lower costs.

Territorializing Economic Governance, but to What End?

SEZs represent enclaved economic and governance interventions that came to be valorized within the milieu of India's federalism and multi-party democracy, since liberalization. The role of such incentivized zones to achieve exceptional economic outcomes remains debatable, since only a limited number of SEZs have been operationalized and economic performance of operational SEZs reflect general growth patterns, despite being selectively located in economically dynamic areas, catering to economically dynamic sectors (such as the IT sector), and being provided preferential tax incentives and infrastructure. The original seven zones that were promoted as a part of the EPZ policy continue to be the dominant contributors amongst SEZs.

Private sector participation in SEZ development has encouraged the concentration of SEZs around existing economic hubs, with

developers hedging risks and accentuating rather than diminishing spatial economic inequality. SEZs located in economically dynamic areas have deflected attention from comprehensive economic development, allowed systemic and accessible market reforms to be side-stepped, consumed infrastructure investments, and put pressure on existing infrastructure, without generating commensurate taxes. The limited success of SEZs has called into question their significant tax write-offs and their role in achieving broader welfare outcomes.

SEZs reveal continuity in economic planning regarding autonomous economic zones, with predominantly sectoral and rural-focused economic planning and urban spatial planning without clear economic objectives. They reveal a continuing trend of local urban bodies not governing and planning high-value economic zones, even when they are co-located, and inadequate local-level economic planning. However, the importance of local economies and development aspirations has been highlighted by public protests against SEZs, which have emerged around land aggregation and land transfers. SEZ experiences highlight the lack of participation of local communities translating into oft-violent politics of coercion and consent around land aggregation. Relationships between state governments and local landed elites, developers, and community groups have been important for successfully operationalizing SEZs. Despite their lack of success, SEZs have encouraged imaginations of incentivized, exclusive enclaves, separated from the potentialities and barriers of local economies. Although SEZs are now de-prioritized, greenfield and enclaved visions continue to resurface across new formats, including new capital cities, smart cities, industrial corridors, and new townships focused on high-end service sectors.

With policies such as Make in India and Skill India, there is a resurgent national industrial agenda. The SEZ experience highlights the need for economic planning beyond prominent investors and corporates, and engagement with local land and labour dynamics. India's current economic profile is characterized by the growing significance of small- and medium-sized cities, informality in the production chains of both formal and informal units, informality in labour sourcing and work contracts, and the increasing role of women in the workforce. Moreover, much of the country's production and growth is supported by a broad land tenure spectrum, with

high values of land creating entry barriers for small and medium scale enterprises. Operationalizing successful and relevant economic growth is dependent upon nuanced engagement with these dynamics through local planning, integrated with existing spatial planning processes, and participation of local bodies, communities, and other stakeholders.

Conclusions and Suggestions: Looking Forward

Academic books routinely conclude by calling for more research on the subject at hand. We do not wish to break with this fine tradition, but would like to end on a more useful note. In this section, we briefly summarize our key findings, followed by some suggestions highlighting the significance of field-based research for future researchers studying the changing nature and scope of India's approach to spatial planning and development.

Tracking Independent India's Approach to Spatial Planning and Development

As described in this volume, the domain of spatial planning and development has witnessed noticeable changes since the country's Independence in 1947. For example, writing just a few years after Independence, Wayne Wilcox (1965) noted the remarkable lack of government reach in non-metropolitan India, and especially the hinterland. Here, an itinerant chowkidar, usually an ill-trained watchman equipped with a lathi or a heavy wooden stick, was often the only symbol of government, if at all. Watching over several remote villages, the chowkidar routinely walked many miles (often over several days and treacherous terrain) to report unusual events (floods, riots, epidemics) to the nearest officials located in larger settlements who took (or not) follow-up action as per political contingency and bureaucratic convenience. Describing the recent regime change from the imperial to the developmental state, Wilcox (1965: 114) also explained how the 'administrative machinery of the state is relatively weak in comparison

to the problems of stimulating development or using high levels of coercion in change, but strong enough to continue to dominate the decision-making process in the central government'.

Almost 50 years later, the elite-led centralized planning and development model, focusing more on economic progress and nation-building in comparison to the local people and their practices and places, has apparently 'succeeded', if 'development', among other things, is to be measured in terms of how well-linked many of these remote areas and culturally diverse communities are to the rest of the nation, through utility and communication networks of various kinds including all-weather roads. As described in this volume, the enhanced government presence, especially when seen in the light of Wilcox's observations, in many of India's smaller settlements and remote areas is now increasingly evident in state-sponsored schools and health centres as much as in centrally- funded welfare programmes providing employment to rural residents, midday meals to school-going children, and state pensions to the disabled and elderly. Although national economic progress remains a cornerstone of India's public policy, we find that paying attention to local people and places is also increasingly important due to the invisible, messy, and often complex nature of India's ongoing urbanization.

Chapters 5 and 6 of this volume take up this story, describing the manner in which many rural areas in India are slowly but steadily becoming urban. Mediated by a combination of larger demographic, social, and economic changes, the transformation of these smaller settlements is also a result of broader policy interventions. But these places are often afflicted with high rates of unemployment, poverty, outward migration, and shifting economic base from agricultural to non-agricultural activities. Physical and social amenities, civic infrastructure, as well as various government social programmes, for the most part, have not kept pace with residents' needs, so much so, that at times it has resulted in major social conflicts over very basic human needs such as drinking water and drainage.

Thus, properly planned provision of basic infrastructure such as internal roads, regular electricity supply, adequately staffed schools and hospitals in both rural and not-so-rural areas is as important as providing civic infrastructure in urban areas. Most importantly, judiciously conceived spatial plans by local people for these remote

places, rather than centrally imposed development ideas, can help in important ways. Local governments in the rural areas (or the so called village councils or panchayats) already have some experience in this regard. Not only do they approve and help implement almost all the development projects and social welfare schemes in their jurisdictions, they are also institutionally capable of receiving and using funds from both the central and state governments. Many panchayats, however, do not have the capacity to conceive and develop spatial plans and downstream projects in-house, at a time when it is becoming increasingly clear that they should be undertaking such activities.

Along similar lines, many of the ongoing shifts in India's largest cities could be positively harnessed by strengthening the urban local bodies (ULBs), finding ways to devolve urban planning and development responsibilities to local planning actors, and developing processes and frameworks to coordinate different kinds of planning efforts. This is especially important because as described in Chapter 1, the mega-project-based Nehruvian economic development model of the first phase (1947–67) focusing on the country's economic, infrastructure, and spatial development landscape appears to have come full circle in the fourth phase (1991 to present). There is a renewed focus on mega projects, exemplified by the interstate industrial corridor projects such as the Delhi–Mumbai Industrial Corridor (DMIC) and the Smart Cities initiative, but with four crucial differences this time around.

First, many actors—central and state governments, quasi-governmental agencies such as industrial development corporations, private and public financial institutions, and the residents living in the project area—are beginning to influence the processes of planning and development rather than only the Indian State. Second, there is an increasing recognition that cities are the engines of national economic growth and that the development of supporting infrastructure is critical for sustaining this growth. Third, the sizable, growing, and increasingly globally connected middle class and an activist judiciary are demanding better-quality infrastructure, services, and environmental stewardship. Fourth, popular resistance to 'top–down' policies like those evident in the cases of compulsory land acquisition combined with the ongoing empowerment of historically suppressed socio-economic classes has begun to shift the polity's attention towards marginalized groups and the persistent rural–urban

economic divide. This divide, for instance, has emerged sharply in the national discourse following the reportage of widespread resistance to the compulsory acquisition of land for the development of private special economic zones (SEZs).

The urban- and infrastructure-development-oriented shift, however, has not led to the integration of physical infrastructure and economic development with the planning and development of places. Presently, the focus seems primarily on individual infrastructure and economic development projects, and not on linking these activities with place-based planning for local people. We find that this is largely because of the following two reasons: First, local governments are neither empowered nor do they posses the capacity to conceive, manage, and fund the development of spatial plans and downstream projects. More than two decades have passed since the passage of the 74th Constitutional Amendment that called for devolution of spatial planning and development functions and powers to local governments. However, these functions are still predominantly controlled by the state governments, which seek to retain their authority over both urban and rural areas. Even where these functions are performed by a local elected or semi-autonomous institution, such as a municipal corporation or a development agency, these organizations are often headed by bureaucrats answerable to the state governments and not to the organizations they lead. We argue, that while these institutional arrangements might have been suitable for the first few decades after India's Independence, when planning and implementation capacities were lacking at the local level, these arrangements have gradually led to a widespread neglect of and underinvestment in local governments and, in turn, in both urban and rural settlements.

Second, and related to the preceding issue, is the lack of mechanisms to link larger-scale national- and state-level infrastructure plans with planning for urban regions and local places. Strong local governments that have the power and capacity to plan and fund local development can help achieve coherence between different kinds of planning efforts targeting various sectors and spatial scales. For instance, Chapter 3 describes how the master-planning-based planning approach in the city of Jaipur has gradually shifted from the government-led planning model to a multi-actor one with additional oversight provided by non-governmental organizations (NGOs) and

the judiciary. Further, the largely physical-planning-focused master plans are not only attempting to include other—social, economic, and environmental—dimensions, but also beginning to pay attention to the changes at the regional scale.

We argue that administratively, technically, and financially strong local governments, rather than a distant state or central government, would be better able to anticipate and respond to the larger and ongoing shifts shaping local places. Understanding the local, historical, and geographical contexts and political economy is important for successfully engaging multiple local players in the planning and development processes, and to plan for non-physical dimensions. Strong local governments would also be better able to integrate their local plans with regional-, state-, and national-level initiatives, such as the DMIC, in a manner where these centrally sponsored programmes do not run roughshod over settlements crossing their path. Finally, significant local capacity would also be required to make and pursue spatial development plans for the rapidly growing rural settlements, small towns, and surrounding areas as described in Chapters 5 and 6. Here, it is especially important to note that, instead of treating local governments in rural and urban areas separately, ULBs and panchayats should be encouraged to work together, for instance, when making plans for regional development.

Additionally, strong local governments can also help fund local spatial development. As noted in the Introduction to the volume and Chapter 1, Indian cities charge little or no property taxes; in part because they lack the political support and institutional capacity to develop a robust tax roll and collect due taxes. Many of the non-traditional revenue sources, such as an impact fee or the sale of development rights, require detailed knowledge of local real estate markets, infrastructure requirements, and the legal environment; and the technical capacity to design and implement long-range financial models. Strong local governments are a prerequisite for building such revenue streams required to fund local plans and projects.

Lack of effective processes to coordinate local place-based planning with large-scale infrastructure plans often leads to unsatisfactory implementation, and in many cases, rampant violations, of a city's master plan. The Jawaharlal Nehru National Urban Renewal Mission (JnNURM) tried to address this problem by requiring the largest

Indian cities to develop city development plans (CDPs). The decision-makers hoped that these CDPs would cater to the infrastructure requirements and, in the short term, ensure that the JnNURM-funded projects are well-integrated with the cities' overall planning efforts, while, in the long term, develop a culture of preparing locally sensitive infrastructure plans that would work smoothly with existing city-level master plans. Given the poor quality of many CDPs, decision-makers need to pay attention to the ULBs' inadequate capacity to prepare such plans and to develop attendant legal and institutional frameworks.

Suggestions for Future Researchers

Irrespective of ideological commitments and disciplinary orienta-tions, many readers would have noticed the substantial scope and sizable extent of ongoing changes in India's spatial planning and development practices across varied domains such as infrastructure policy, local plan-making practice, and the on-the-ground outcomes. We believe that these shifts necessitate carefully conceptualized field-based research to further our understanding of the many other salient, yet unstudied, shifts shaping India's numerous settlements that routinely escape scholarly attention. It is to this group that we direct the following suggestions:

1.   There is no substitute for field-based research for studying India's fast-growing settlements that are spread across regionally diverse and culturally varied contexts. Turning the attention from the largest urban centres, such as Kolkata, Mumbai, and Delhi that dominate the discourse on urban India, and paying attention to smaller cities and remote settlements can help uncover, as this volume has shown, how the spatial planning and development of some of India's lesser-known settlements is taking place. As Chapter 6 that examines Bihar's remote settlements has clearly demonstrated, carefully conceived and empirically sound field-based research work not only helps us see through established yet, at some level, empirically less-useful categories such as 'rural' and 'urban', but also helps us comprehend how the processes of urbanization are shaping the very edges of the country's spatial landscape.

2. If the purpose of field-based planning research is to map and com-
    prehend 'real-world' phenomena (and not really to demonstrate the
    coherence or efficacy of theoretical ideas or abstract frameworks),
    then the importance of employing practically useful conceptual
    and analytical approaches cannot be understated. As demonstrated
    in this volume, using an eclectic mix of theoretical insights from a
    variety of disciplines such as history, political science, economics,
    and cultural studies; and a diligent mix of methods such as archival
    research, content analysis, interviews, and analyses of population
    censuses and other empirical data can help uncover the hidden
    facets of human settlements that are intrinsically complex.

3. Locating the object of study in its historical trajectory of
    development, as we have shown, not only helps make sense of
    how we got to where we are but also how we might do better
    than the past efforts. In the case of post-Independence India,
    for example, it is clear that that the founding fathers imagined
    and positioned planning as a state-centered scientific tool
    for building the new nation. On the one hand, the adopted
    approach made India self-reliant in food production and lifted
    millions out of poverty but, on the other hand, the abiding
    trust in scientific expertise and centralized control meant that
    a large majority of people were excluded from the decision-
    making process. Notwithstanding the variety of oppressions and
    historical structures of subjugation, however, many sections of
    marginalized populations have shaped post-Independence India
    and its settlements in crucial ways. As an ever-increasing number
    of Indians search for livelihoods, shelter, and amenities in its
    rapidly growing settlements, spatial planning for places could
    actually help in small but significant ways. We do not precisely
    know what the future will bring. But we do know that a large,
    diverse, and rapidly growing India would need social solidarity to
    face an uncertain future. An inclusive and just planning process
    promoting access to basic public amenities such as regular
    electricity supply, parks, and schools, and common goods such
    as clean air and water would definitely help foster such social
    solidarity.

Bibliography

Adhvaryu, B. 2011. 'The Ahmedabad Urban Development Plan-making Process: A Critical Review', *Planning Practice and Research*, 26(2): 229–50.

Administrative Staff College of India (ASCI). 2010. *ASCI Training Manual*. Hyderabad: Administrative Staff College of India.

Afshar, F. 1994. 'Globalization: The Persistent Rural–Urban Question and the Response of Planning Education', *Journal of Planning Education and Research*, 13(4): 271–83.

Aggarwal, A. 2004. 'Export Processing Zones in India: Analysis of the Export Performance'. Working Paper No. 148. New Delhi: Indian Council for Research on International Economic Relations.

———. 2006. 'Special Economic Zones: Revisiting the Policy Debate', *Economic and Political Weekly*, 41(43–4): 4533–6.

———. 2012. *Social and Economic Impact of SEZs in India*. New Delhi: Oxford University Press.

Ahluwalia, I and P.K. Mohanty. 2014. 'Planning and Markets for Urban Development in India', in I. Ahluwalia, R. Kanbur, and P. Mohanty (eds), *Urbanisation in India: Challenges, Opportunities and the Way Forward*, pp. 56–81.

Ahluwalia, M. 1994. 'India's Economic Reforms', Planning Commission, New Delhi. Available at http://planningcommission.nic.in/aboutus/speech/spemsa/msa012.doc (accessed 11 October 2014).

Ahmed, S. and A. Varshney. 2012. 'Battles Half Won: Political Economy of India's Growth and Economic Policy since Independence', in C. Ghate (ed.), *The Oxford Handbook of the Indian Economy*, pp. 56–102. New York: Oxford University Press.

Ahmed, W., A. Kundu, and R. Peet (eds). 2011. *India's New Economic Policy: A Critical Analysis*. New Delhi: Routledge.

Ahmedabad Janmarg Limited (AJL). 2012. 'Janmarg: Revolutionizing Public Transit'. Available at http://jnnurm.nic.in/wp-content/uploads/2011/01/Brochures_Published_Janmarg.pdf (accessed 17 January 2015).

Ahmedabad Municipal Corporation (AMC). 2006. Stamp Duty: Annual Statement of Rates, 2006 (Draft). Available at http://www.egovamc.com/gruda/6_1_AMC_NEW_LIMIT_TP.PDF (accessed 16 April 2015).

Aijaz, R. 2008. 'Form of Urban Local Government in India', *Journal of Asian and African Studies*, 43(2): 131–54.

Alfaro, L. and L. Iyer. 2012. *Special Economic Zones in India: Public Purpose and Private Property*. Harvard Business School Case Studies. Boston: Harvard Business School.

Altshuler, A. and S. Gomez-Ibanez. 1993. *Regulation for Revenue: The Political Economy of Land Use Exactions*. Washington, DC: The Brookings Institute.

Amado, J. 1989. 'Free Industrial Zones: Law and Industrial Development in the New International Division of Labor', *Journal of International Law*, 11(1): 81–150. Available at http://scholarship.law.upenn.edu/jil/vol11/iss1/2 (accessed 29 August 2015).

Amsden, A. 1989. *Asia's Next Giant*. New York: Oxford University Press.

Anadkat, V. 2013. 'Rajkot BRTS'. Available at http://www.slideshare.net/EMBARQNetwork/004-vijay-anadkat (accessed 26 February 2015).

———. 2015. Telephone Communication with Shishir Mathur, 24 March.

Anand, Anu. 2014. 'Lack of Toilets Puts India's Health and Rural Women's Safety at Risk', *The Guardian*, 28 August. Available at https://www.theguardian.com/global-development/2014/aug/28/toilets-india-health-rural-women-safety (accessed on 7 January 2017).

Anand, N. 2012. 'Municipal Disconnect: On Abject Water and Its Urban Infrastructures', *Ethnography*, 13(4): 487–509.

———. 2015. 'Leaky States: Water Audits, Ignorance, and the Politics of Infrastructure', *Public Culture*, 27(2): 305–29.

Anjaria, J. and C. McFarlane (eds). 2011. *Urban Navigations: Politics, Space and the City in South Asia*. New Delhi: Routledge.

Ansari, J.H. 1977. 'Evolution of Town Planning Practice and System of Urban Government in India', *Urban and Rural Planning Thought*, 20(1): 9–23.

———. 1977. 'Evolution of Town Planning Practice and System of Urban Government in India', *Urban and Rural Planning Thought*, 20(1): 9–23.

Aranya. 2003. 'Globalisation and Urban Restructuring of Bangalore, India: Growth of the IT Industry, Its Spatial Dynamics and Local Planning Responses'. Presented at the 39th ISOCARP Congress, Cairo, Egypt, 17–22 October. Available at http://www.isocarp.net/Data/case_studies/255.pdf (accessed 16 January 2015).

Armstrong, R.J. and D.A. Rodriguez. 2006. 'An Evaluation of the Accessibility Benefits of Commuter Rail in Eastern Massachusetts Using Spatial Hedonic Price Functions', *Transportation*, 33(1): 21–43.

Asher, M. 2008. 'Land from Landless', *Tehelka*. Available at http://www.tehelka.com/story_main40.asp?filename=cr090808landfrom_landless.asp (accessed 20 August 2015).

Asian Development Bank (ADB). 2007. *Asian Development Outlook*. Manila: Asian Development Bank.

———. 2012. *Infrastructure for Supporting Inclusive Growth and Poverty Reduction in Asia*. Manila: ADB. Available at http://www.adb.org/sites/default/files/publication/29823/infrastructure-supporting-inclusivegrowth.pdf (accessed 7 January 2015).

Austin, G. 1999. *Working a Democratic Constitution: A History of the Indian Experience*. New Delhi: Oxford University Press.

Aziz, A. and S. Shah. 2012. *Public Private Partnerships in Urban Water Sector: Potential and Strategies*. Chennai: Athena Infonomics. Available at https://www.gov.uk/government/uploads/system/uploads/attachment_data/file/186992/PublicPrivatePartnershipsUrbanWaterSupply.pdf (accessed 5 March 2015).

Banerjee, A., S. Cole, and E. Duflo. 2005. 'Banking Financing in India', in W. Tseng and D. Cowen (eds), *India's and China's Recent Experience with Reform and Growth*, pp. 138–57. Washington, DC: International Monetary Fund (IMF).

Banerjee, T. 2005. 'Understanding Planning Cultures: The Kolkata Paradox', in Bishwapriya Sanyal (ed.), *Comparative Planning Cultures*, pp. 145–64. New York: Routledge.

———. 2009. 'US Planning Expeditions to Postcolonial India: From Ideology to Innovation in Technical Assistance', *Journal of the American Planning Association*, 75(2): 193–208.

Bangalore Development Authority (BDA). 2012a. *Proceedings of the Pre-proposal Conference on RfP for the Preparation of the Revised Master Plan for Bangalore-2031*. Bangalore: Bangalore Development Authority (BDA).

Bangalore Development Authority (BDA). 2012b. 'Request for Proposals (Revised) for the Consultancy Assignment "Preparation of Revised Master Plan for Bangalore-2031"', Bangalore Development Authority (BDA), Bangalore.

Bapat, M. 1983. 'Hutments and City Planning', *Economic and Political Weekly*, 18(11): 399–406.

Bardhan, P. 1984. *The Political Economy of Development in India*. New Delhi: Oxford University Press.

Basu, A. 1988. *Urban Squatter Housing in Third World*. Delhi: Mittal Publications.

Basu, K. and A. Maertens. 2007. 'The Pattern and Causes of Economic Growth in India', BREAD Working Paper No. 149. Bureau for Research and Economic Analysis of Development.

Batra, L. 2009. 'A Review of Urbanisation and Urban Policy in Post-independent India'. New Delhi: Centre for the Study of Law and Governance, Jawaharlal Nehru University. Available at http://www.jnu.ac.in/cslg/workingPaper/12-A%20Review%20of%20Urban%20%28Lalit%20Batra%29.pdf (accessed 5 January 2015).

Baud, I.S.A. and J. de Wit (eds). 2008. *New Forms of Urban Governance in India: Shifts, Models, Networks and Governance*. New Delhi; Thousand Oaks, Calif; London; and Singapore: Sage.

Bayley, C.A. 1879. *Imperial Gazetteer of India: Rajputana*, Volumes 1 and 2. Oxford: Clarendon Press.

Beneria, L. 2001. 'Shifting the Risk: New Employment Patterns, Informalization and Women's Work', *International Journal of Politics, Culture and Society*, 15(1): 27–53.

Benjamin, S. 2008. 'Occupancy Urbanism: Radicalizing Politics and Economy beyond Policy and Programs', *International Journal of Urban and Regional Research*, 32(3): 719–29.

Bhagat, R.B. 2002. 'Challenges of Rural–Urban Classification for Decentralised Governance', *Economic and Political Weekly*, 37(25): 2413–16.

———. 2005. 'Rural–Urban Classification and Municipal Governance in India', *Singapore Journal of Tropical Geography*, 26(1): 61–73.

Bhagwati, J. 2007. 'India Doesn't Need SEZs', *The Times of India*, 19 October. Available at http://timesofindia.indiatimes.com/india/India-doesnt-need-SEZs-Bhagwati/articleshow/2201326.cms (accessed 20 January 2017).

Bhagwati, J. and A. Panagariya. 2013. *Why Growth Matters: How Economic Growth in India Reduced Poverty and the Lessons for Other Developing Countries*. New York: Public Affairs.

Bhan, G. 2010. 'Urban Citizenship in the Juridical City: Tentative Propositions for Millennial Delhi'. Mimeo. Paper presented at the 'Contesting the Indian City: State, Space and Citizenship in the Global Era' symposium held at the Centre for Studies in Social Sciences, Calcutta.

Bhardwaj, A.K.V. 2014a. 'Experts Question BDA's Move to Draw Master Plan-2031', *The Hindu*, 20 March. Available at http://www.thehindu.com/news/cities/bangalore/experts-question-bdas-move-to-draw-master-plan2031/article5811218.ece (accessed 25 February 2015).

———. 2014b. 'Who Will Plan for Bengaluru?', *The Hindu*, 15 November. Available at http://www.thehindu.com/news/cities/bangalore/who-will-plan-for-bengaluru/article6600203.ece (accessed 11 March 2015).

Bhat, T.P. 2011. *Structural Changes in India's Foreign Trade*. New Delhi: Institute for Studies in Industrial Development. Available at http://isidev.nic.in/pdf/icssr_tpb.pdf (accessed 4 January 2015).

Bhattacharya, R. and K. Sanyal. 2011. 'Bypassing the Squalor: New Towns, Immaterial Labour and Exclusion in Post-colonial Urbanisation', *Economic and Political Weekly*, 46(31): 41–8.

Bjorkman, L. 2014. 'Becoming a Slum: From Municipal Colony to Illegal Settlement in Liberalization-era Mumbai', *International Journal of Urban and Regional Research*, 38(1): 36–59.

Boarnet, M. and S. Chalermpong. 2001. 'New Highways, House Prices, and Urban Development: A Case Study of Toll Roads in Orange County, CA', *Housing Policy Debate*, 12(3): 575–605.

Bose, A.B. 1992. 'The Disadvantaged Urban Child in India'. New Delhi: UNICEF. Available at http://www.unicef-irc.org/publications/pdf/ucs1_low.pdf (accessed 16 December 2014).

Bourne, L. and J. Simmons. 2004. 'The Conceptualizations and Analysis of Urban Systems: A North American Perspective', in T. Champion and G. Hugo (eds), *New Forms of Urbanization: Beyond the Urban–Rural Dichotomy*, pp. 249–68. Aldershot: Ashgate Publishing.

Brenner, N. 2004. *New State Spaces: Urban Governance and the Rescaling of Statehood*. Oxford; New York: Oxford University Press.

Brosius, C. 2009. 'The Gated Romance of "India Shining": Visualising Urban Lifestyle in Images of Residential Housing Development', in K.M. Gokulsing, A.F.E.W.C. Hawaii, and W. Dissanayake (eds), *Popular Culture in a Globalised India: A Reader*, pp. 174–91. London: Routledge.

Buch, M.N. 1987. *Planning the Indian City*. New Delhi: Vikas Publishing.

Burt, Z. and I. Ray. 2014. 'Storage and Non-payment: Persistent Informalities within the Formal Water Supply of Hubli-Dharwad, India', *Water Alternatives*, 7(1): 106–20.

Bussolo, M. and A. Nicita. 2005. 'Trade Policy Reforms', in A. Coudouel and S. Paternostro (eds), *Analyzing the Distributional Impacts of Reforms: A Practitioner's Guide to Trade, Monetary and Exchange Rate Policy, Utility Provision, Agricultural Markets, Land Policy, and Education*, pp. 1–38. Washington, DC: The World Bank.

Butler, M.A. and C.A. Beale. 1994. *Rural–Urban Continuum Codes for Metropolitan and Nonmetropolitan Counties*. Washington, DC: US Economic Research Service.

Campbell, M. 2002. *Maquiladoras: Rethinking NAFTA* [video]. PBS.

Carmel, E. and P. Tjia. 2005. *Offshoring Information Technology*. Cambridge: Cambridge University Press.

Castells, M. 1977. *The Urban Question: A Marxist Approach*. Berkeley: University of California Press.

Census of India. 1991. Primary Census Abstract and Village Data Abstract. Available on file with the author.

————. 2001. Primary Census Abstract and Village Data Abstract. Available at http://www.censusindia.gov.in/2011-common/census_data_2001.html (accessed 7 January 2017).

————. 2011a. Census data for Kerala. Available at http://censusindia.gov.in/2011-prov-results/paper2/data_files/kerala/13-concept-34.pdf (accessed 28 December 2016).

————. 2011b. Census data. Available at www.census2011.co.in/density.php (accessed 5 January 2017).

Centre for Symbiosis of Technology, Environment and Management (STEM). 1992. *An Objective Review of Implementation of Master Plans in Selected Class I Cities and Other Towns.* Bangalore: STEM.

Centre of Excellence in Urban Transport (CEUT). 2015. *Janmarg-BRTS: Ahmedabad Bus Rapid Transit System.* Available at http://www.unescap.org/sites/default/files/4.2% Institutional issues and coordination in sustainable transport—CEPT.pdf (accessed 26 February 2015).

Cerra, V. and S. Saxena. 2000. 'What Caused the 1991 Currency Crisis in India?'. IMF Working Paper WP/00/157. Washington, DC: IMF. Available at http://www.imf.org/external/pubs/ft/wp/2000/wp00157.pdf (accessed 2 December 2014).

Chacko, E. 2007. 'From Brain Drain to Brain Gain: Reverse Migration to Bangalore and Hyderabad, India's Globalizing High Tech Cities', *GeoJournal*, 68(2–3): 131–40.

Chakrabarti, V. 1998. *Indian Architectural Theory: Contemporary Uses of Vastu Vidya.* Surrey: Curzon Press.

Chakravorty, S. 2000. 'From Colonial City to Globalizing City? The Far from Complete Spatial Transformation of Calcutta', in P. Marcuse and R. van Kempen (eds), *Globalizing Cities: A New Spatial Order*, pp. 56–77. London: Wiley-Blackwell.

————. 2013. *The Price of Land: Acquisition, Conflict, Consequence.* New Delhi: Oxford University Press.

Champion, T. and G. Hugo. 2003. 'Beyond the Urban–Rural Dichotomy: Towards a New Conceptualization of Settlement for Demographers'. Paper presented at the 'PAA 2003 Annual Meeting', 1–3 May, Minneapolis.

———— (eds). 2004. *New Forms of Urbanization: Beyond the Urban–Rural Dichotomy.* Aldershot: Ashgate Publishing.

Chatterjee, P. 2004. *The Politics of the Governed.* New York: Columbia University Press.

————. 2008. 'Democracy and Economic Transformation in India', *Economic and Political Weekly*, 43(16): 53–62.

Chawla, B.S. 1995. *The Haryana Municipal Act 1973* (Commentary with Allied Rules and Bye-laws, Amended Up-to-date). Chandigarh: Chawla Publications.

Chief Town Planner and Architectural Advisor. 1976. *Master Plan for Jaipur*. Jaipur: Government press.

Chopra, S. and J. Pudussery. 2014. 'Social Security Pensions in India: An Assessment', *Economic and Political Weekly*, 49(19): 68–74.

City Managers' Association Rajasthan. 2003. 'Best Practices of the Cities of Rajasthan'. Mimeo. Jaipur: Directorate of Local Bodies, Government of Rajasthan.

City of Kanchipuram. 2014a. The Planning Authority (Levy of Development Charges) Rules, 1975. Available at http://www.kanchi.nic.in/mlpa_final/LPA%20rules/Levy_Dev_Charges_Appeal_Rules.pdf (accessed 18 June 2014).

———. 2014b. Tamil Nadu Town and Country Planning Act, 1971. Available at http://www.kanchi.nic.in/mlpa_final/Act/Town%20&%20Country%20Planning%20Act%201971.pdf (accessed 18 June 2014).

CNBC TV-18. 2010. 'IT Industry Does Not Need Tax Exemption: Narayana Murthy', 31 March. Available at http://www.moneycontrol.com/news/business/it-industry-does-not-need-tax-exemption-narayana-murthy_449125.html (accessed 15 January 2017).

Coelho, K., L. Kamath, and M. Vijaybaskar. 2011. 'Infrastructures of Consent: Interrogating Citizen Participation Mandates in Indian Urban Governance', IDS Working Papers 362, Institute of Development Studies.

Cohen, B. 2014. 'Negotiating Differences: India's Language Policy', in S. Williams (ed.), *Social Difference and Constitutionalism in Pan-Asia*, pp. 27–52. Cambridge: Cambridge University Press.

Communicate Karo. 2013. 'Rajpath, the Second BRT System in Gujarat, Chugs into Rajkot City'. Available at https://communicatekaro.wordpress.com/2013/09/17/rajpath-the-second-brt-system-in-gujarat-chugs-into-rajkot-city/ (accessed 26 February 2015).

Comptroller and Auditor General of India (CAG). 2012. *Performance Audit on Jawaharlal Nehru National Urban Renewal Mission (Ministry of Urban Development, Ministry of Housing and Urban Poverty Alleviation)*. New Delhi: CAG. Available at http://saiindia.gov.in/english/home/Our_Products/Audit_report/Government_Wise/union_audit/recent_reports/union_performance/2012_2013/Commercial/Report_15/Report_15.html (accessed 17 January 2015).

———. 2013. *Audit of Revenue Receipts: Indirect Taxes (Customs Duties)*. Report No. 14 of 2013. New Delhi: Union Government, Department of Revenue—Customs (Compliance Audit).

———. 2014. *Performance of Special Economic Zones (SEZs)*. Report No. 21 of 2014. New Delhi: CAG, Union Government, Department of Revenue. Available at http://www.saiindia.gov.in/english/home/Our_Products/Audit_Report/Government_Wise/union_audit/recent_reports/

union_performance/2014/INDT/Report_21/21of2014.pdf (accessed 21 January 2015).

Coombes, M. and S. Raybould. 2001. 'Commuting in England and Wales', in D. Pitfield (ed.) *Transport Planning, Logistics and Spatial Mismatch*. European Research in Regional Science 11, pp. 111–33. London: Pion.

Cromartie, J. and L.L. Swanson. 1996. 'Census Tracts more Precisely Define Rural Populations and Areas, *Rural Development Perspectives*, 11(3): 31–9.

Dainik Bhaskar. 2009. 'Naye Mayor ki Pehli Prathamikta Virasat Bachana' [New Mayor Identifies Heritage as the First Priority], Jaipur edition, 27 November.

Datta, A. and S.K. Mishra. 2011. 'Glimpses of Women's Lives in Rural Bihar: Impact of Male Migration', *The Indian Journal of Labour Economics*, 54(3): 457–77.

Datta, S. 2012. 'The Impact of Improved Highways on Indian Firms', *Journal of Development Economics*, 99(1): 46–57.

Debrezion, G., E. Pels, and P. Rietveld. 2006. 'The Impact of Rail Transport on Real Estate Prices: An Empirical Analysis of the Dutch Housing Market'. Tinbergen Institute Discussion Paper, TI 2006-031/3. Amsterdam: Tinbergen Institute.

Deccan Chronicle. 2010. 'Another 260-km Ring Road Planned for City', 4 December. Available at https://web.archive.org/web/20101206032311/http://www.deccanchronicle.com/hyderabad/another-260-km-ring-road-planned-city-784 (accessed 22 January 2017).

Delhi Mumbai Industrial Corridor (DMIC). 2014. Delhi Mumbai Industrial Corridor. Available at http://www.dmic.co.in/ (accessed 17 January 2015).

Denis, E. and K. Marius-Gnanou. 2011. 'Toward a Better Appraisal of Urbanization in India', *Cybergeo: European Journal of Geography*, 569. doi: 10.4000/cybergeo.24798.

Department of Industrial Policy and Promotion (DIPP). 2002. 'Industrial Policy Highlights'. New Delhi: Ministry of Commerce and Industry, Government of India. Available at http://eaindustry.nic.in/handbk/chap001.pdf (accessed 6 December 2014).

Desai, N. 2007. 'Are SEZs A Good Idea?', *The Business Standard*, 15 March. Available at http://www.business-standard.com/article/opinion/nitin-desai-are-sezs-a-good-idea-107031501100_1.html (accessed 15 January 2017).

Desai, R. and R. Sanyal (eds). 2012. *Urbanizing Citizenship: Contested Spaces in Indian Cities*. Delhi: Sage.

Devi, Gayatri. 1996. *A Princess Remembers: The Memoirs of the Maharani of Jaipur*. Delhi: Rupa and Co.

Dhoot. V. 2006. 'Treat SEZs Like Real Estate, Says RBI Governor', *The Indian Express*, 22 September.

Dobbs, Z. 2009. 'Fabian Socialism', in *Keynes at Harvard: Economic Deception as a Political Credo*. Austin: Perry Press. Available at http://www.keynesatharvard.org/ (accessed 21 November 2014).

Drèze, J. 2013. 'How Life is Improving in India's Poorest Regions', BBC News, 23 December. Available at http://www.bbc.com/news/world-asia-india-25315528 (accessed 24 December 2013).

Dupont, V. 2004. 'Urban Development in Delhi', in T. Champion and G. Hugo (eds), *New Forms of Urbanization: Beyond the Urban–Rural Dichotomy*, pp. 171–190. Aldershot: Ashgate Publishing.

Dupont, V. and N. Sridharan. 2007. 'Peri-urban Dynamics: Case Studies in Chennai, Hyderabad and Mumbai'. eSocialSciences Working Paper Series No. 974. eSocialSciences. Available at https://ideas.repec.org/p/ess/wpaper/id974.html (accessed 15 January 2017).

Dutt, A.K., I. Pomeroy, I. Islam, and I. Chatterjee. 2016. 'Cities of South Asia', in Stanley D. Brunn Jessica K. Graybill, Maureen Hays-Mitchell, and Donald J. Zeigler (eds), *Cities of the World: World Regional Urban Development*, 6th edition, pp. 316–412. New York: HarperCollins.

Economic Times. 2012. 'A P J Kalam's PURA project a "complete failure": Jairam Ramesh', 24 February. Available at http://economictimes.indiatimes.com/news/politics-and-nation/a-p-j-kalams-pura-project-a-complete-failure-jairam-ramesh/articleshow/12021823.cms (accessed 7 January 2017).

Exim Bank. 2014. *Annual Report 2013–2014*. New Delhi: Export-Import Bank of India.

Fahim, M. 2009. 'Local Government in India Still Carries Characteristics of Its Colonial Heritage'. Available at http://www.citymayors.com/government/india_government.html (accessed 24 May 2009).

Fernandes, L. 2006. *India's New Middle Class: Democratic Politics in an Era of Economic Reform*. Minneapolis: University of Minnesota Press.

Frankel, F.R. 2009. *India's Political Economy 1947–2004*, 2nd edition. New Delhi: Oxford University Press.

Frey, R. 2003. 'The Transfer of Core-based Hazardous Production Processes to the Export Processing Zones of the Periphery: The Maquiladora Centers of Northern Mexico', *Journal of World-Systems Research*, 9(2): 317–54.

Friedman, T. 2005. *The World is Flat*. New York: Farrar, Straus and Giroux.

Friedmann, J. 2011. 'The Transactive Style of Planning', in J. Friedmann (ed.), *Insurgencies: Essays in Planning Theory*, pp. 15–28. UK, USA, and Canada: Routledge.

Frobel, F., J. Heinrichs, and O. Kreye. 1980. *The New International Division of Labour*. Cambridge: Cambridge University Press.

Gandhi, S. 2002. *The Tilt: The U.S. and the South Asian Crisis of 1971*, National Security Archive Electronic Briefing Book No. 79. Washington, DC: National Security Archives. Available at http://www2.gwu.edu/~nsarchiv/NSAEBB/NSAEBB79/ (accessed 13 December 2014).

Gandhinagaronline. 2014. History of Gandhinagar. Available at http://www.gandhinagaronline.in/city-guide/history-of-gandhinagar (accessed 12 November 2014).

Gereffi, G. 2001. 'Shifting Governance Structures in Global Commodity Chains, With Special Reference to the Internet', *American Behavioral Scientist*, 44(10): 1616–37.

Gereffi, G. and M. Korzeniewicz. 1994. *Commodity Chains and Global Capitalism*. Westport: Greenwood Press.

Ghani, E., A. Goswami, and W. Kerr. 2014. 'Highway to Success: The Impact of the Golden Quadrilateral Project for the Location and Performance of Indian Manufacturing'. Paper presented at the 2nd Urbanization and Poverty Reduction Research Conference, Washington, DC, 12 November Available at http://www.worldbank.org/content/dam/Worldbank/Event/DEC/Urbanization-Conf-2014/GGK-GQEntry.pdf (accessed 16 January 2015).

Ghate, C. (ed.). 2012. *The Oxford Handbook of the Indian Economy*. New York: Oxford University Press.

Ghertner, D.A. 2011. 'Gentrifying the State, Gentrifying Participation: Elite Governance Programs in Delhi', *International Journal of Urban and Regional Research*, 35(3): 504–32.

Ghosh, A. 2005. 'Public–Private or a Private Public: Promised Partnership of the Bangalore Agenda Task Force', *Economic and Political Weekly*, 40(47): 4914–22.

———. 2006. 'Working of the BATF', *Economic and Political Weekly*, 41(14): 1376–7.

Ghosh, S. 1997. *Indian Democracy Derailed: Politics and Politicians*. New Delhi: A.P.H. Publishing Corporation.

Gibbons, S. and S. Machin. 2006. 'Paying for Primary Schools: Admission Constraints, School Popularity or Congestion', *The Economic Journal*, 116(510): C77–C92.

Gill, L.S. 2007. 'Economic and Social Implications of Special Economic Zones', *The Economic Challenger*, 9(36): 37–41.

Ginsburg, N. 1991. 'The Extended Metropolis: Settlement Transition in Asia', in N. Ginsburg, B. Koppel, and T.G. McGee (eds), *The Extended Metropolis*, pp. 27–46. Honolulu: University of Hawaii Press.

Godschalk, D.R. and W.R. Anderson. 2012. *Sustaining Places: The Role of the Comprehensive Plan*. Planning Advisory Service (PAS report #567). Chicago: American Planning Association.

Gold, Ann and Bhoju Ram Gujar. 2002. *In the Time of Trees and Sorrow: Nature, Power, and Memory in Rajasthan*. Durham: Duke University Press.

Goldman, M. 2010. 'Speculative Urbanism and the Making of the Next World City', *International Journal of Urban and Regional Research*, 35(3): 555–81.

Gooptu, N. 2011. 'Economic Liberalization, Urban Politics, and the Poor', in S. Ruparelia, T. Reddy, J. Harriss, and S. Corbridge (eds), *Understanding India's New Political Economy: A Great Transformation*, pp. 35–48. London: Routledge.

Gopakumar, G. 2014. 'Experiments and Counter-experiments in the Urban Laboratory of Water-supply Partnerships in India', *International Journal of Urban and Regional Research*, 38(2): 393–412.

Government of Gujarat. 2011. ASR-2011 Final. Available at http://revenuedepartment.gujarat.gov.in/downloads/RAJKOT-NAGARPALIKA.pdf (accessed 17 April 2015).

Government of India. 2005. *The Special Economic Zones Act*. New Delhi: Ministry of Law and Justice, Government of India.

———. 2011. 'Fact Sheet on Foreign Direct Investment (FDI) from August 1991 to April 2011'. New Delhi: Department of Industrial Policy and Promotion, Ministry of Commerce and Industry.

Government of Karnataka. 2010. Karnataka Urban Drinking Water and Sanitation Policy, 2002. Bangalore: Urban Development Department, Government of Karnataka. Available at http://www.uddkar.gov.in/watersanitation (accessed 29 March 2015).

———. 2011. '24X7 Water Supply in 3 Cities of Karnataka'. Bangalore: Infrastructure Development Department, Government of Karnataka. Available at http://www.iddkarnataka.gov.in/docs/CS_Karnataka.pdf (accessed 2 April 2015).

———. 2014. *Bangalore Metropolitan Planning Committee Rules*. Bangalore: Urban Development Department, Government of Karnataka.

Government of Tamil Nadu. 2009. 'Creation of Tamil Nadu Town and Country Planning State Infrastructure and Amenities Fund'. Available at http://www.tniuscbe.org/download/go/go1530.pdf (accessed 18 June 2014).

———. 2012. 'Infrastructure and Amenities Charges: Increase by 50% of the Present Prevailing Rates in Town and Country Planning and CMDA Areas'. Available at http://cms.tn.gov.in/sites/default/files/gos/hud_e_86_2012.pdf (accessed 18 June 2014).

Graham, S. and S. Marvin. 2001. *Splintering Urbanism*. London: Routledge.

Graham, S., R. Desai, and C. McFarlane. 2013. 'Water Wars in Mumbai', *Public Culture*, 25(1 69): 115–41.

Grasset, J. and F. Landy. 2007. 'Special Economic Zones in India: Between International Integration and Real Estate Speculation', *Man and Development*, 29(4): 63–74.

Guha, R. and G.C. Spivak (eds). 1988. *Selected Subaltern Studies*. New York: Oxford University Press.

Gupta, A. 1995. 'Blurred Boundaries: The Discourse of Corruption, the Culture of Politics, and the Imagined State', *American Ethnologist*, 22(2): 375–402.

Gupta, A. and K. Sivaramakrishnan. 2010. *The State in India after Liberalization*. New York: Routledge.

Gupta, Ramesh Chandra. 1992. *Land Assembly in the Indian Metropolis*. New Delhi: Uppal Publishing House.

Guru, S. 2014. 'Mahalanobis Growth Model and Heavy-industry Strategy of Development!'. Available at http://www.yourarticlelibrary.com/economics/mahalanobis-growth-model-and-heavy-industry-strategy-of-development/38376/ (accessed 16 December 2014).

Harriss, J. 2000. 'How Much Difference Does Politics Make? Regime Differences across Indian States and Rural Poverty Reduction'. Mimeo. London: London School of Economics, Development Studies Institute.

Harriss-White, B. 2002. *India Working: Essays on Society and Economy*. Cambridge: Cambridge University Press.

Harvey, D. 1981. 'The Spatial Fix: Hegel, Von Thunen, and Marx', *Antipode*, 13(3): 1–12.

———. 1985. *The Urban Experience*. Baltimore: The Johns Hopkins University Press.

———. 2001. *Spaces of Capital*. New York: Routledge.

Haryana Government Gazette. 2014. Rates of Conversion Charges in the Controlled Areas in the State. Available at http://tcpharyana.gov.in/CIM/DOC/Conversion%20charges.pdf (accessed 2 June 2015).

haryana-online.com. 2009. 'History of Haryana-Haryana Day: A New State is Born!'. Available at http://www.haryana-online.com/History/history_1966-.htm (accessed 22 October 2014).

Haynes, Douglas. 1991. *Rhetoric and Ritual in Colonial India: The Shaping of a Public Culture in Surat City, 1852–1928*. Berkeley: University of California Press.

Henneberry, J. 1998. 'Transport Investment and House Prices', *Journal of Property Valuation and Investment*, 16(2): 144–58.

High Powered Expert Committee (HPEC). 2011. *Report on Indian Urban Infrastructure and Services*. Report for the Government of India by the High Powered Expert Committee for Estimating the Investment Requirements

for Urban Infrastructure Services. New Delhi: HPEC, niua.org/projects/
hpec/finalreport-hpec.pdf (accessed 15 February 2012).

Hindustan Times. 2014. 'Badaun Girls' Tragic Story Points to Risks Women
Face in Rural India' 1 June. Available at http://www.hindustantimes.
com/india/badaun-girls-tragic-story-points-to-risks-women-face-in-
rural-india/story-KyeVJGfF3yyxmeZOEYWW9J.html (accessed 7
January 2017).

Hiro, D. 2014. *Indians in a Globalizing World: Their Skewed Rise.* Noida:
HarperCollins.

Huntington, S. 1987. 'The Goals of Development', in Myron Weiner
and Samuel Huntington (eds), *Understanding Political Development*,
pp. 3–30. Boston: Little Brown.

Hussain, M. 2011. *The Geography of India.* New Delhi: Tata McGraw-Hill.

India Infoline News Service. 2012. 'Central Subsidies to be Brought Down
to 1.75% of GDP in Three Years: FM'. Available at http://www.indi-
ainfoline.com/article/news/central-subsidies-to-be-brought-down-to-
175-percent-of-gdp-in-three-years-fm-5377266664_1.html (accessed
6 January 2015).

Indian Institute of Technology Delhi (IIT Delhi). 2014. History of the
Institute. Available at http://www.iitd.ac.in/content/history-institute
(accessed 21 December 2014).

Indian Kanoon. 2014. The States Reorganisation Act, 1956. Available at
http://indiankanoon.org/doc/1211891/ (accessed 23 November 2014).

Institute of Human Development (IHD). 2009. *Inclusive Development in
Rural Bihar: Household Survey.* New Delhi: IHD.

———. 2011. *Inclusive Development in Rural Bihar: Village Survey.* New
Delhi: IHD.

———. 2012a. *Social and Economic Change in Rural Bihar and the Emerging
Policy Framework.* New Delhi: Institute for Human Development.

———. 2012b. *Gender and Poverty in Rural Bihar.* New Delhi: Institute for
Human Development.

Institute of Town Planners, India (ITPI). 1955. 'Autumn Planning Seminar
and State Planning Officials' Conference at Lucknow', *Journal of the
Institute of Town Planners, India*, November: 8–28.

———. 1976. *Silver Jubilee Year Book.* New Delhi: ITPI.

International Monetary Fund. 2000. 'Offshore Financial Centers', IMF
Background Paper. Available at https://www.imf.org/external/np/mae/
oshore/2000/eng/back.htm (accessed 20 February 2016).

———. 2002. At a Glance—India and the IMF. Washington, DC: IMF.
Available at http://www.imf.org/external/country/ind/rr/glance.htm
(accessed 2 January 2015).

————. 2015. SDR Valuation. Available at http://www.imf.org/external/np/fin/data/rms_sdrv.aspx (accessed 4 January 2015).

Ismail, Mirza. 1954. *My Public Life: Recollections and Reflections*. London: Allen & Unwin.

Jacob, S. 2008. 'Master Plan Not Legal: PIL in High Court', *Citizen Matters, Bangalore*. Available at http://bangalore.citizenmatters.in/articles/view/270-cdp-charged (accessed 13 March 2015).

Janardhan, A. 2015. 'Explained: Why is Chennai under water?', *Indian Express*, 4 December. Available at http://indianexpress.com/article/explained/why-is-chennai-under-water/ (accessed 5 December 2015).

Jawaharlal Nehru National Urban Renewal Mission (JnNURM). 2005. Program Brochure. New Delhi: Ministry of Urban Development, Government of India.

————. 2010. *Repeal of Urban Land Ceiling & Regulation Act (ULCRA): State Level Reform*. New Delhi: Ministry of Urban Development, Government of India. Available at http://jnnurm.nic.in/wp-content/uploads/2011/01/Mandatory_Primer_5-RepealULCRA.pdf (accessed 12 January 2015).

Jeffery, Robin. 2000. *India's Newspaper Revolution: Capitalism, Technology, and the Indian Language Press*. New York: Palgrave Macmillan.

Jeffrey, C. 2002. 'Caste, Class and Clientelism: A Political Economy of Everyday Corruption in Rural North India', *Economic Geography*, 78(1): 21–41.

Jenkins, R., L. Kennedy, and P. Mukhopadhyay. 2014. *Power, Policy, and Protest*. New Delhi: Oxford University Press.

Joshi, V. and I.M.D. Little. 1996. *India's Economic Reforms, 1991–2001*. New Delhi: Oxford University Press.

Kalia, R. 1985. 'Chandigarh: A Planned City', *Habitat International*, 9(3–4): 135–50.

————. 1999. *Chandigarh: The Making of an Indian City*. New Delhi: Oxford University Press.

————. 2004. *Gandhi Nagar: Building National Identity in Postcolonial India*. Columbia: University of South Carolina Press.

————. 2006. 'Modernism, Modernization and Post-colonial India: A Reflective Essay', *Planning Perspectives*, 21(2): 133–56.

Kamat, S. 2011. 'Neoliberalism, Urbanism and the Education Economy: Producing Hyderabad as a "Global City"', *Discourse: Studies in the Cultural Politics of Education*, 32(2): 187–202.

Kamath, L. 2006. *Achieving Global Competitiveness and Local Poverty Reduction? Examining the Public–Private Partnering Model of Governance in Bangalore, India*. Doctor of Philosophy. Rutgers, The State University of New Jersey.

Kamath, L. and M. Vijayabaskar. 2009. 'Limits and Possibilities of Middle Class Associations as Urban Collective Actors', *Economic and Political Weekly*, 44(26–7): 368–76.

Karatchkova, E. 2007. 'Ghost Towns and Bustling Cities: Constructing a Master Narrative in Nineteenth Century Jaipur', in C. Henderson and M. Weisgrau (eds), *Raj Rhapsodies: Tourism, Heritage and the Seduction of History*, pp. 27–45. Hampshire: Ashgate.

Kasturi, K. 2008. 'Of Public Purpose and Private Profit', in 'Special Economic Zones: A Symposium on the Recent Economic Policy Initiatives'. Available at http://www.india-seminar.com/2008/582/582_kannan_kasturi.htm (accessed 15 January 2017).

Katano, H. 1965. 'Some Characteristics of Professor Mahalanobis' Growth Model', *The Developing Economies*, 3(1): 34–47. Available at http://www.ide.go.jp/English/Publish/Periodicals/De/pdf/65_01_03.pdf (accessed 15 December 2014).

Keeble, L. 1959. *Principles and Practice of Town and Country Planning*. London: The Estates Gazette Ltd.

Kennedy, L. 2007. 'Regional Industrial Policies Driving Peri-urban Dynamics in Hyderabad, India', *Cities*, 24(2): 95–109.

Kennedy, L. and M.H. Zérah. 2008. 'The Shift to City-centric Growth Strategies: Perspectives from Hyderabad and Mumbai', *Economic and Political Weekly*, 43(39): 110–17.

Khan, S. 2014. 'The Other JNNURM: What Does it Mean for Small Towns in India?', CPR Urban Working Paper 4. New Delhi: Centre for Policy Research. Available at http://www.cprindia.org/sites/default/files/The%20Other%20JNNURM.pdf (accessed 20 January 2015).

Khanna, B. 2014. 'Fast-paced BDA Prepares for CDP-2031', *Deccan Herald*, 28 February. Available at http://www.deccanherald.com/content/389050/fast-paced-bda-prepares-cdp.html (accessed 13 March 2015).

Khilnani, S. 1999. *The Idea of India*. New York: Farrar, Straus and Giroux.

Kohli, A. 1989. 'Politics of Economic Liberalization in India', *World Development*, 17(3): 305–28.

Kotwal, A. and B. Ramaswami. 1999. 'Economic Reforms in Agriculture and Rural Growth', in J. Sachs, A. Varshney, and N. Bajpai (eds), *India in the Era of Economic Reforms*, pp. 121–59. New Delhi: Oxford University Press.

Kumar, A. 2002. *The Black Economy in India*. Gurgaon: Penguin Books.

———. 2006. 'Trends of Planning and Governance in Metropolitan India', *ITPI Journal*, 3(2): 10–20.

Kumar, D. 2011. 'Competition and Road Transport Sector'. Available at http://cci.gov.in/images/media/speeches/CompRoadTranRITESArticle. pdf (accessed 15 January 2015).

Kundra, A. 2000. *The Performance of India's Export Zones*. London: Sage.

Kundu, A. 2000. 'Urban Poverty in India: Issues and Perspectives in Development', *Social Change*, 30(1–2): 8–32.

Kundu, D. 2011. 'Elite Capture in Participatory Urban Governance', *Economic and Political Weekly*, 46(10): 23–5.

Lall, R. and A. Rastogi. 2007. 'The Political Economy of Infrastructure Development in Post-independence India'. IDFC Occasional Paper Series 2007/1. Mumbai: IDFC. Available at http://www.idfc.com/pdf/ publications/the_political_economy_of_infrastructure_development_ in_post_independence_india.pdf (accessed 2 January 2015).

Lalvani, M. 2010. 'Bharat Nirman: A Stocktaking', *Economic and Political Weekly*, 45(17): 19–24.

LegalCrystal. 2014. Judgment: *D. Manikandan v. State of Tamil Nadu*. Available at http://www.legalcrystal.com/1022867 (accessed 12 May 2014).

Liechty, M. 2003. *Suitably Modern: Making Middle-class Culture in a New Consumer Society*. Princeton: Princeton University Press.

Lochl, M. and K.W. Axhausen. 2010. 'Modeling Hedonic Residential Rents for Land Use and Transport Simulation While Considering Spatial Effects', *Journal of Transport and Land Use*, 3(2): 39–63.

Lok Sabha Secretariat. 2013. 'National Highways Development Project: An Overview'. Reference Note No. 23/RN/Ref./August/2013. Available at http://164.100.47.134/intranet/NHDP.pdf (accessed 16 January 2015).

Mahadevia, D. 2006. 'NURM and the Poor in Globalising Mega Cities', *Economic and Political Weekly*, 41(31): 3399–403.

———. 2011. 'Branded and Renewed? Policies, Politics and Processes of Urban Development in the Reform Era', *Economic and Political Weekly*, 46(31): 56–64.

Manjusainath, G. 2013. 'BDA's Drushti Goes Out of Sight', *Deccan Herald*, 8 December. Available at http://www.deccanherald.com/content/373563/ bda039s-drushti-goes-sight.html (accessed 12 March 2015).

Markusen, A. 1996. 'Sticky Places in Slippery Space: A Typology of Industrial Districts', *Economic Geography*, 72(3): 293–313.

Massey, D., P. Quintas, and D. Wield. 1992. *High-tech Fantasies*. London: Routledge.

Mathur, O.P., D. Thakur, and N. Rajadhyaksha. 2009. *Urban Property Tax Potential in India*. New Delhi: National Institute of Public Finance and Policy.

Mathur, S. 2008. 'Impact of Transportation and Other Jurisdictional-level Infrastructure and Services on Housing Prices', *Journal of Urban Planning and Development*, 134(1): 32–41.

———. 2013. 'Use of Land Pooling and Reconstitution for Urban Development: Experiences from Gujarat, India', *Habitat International*, 38: 199–206.

McGee, T.G. 1991. 'The Emergence of *Desakota* Regions in Asia: Expanding a Hypothesis', in N. Ginsburg, B. Koppel, and T.G. McGee (eds), *The Extended Metropolis*, pp. 3–25. Honolulu: University of Hawaii Press.

McMillen, D.P. and J.F. McDonald. 2004. 'Reaction of House Prices to a New Rapid Transit Line: Chicago's Midway Line, 1983–1999', *Real Estate Economics*, 32(3): 463–86.

Mehta, P.B. 2003. *The Burden of Democracy*. New Delhi: Penguin Books.

Ministry of Commerce and Industry. 2014a. List of State-wise Exporting SEZs (as on 05.12.2014). New Delhi: Department of Commerce, Ministry of Commerce and Industry, Government of India. Available at http://sezindia.nic.in/writereaddata/pdf/ListofoperationalSEZs.pdf (accessed 21 January 2015).

———. 2014b. Formal Approvals Granted in the Board of Approvals after Coming into Force of SEZ Rules as on 05.12.2014. New Delhi: Department of Commerce, Ministry of Commerce and Industry, Government of India. Available at http://www.sezindia.nic.in/writeread-data/pdf/ListofFormalapprovals.pdf (accessed 21 January 2015).

———. 2015a. Fact Sheet on Special Economic Zones. New Delhi: Department of Commerce, Ministry of Commerce and Industry, Government of India. Available at http://sezindia.gov.in/about-fsheet.asp (accessed 20 January 2015).

———. 2015b. List of Operational SEZs. New Delhi: Department of Commerce, Ministry of Commerce and Industry, Government of India. Available at http://sezindia.gov.in/about-osi.asp (accessed 20 January 2015).

———. 2015c. About SEZs Introduction. New Delhi: Department of Commerce, Ministry of Commerce and Industry, Government of India. Available at http://sezindia.gov.in/about-introduction.asp (accessed 20 January 2015).

Ministry of Finance (MoF). 2004. *Central Government Subsidies in India*. New Delhi: Ministry of Finance, Government of India. Available at http://finmin.nic.in/reports/cgsi-2004.pdf (accessed 2 January 2015).

Ministry of Housing and Urban Poverty Alleviation (MHUPA). 2004. 'Performance of Programmes/Schemes—Urban Development', in *Government of India Performance Budget 2002–2003*. New Delhi: Ministry

of Housing and Urban Poverty Alleviation. Available at http://mhupa.gov. in/pdf/performance/2002-2003/3.pdf (accessed 1 December 2014).

Ministry of Shipping, Road Transport and Highways (MSRTH). 2007. *Roads (2007–2012)*. The Report of the Working Group on Roads for the 11th Five Year Plan. Available at http://planningcommission.nic.in/ aboutus/committee/wrkgrp11/wg11_road.pdf (accessed 15 January 2015).

Ministry of Statistics and Programme Implementation (MoSPI). 2013. 'Five Year Plans', in *Statistical Year Book India 2014*. New Delhi: Ministry of Statistics and Programme Implementation (MoSPI), Government of India. Available at http://mospi.gov.in/statistical-year-book-india/2014/176 (accessed 1 February 2015).

———. 2014. Agenda Item-2: Service Sector Statistics. New Delhi: MoSPI, Government of India. Available at http://mospi.nic.in/mospi_new/ upload/cocsso_data/Agenda_2%20final_service_11nov14.pdf (accessed 7 January 2015).

Ministry of Urban Development (MoUD). 2005. Jawaharlal Nehru National Urban Renewal Mission Guidelines. New Delhi: Ministry of Urban Development, Urban Development Division.

———. 2006. Jawaharlal Nehru National Urban Renewal Mission. New Delhi: Ministry of Urban Development, Government of India. Available at http://jnnurm.nic.in/ (accessed 22 February 2011).

———. 2010a. Water Supply. New Delhi: Ministry of Urban Development, Government of India. Available at http://moud.gov.in/sites/upload_ files/moud/files/pdf/Indicators&Benchmarks.pdf (accessed 29 March 2015).

———. 2010b. *User Charges: ULB Level Reform*. New Delhi: Ministry of Urban Development, Government of India. Available at http://jnnurm. nic.in/wp-content/uploads/2011/01/Mandatory_Primer_4-UC.pdf (accessed 30 April 2015).

———. 2015. The Constitution (Seventy-fourth Amendment) Act, 1992: Background. Available at http://moud.gov.in/legislation/constiution (accessed 2 January 2015).

Mitra, S. 2015. 'Anchoring Transnational Flows: Hypermodern Spaces in the Global South', in F. Miraftab and N. Kudva (eds), *Cities of the Global South Reader*, pp. 106–14. Oxon; New York: Routledge.

Mody, A. 2010. 'Special Economic Zones: A Briefing Note', Research Project: The Politics of India's Special Economic Zones. Avilable at http://www.indiaSEZpolitics.org (accessed 20 August 2015).

Mohan, R. and S. Dasgupta. 2004. 'Urban Development in India in the 21st Century: Policies for Accelerating Urban Growth'. Working Paper No. 231. Stanford: Stanford Center for International Development,

Stanford University. Available at http://web.stanford.edu/group/siepr/cgi-bin/siepr/?q=system/files/shared/pubs/papers/pdf/SCID231.pdf (accessed 2 December 2015).

Mohanty, P. 2005. 'Urban Sector Reform Agenda: Financing Civic Services and Development'. New Delhi: Centre for Good Governance. Available at http://www.cgg.gov.in/workingpapers/ASCII_Collectors.pdf (accessed 17 January 2015).

Mohanty, Prasanna K. 2014. *Cities and Public Policy: An Urban Agenda for India*. New Delhi: Sage.

Morris, S. and A. Pandey. 2007. 'Towards Reform of Land Acquisition Framework in India', *Economic and Political Weekly*, 42(22): 2083–90.

Mukherji, R. 2010. 'Regulation and Infrastructure Development in India: Comparing Telecommunications, Ports and Power', in V. Chand (ed.), *Public Service Delivery in India: Understanding the Reform Process*, pp. 177–225. New Delhi: Oxford University Press.

Mukhopadhyay, P. 2009. 'Promised Land of SEZs', CPR Occasional Paper Series, No. 2. New Delhi: Centre for Policy Research.

Mukhopadhyay, P. and K. Pradhan. 2009. 'Location of SEZs and Policy Benefits: What Does the Data Say?', CPR Discussion Paper Series, No. 3. New Delhi: Centre for Policy Research.

Mumbai First. 2012. Homepage. Available at http://www.mumbaifirst.org/index.php (accessed 11 March 2015).

NASSCOM. 2012. Homepage. http://www.nasscom.in (accessed 12 May 2013).

NASSCOM–McKinsey. 2005. *Extending India's Leadership of the Global IT and BPO Industries*. New Delhi: McKinsey. Available at http://www.mckinsey.com/locations/india/mckinseyonindia/pdf/nasscom_mckinsey_report_2005.pdf (accessed 11 January 2010).

Nataraj, G. 2013. 'Infrastructure Challenges in India: The Role of Public–Private Partnerships'. Paper presented at the Workshop on Sustaining High Growth in India. Delhi: Institute of Economic Growth, Delhi University. Available at http://iegindia.org/wshop2526july/paper5.pdf (accessed 3 January 2015).

National Council of Applied Economic Research (NCAER). 2011. 'India's Middle Class Population to Touch 267 Million in 5 Years', *The Economic Times*, 6 February, http://articles.economictimes.indiatimes.com/2011-02-06/news/28424975_1_middle-class-households-applied-economic-research (accessed 5 February 2015).

National Highways Authority of India (NHAI). 2014a. Indian Road Network. New Delhi: Ministry of Road Transport & Highways,

Government of India. Available at http://www.nhai.org/roadnetwork. htm (accessed 7 January 2015).

―――. 2014b. National Highway Development Project (NHDP). New Delhi: Ministry of Road Transport & Highways, Government of India. Available at http://www.nhai.org/nhdpdates.htm (accessed 7 January 2015).

National Institute of Urban Affairs (NIUA). 1991. *Jawaharlal Nehru on Building a New India*. New Delhi: NIUA.

―――. 2004. 'Urban Reform Incentive Fund (URIF): An Update', *Urban Finance*, 7(1): 1–12. Available at http://www.niua.org/sites/default/files/Urb_fin_mar_04_0.pdf (accessed 17 January 2015).

National Urban Transport Policy (NUTP). 2006. *National Urban Transport Policy*. New Delhi: Ministry of Urban Development, Government of India. Available at http://www.indiaenvironmentportal.org.in/files/TransportPolicy.pdf (accessed 6 January 2015).

Navlakha, G. 2000. 'Urban Pollution: Driving Workers to Desperation', *Economic and Political Weekly*, 35(51): 4469–71.

Nelson, A.C., J.C. Nicholas, and J.C. Juergensmeyer. 2009. *Impact Fees: Principles and Practice of Proportionate-share Development Fees*. Chicago: American Planning Association.

Nelson, A.C., L.K. Bowles, J.C. Juergensmeyer, and J.C. Nicholas. 2008. *A Guide to Impact Fees and Housing Affordability*. Washington, DC: Island Press.

Office for National Statistics (UK). 2013. '2011 Census: Characteristics of Built-up Areas'. Available at http://www.ons.gov.uk/peoplepopulationandcommunity/housing/articles/characteristicsofbuiltupareas/2013-06-28 (accessed on 28 December 2016).

Ong, A. 2000. 'Graduated Sovereignty in South-east Asia', *Theory, Culture & Society*, 17(4): 55–75.

Palit, A. and S. Bhattacharjee. 2008. *Special Economic Zones in India*. London: Anthem Press.

Panagariya, A. 2004. 'India's Trade Reform: Progress, Impact and Future Strategy'. Columbia University Policy Paper. New York: Columbia University. Available at http://www.columbia.edu/~ap2231/Policy%20Papers/IPF_India.pdf (accessed 2 January 2015).

Pani, N. 2006. 'Icons and Reform Politics in India: The Case of S.M. Krishna', *Asian Survey*, 46(2): 238–56.

PAR-FORE. 2007. 'Special Economic Zones (SEZs) in India'. Available at http://www.parfore.in/pdf/2-2007SEZs_In_India.pdf (accessed 20 February 2016).

Parnell, S. and J. Robinson. 2006. 'Development and Urban Policy: Johannesburg's City Development Strategy', *Urban Studies*, 43(2): 337–55.

Planning Commission. 2010a. *Third Five Year Plan*. New Delhi: Planning Commission. Available at http://planningcommission.gov.in/plans/planrel/fiveyr/index3.html (accessed 2 January 2015).

———. 2010b. *Seventh Five Year Plan*. New Delhi: Planning Commission. Available at http://planningcommission.gov.in/plans/planrel/fiveyr/index7.html (accessed 2 January 2015).

———. 2011. 'Faster, Sustainable and More Inclusive Growth: An Approach to the Twelfth Five Year Plan (2012–2017)'. Government of India, Planning Commission. Available at http://planningcommission.nic.in/plans/planrel/12appdrft/approach_12plan.pdf (accessed on 28 December 2016).

Pradhan Mantri Gram Sadak Yojana (PMGSY). 2011. Pradhan Mantri Gram Sadak Yojana (PMGSY). New Delhi: Ministry of Rural Development, Government of India. Available at http://pmgsy.nic.in/Intr_E.pdf (accessed 7 January 2015).

Pradhan, Kanhu Charan. 2013. 'Unacknowledged Urbanisation: The New Census Towns of India', *Economic and Political Weekly*, 48(36): 43–51.

Prakash, G. 1999. *Another Reason: Science and the Imagination of Modern India*. Princeton: Princeton University Press.

Prakash, Ved. 1969. *New Towns in India*. Durham: Program in Comparative Studies on Southern Asia, Duke University.

Prasad, R. and R. Ray. 2010. 'Special Economic Zones in India: Following Well-trodden Paths', *Indian Journal of Economics and Business*, 9(3): 559–83.

PricewaterhouseCoopers (PWC). 2012. *The Road Ahead: Highways PPP in India*. Available at http://www.pwc.in/en_IN/in/assets/pdfs/publications-2012/the-road-ahead-highways-ppp.pdf (accessed 15 January 2015).

Pyle, J. 2001. 'Sex, Maids and Export Processing: Risks and Reasons for Gendered Global Production Networks', *International Journal of Politics, Culture, and Society*, 15(1): 55–76.

Qadeer, M.A. 2000. 'Ruralopolis: The Spatial Organisation and Residential Land Economy of High-density Rural Regions in South Asia', *Urban Studies*, 37(9): 1583–1603.

———. 2004. 'Urbanization by Implosion', *Habitat International*, 28(1): 1–12.

Rajasthan Patrika. 2009. 'Oonchi Udaan ko Tayyar' [Ready to Fly High], Jaipur edition, 26 December.

Rajkot Municipal Corporation (RMC). 2007. *Detailed Project Report (DPR)-1 for Rajkot Bus Rapid Transit System Phase-1: Development of*

Blue Corridor (Part-1). Available at http://117.240.112.170/jnnurm/BRTS_DPR.pdf (accessed 26 February 2015).

———. 2010. Rajkot Municipal Corporation. Available at http://jnnurm.nic.in/wp-content/uploads/2011/01/Brochures_Published_Rajkot.pdf (accessed 26 February 2015).

Rajkot Rajpath Limited (RRL). 2012. Project Highlight. Available at http://www.rajkotrajpath.com/project-highlight.php (accessed 26 February 2015).

Rajkumar, D. and J. Hanley. 2007. 'Growth and Persistence of Large Business Groups in India', *Journal of Comparative International Management*, 10(1): 3–24. Available at http://www.academia.edu/1609066/GROWTH_AND_PERSISTENCE_OF_LARGE_BUSINESS_GROUPS_IN_INDIA (accessed 15 January 2015).

Ramachandraiah, C. 2003. 'Information Technology and Social Development', *Economic and Political Weekly*, 38(12–13): 1192–7.

———. 2008. 'Urban Growth, Loss of Water Bodies and Flooding in Indian Cities: The Case of Hyderabad', in J. Feyen, K. Shannon, and M. Neville (eds), *Water and Urban Development Paradigms: Towards an Integration of Engineering, Design and Management Approaches*, pp. 121–5. Boca Raton, Florida: CRC Press.

Ranganathan, M. 2014. 'Paying for Pipes, Claiming Citizenship: Political Agency and Water Reforms at the Urban Periphery', *International Journal of Urban and Regional Research*, 38(2): 590–608.

Rawat, V., M. Bhushan, and S. Surepally. 2011. 'The Impact of Special Economic Zones in India: A Case Study of Pollepally SEZ'. *Social Development Foundation Working Paper Series*. New Delhi: Social Development Foundation. Available at http://www.indiaenvironmentportal.org.in/files/WEB_SDF_India_final_layout.pdf (accessed 15 January 2017).

Raychaudhuri, Tapan. 1999. *Perceptions, Emotions, Sensibilities: Essays on India's Colonial Past and Post-colonial Experiences*. New Delhi: Oxford University Press.

Redfearn, C.L. 2009. 'How Informative are Average Effects? Hedonic Regression and Amenity Capitalization in Complex Urban Housing Markets', *Regional Science and Urban Economics*, 39(3): 297–306.

Reference for Business. 2014. History of Steel Authority of India Ltd. Available at http://www.referenceforbusiness.com/history2/90/STEEL-AUTHORITY-OF-INDIA-LTD.html (accessed 2 December 2014).

Rex, J. and R. Moore. 1967. *Race, Community and Conflict: A Study of Sparkbrook*. Harmondsworth: Penguin.

Rohith, B.R. 2014. 'CDP 2015 Still Stuck, but BDA Ready for Master Plan 2031', *The Times of India*. Available at http://timesofindia.indiatimes.com/city/bengaluru/CDP-2015-still-stuck-but-BDA-ready-for-master-plan-2031/articleshow/29172751.cms (accessed 11 March 2015).

Rowland, A.M. 2001. 'Population as Determinant of Local Outcomes under Decentralisation: Illustrations from Small Municipalities in Bolivia and Mexico', *World Development*, 29(8): 1373–89.

Roy, A. 2009. 'Strangely Familiar: Planning and the Worlds of Insurgence and Informality', *Planning Theory*, 8(1): 7–11.

———. 2009. 'Why India Cannot Plan Its Cities: Informality, Insurgence, and the Idiom of Urbanization', *Planning Theory*, 8(1): 76–87.

———. 2014. *Capitalism: A Ghost Story*. Chicago: Haymarket Books.

Roy, Ashim Kumar. 1978. *History of the Jaipur City*. New Delhi: Manohar.

Roy, T. 2012. 'India and the World Economy, 1757–1947', in C. Ghate (ed.), *The Oxford Handbook of the Indian Economy*, pp. 33–55. New York: Oxford University Press.

Rudolph, Susanne and Lloyd Rudolph. 1984. *The Modernity of Tradition: Political Development in India*. Chicago: University of Chicago Press.

Ruparelia, S., T. Reddy, J. Harriss, and S. Corbridge. 2011. *Understanding India's New Political Economy*. London: Routledge.

Ryan, B. 2011. 'Reading through a Plan', *Journal of the American Planning Association*, 77(4): 309–27.

Sachdev, Vibhuti and Giles Tillotson. 2002. *Building Jaipur: The Making of an Indian City*. London: Reaktion Books.

Sachs, J.D., A. Varshney, and N. Bajpai. 1999. *India in the Era of Economic Reforms*. New Delhi: Oxford University Press.

Samanta, G. 2014. 'The Politics of Classification and the Complexity of Governance in Census Towns', *Economic and Political Weekly*, 49(22): 55–62.

Sami, N. 2012. *Building Alliances: Power and Politics in Urban India*. Doctor of Philosophy. University of Michigan.

———. 2013a. 'From Farming to Development: Urban Coalitions in Pune, India', *International Journal of Urban and Regional Research*, 37(1): 151–64.

———. 2013b. 'Power to the People? A Study of Bangalore's Urban Task Forces', in G. Shatkin (ed.), *Contesting the Indian City: Global Visions and the Politics of the Local*, pp. 121–44. West Sussex: Wiley Blackwell.

Sampat, P. 2013. 'The "Goan Impasse": Land Rights and Resistance to SEZs in Goa, India'. LDPI Working Paper 53. The Land Deal Politics Initiative.

Sangameswaran, P., R. Madhav, and C. D'Rozario. 2008. '24/7, "Privatisation", and Water Reform: Insights from Hubli-Dharwad'. Available at http://www.ielrc.org/content/a0801.pdf (accessed 2 April 2015).

Sankhe, S., I. Vittal, R. Dobbs, A. Mohan, A. Gulati, J. Ablett, S. Gupta, A. Kim, S. Paul, A. Sanghvi, and G. Sethy. 2010. *India's Urban Awakening: Building Inclusive Cities, Sustaining Economic Growth*. McKinsey & Company. Available at http://www.mckinsey.com/~/media/McKinsey/dotcom/Insights%20and%20pubs/MGI/Research/Urbanization/Indias%20urban%20awakening%20Building%20inclusive%20cities/MGI_Indias_urban_awakening_full_report.ashx (accessed 3 January 2015).

Sanyal, B. 2005. *Comparative Planning Cultures*. New York: Routledge.

Sarin, M. 1982. *Urban Planning in the Third World: The Chandigarh Experience*. London: Mansell Publishing.

Sarkar, Jadunath. 1984. *A History of Jaipur*. Delhi: Manohar Publications.

Saxenian, A. 2002. 'Transnational Communities and the Evolution of Global Production Networks: The Cases of Taiwan, China and India', *Industry & Innovation*, 9(3): 183–202.

————. 2006. *The New Argonauts*. Cambridge: Harvard University Press.

Schaffer, T. 2009. *India and the United States in the 21st Century: Reinventing Partnership*. New Delhi: India Research Press.

Schulczova, L. 2014. 'India's Budget: State of the Economy', *WBP Online*, 10 July. Available at http://wbponline.com/Articles/View/32455/indias-budget-state-of-the-economy (accessed 7 January 2015).

Scott, J.C. 1998 [1985]. *Seeing like a State*. New Haven: Yale University Press.

Searle, L. 2010. *Making Space for Capital: The Production of Global Landscapes in Contemporary India*. PhD Dissertation, Anthropology Program, University of Pennsylvania.

Sengupta, A., K. Kannan, and R. Srivastava. 2007. 'Growth Pole: A Case for Special Economic Zone for Clusters of Small and Micro Enterprises', *The Indian Journal of Labour Economics*, 50(2): 217–30.

Shatkin, G. (ed.). 2014. *Contesting the Indian City: Global Visions and the Politics of the Local*. West Sussex: Wiley-Blackwell.

Shaw, A. 2013. 'Emerging Perspectives on Small Cities and Towns', in R. Sharma and R. Sandhu (eds), *Small Cities and Towns in Global Era: Emerging Changes and Perspectives*, pp. 36–53. Jaipur: Rawat Publications. Available at http://www.researchgate.net/publication/261958465_Small_Cities_and_Towns_in_Global_Era_Emerging_Changes_and_Perspectives (accessed 15 November 2014).

———— (ed.). 2007. *Indian Cities in Transition*. Chennai: Orient Longman.

Shaw, A. and M. Satish. 2007. 'Metropolitan Restructuring in Post-liberalized India: Separating the Global and the Local', *Cities*, 24(2): 148–63.

Singh, Hira. 1998. *Colonial Hegemony and Popular Resistance: Princes, Peasants and Paramount Power*. Toronto: Canadian Scholars Press.

Singh, N. 2012. 'The Dynamics and Status of India's Economic Reforms', in C. Ghate (ed.), *The Oxford Handbook of the Indian Economy*, pp. 499–525. New York: Oxford University Press.

Sinha, A. 2004. 'The Changing Political Economy of Federalism in India: A Historical Institutionalist Approach', *India Review*, 3(1): 25–63.

Sinha, A. and J. Singh. 2011. 'Jamshedpur: Planning an Ideal Steel City in India', *Journal of Planning History*, 10(4): 263–81.

Sinha, S. 2008. 'Lineages of the Developmentalist State: Transnationality and Village India, 1900–1965', *Comparative Studies in Society and History*, 50(1): 57–90.

Sitapati, V. 2013. 'Hindi Paper Finds Success Going Hyperlocal'. Available at http://india.blogs.nytimes.com/2013/07/04/hindi-paper-finds-success-going-hyperlocal/?_r=0 (accessed 15 March 2015).

Sivaramakrishnan, K. and A. Agrawal (eds). 2003. *Regional Modernities: The Cultural Politics of Development in India*. Stanford: Stanford University Press.

Sivaramakrishnan, K.C. 2011. *Re-visioning Indian Cities: The Urban Renewal Mission*. New Delhi: Sage.

———. 2013. 'Are We Stuck with the 74th CAA?'. Paper presented at the '21st Century Indian City Conference', Bangalore, 26–7 March. Available at http://indiancities.berkeley.edu/2013/Presentations/Sivaramakrishnan.ppt (accessed on 28 December 2016).

Smith, G. 2008. 'Use of Fees or Alternatives to Fund Transit'. Legal Research Digest 28, Transit Cooperative Research Program. Washington, DC: Transportation Research Board. Available at http://onlinepubs.trb.org/onlinepubs/tcrp/tcrp_lrd_28.pdf (accessed 30 October 2011).

Smith, J. and T. Gihring. 2009. 'Financing Transit Systems through Value Capture'. Victoria: Victoria Transport Policy Institute.

Sood, A. 2015. 'Industrial Townships and the Policy Facilitation of Corporate Urbanisation in India', *Urban Studies*, 52(8): 1359–78.

Sridharan, N. 2008. 'New Forms of Contestation and Cooperation in Indian Urban Governance', in I.S.A. Baud and J. de Wit (eds), *New Forms of Urban Governance in India: Shifts, Models, Networks and Governance*, 1st edn, pp. 291–311. New Delhi; Thousand Oaks, Calif; London; Singapore: Sage.

———. 2014. 'Village and Small Town Development through the Provision of Urban Services in India: A New Approach to Help the Rural Poor'. Presented at the Rural–Urban Poverty Linkages Conference held from 2–4 September in Zhejiang, People's Republic of China. Available

at   http://rksi.org/sites/default/files/document/364/34-sridharan-pura-report.pdf (accessed 11 December 2014).

Srivastava, D.K., C. Bhujanga Rao, P. Chakraborty, and T.S. Rangamannar. 2003. *Budgetary Subsidies in India: Subsidising Social and Economic Services*. New Delhi: National Institute of Public Finance and Policy (NIPFP). Available at http://planningcommission.gov.in/reports/sereport/ser/stdy_bgdsubs.pdf (accessed 6 January 2015).

Staples, Eugene. 1992. *Forty Years: A Learning Curve*. New Delhi: The Ford Foundation.

Statistics Canada. 2011. From Urban Areas to Population Centres. Available at http://www.statcan.gc.ca/eng/subjects/standard/sgc/notice/sgc-06 (accessed on 28 December 2016).

Subramanian, T.S.R. 2004. *Journeys through Babudom and Netaland: Governance in India*. New Delhi: Rupa & Co.

Sudhira, H.S., T.V. Ramachandra, and M.H.B. Subrahmanya. 2007. 'Bangalore', *Cities*, 24(5): 379–90.

Sukumar, R. 2003. 'The Future of Indian Cities is Here', *Business Today*, 17 August.

Sundaresan, J. 2013. *Urban Planning in Vernacular Governance: Land Use Planning and Violations in Bangalore*. Doctor of Philosophy. The London School of Economics.

Swamy, M.C.K. 1966. 'New Towns in India', *Journal of the Institute of Town Planners, India*, 49–50: 40–51.

Tamil Nadu Government Gazette. 2008. Tamil Nadu Town and Country Planning (Levy of Infrastructure and Amenities Charges) Rules, 2008. Available at http://www.tn.gov.in/tcp/gos/GOs_IA.pdf (accessed 2 June 2015).

———. 2013. 'Levy of Development Charges by the Kagithapuram New Town Development Authority, Sanctioned'. Available at http://www. stationeryprinting.tn.gov.in/gazette/2013/31-VI-1.pdf (accessed 18 June 2014).

Tangri, S. 1968. 'Urban Growth, Housing, and Economic Development: The Case of India', *Asian Survey*, 8(7): 519–38.

Tantri, M. 2013. 'India's SEZ Policy: A Retrospective Analysis', Institute for Social and Economic Change Working Paper Series: Working Paper 301. Bangalore: Institute for Social and Economic Change.

Telecom Regulatory Authority of India (TRAI). 2014. 'Highlights of Telecom Subscription Data as on 30th September, 2014'. Press Release Number 73/2014. Available at http://www.trai.gov.in/WriteReadData/WhatsNew/Documents/PR-TSD-Sep-14.pdf (accessed 4 January 2015).

The Hindu. 2014a. 'All About Bangalore Metropolitan Planning Committee', 8 September. Available at http://www.thehindu.com/todays-paper/tp-national/tp-karnataka/all-about-bangalore-metropolitan-planning-committee/article6389574.ece (accessed 13 March 2015).

———. 2014b. 'BDA Chickens Out of Public Hearing', 14 November. Available at http://www.thehindu.com/news/cities/bangalore/bda-chickens-out-of-public-hearing/article6595764.ece (accessed 11 March 2014).

The State Institute for Urban Development (SIUD). 2012. '24X7 Urban Water Supply: A PPP Attempt in Karnataka'. Available at http://www.siudmysore.gov.in/pdf/24X7water.pdf (accessed 2 April 2015).

Thirteenth Finance Commission. 2009. *Report of the Thirteenth Finance Commission (2010–2015)*. New Delhi: Fourteenth Finance Commission, Government of India. Available at http://fincomindia.nic.in/ShowContentOne.aspx?id=28&Section=1 (accessed 7 January 2015).

Town and Country Planning Organisation (TCPO). 1962. *Town and Country Planning in India*. New Delhi: TCPO, Ministry of Health, Government of India.

———. 2014. Homepage. Available at http://tcpomud.gov.in/ (accessed 2 December 2014).

Trading Economics. 2015. India Foreign Exchange Reserves. Available at http://www.tradingeconomics.com/india/foreign-exchange-reserves (accessed 6 January 2015).

United Nations (UN). 2015. *Demographic Yearbook: Annuaire Démographique*. New York: United Nations.

United Nations Department of Economic and Social Affairs (UN DESA). 2011. File 3: Urban Population by Major Area, Region and Country, 1950–2050 (thousands). New York: United Nations. Available at esa.un.org/unpd/wup/CD…/WUP2009-F03-Urban_Population.xls (accessed on 15 February 2012).

———. 2014. World Urbanization Prospects: The 2014 Revision. Custom data acquired via website. New York: UN DESA, Population Division. Available at http://esa.un.org/unpd/wup/DataQuery/ (accessed 16 December 2014).

United States Bureau of Census. 2010. 2010 Census Urban and Rural Classification and Urban Area Criteria. Available at https://www.census.gov/geo/reference/ua/urban-rural-2010.html (accessed on 28 December 2016).

US Department of State. 1997. FY 1997 Country Commercial Guide: India. Available at http://www.state.gov/1997-2001-NOPDFS/about_state/business/com_guides/1997/southeast_asia/india97.html (accessed 7 January 2015).

Uttar Pradesh Town Planning Organization (UPTPO). 1952. *Progressive Uttar Pradesh: Town Planning.* Lucknow: New Government Press.

Vadali, S. 2008. 'Toll Roads and Economic Development: Exploring Effects on Property Values', *Annals of Regional Science,* 42(3): 591–620.

Vanaik, A. 2004. 'Unraveling the Self-image of the Indian Bomb Lobby', *Economic and Political Weekly,* 39(46–7): 5006–12.

Vidyarthi, S. 2014. 'Building A "World Class Heritage City": Jaipur's Emergent Elites and New Approach to Spatial Planning', in Gavin Shatkin (ed.), *Contesting the Indian City: Global Visions and the Politics of the Local,* pp. 241–64. West Sussex: Wiley-Blackwell.

Vidyarthi, S., C. Hoch, and C. Basmajian. 2013. 'Making Sense of India's Spatial Plan-making Practice: Enduring Approach or Emergent Variations', *Planning Theory and Practice,* 14(1): 57–74.

Vishwakarma, B. 2015. 'Delhi air pollution: A hara-kiri in waiting!', *The Times of India,* 9 April. Available at http://timesofindia.indiatimes.com/home/environment/pollution/Delhi-air-pollution-A-hara-kiri-in-waiting/articleshow/46860677.cms (accessed 5 December 2015).

Vohra, R. 2012. *The Making of India: A Political History.* New York: M.E. Sharpe.

Voith, R. 1993. 'Changing Capitalization of CBO-oriented Transportation Systems: Evidence from Philadelphia, 1970–1988', *Journal of Urban Economics,* 13: 361–76.

Wallerstein, Immanuel. 1991. 'Braudel on Capitalism, or Everything Upside Down', *The Journal of Modern History,* 63(2): 354–61.

Weinstein, L. 2008. 'Mumbai's Development Mafias: Globalization, Organized Crime and Land Development', *International Journal of Urban and Regional Research,* 32(1): 22–39.

———. 2011. '"Slum-Free Mumbai" and Other Entrepreneurial Strategies in the Making of Mumbai's Global Downtown', in M. Peterson and G. McDonogh (eds), *Global Downtowns,* pp. 234–52. Philadelphia: University of Pennsylvania Press.

Weinstein, L., N. Sami, and G. Shatkin. 2014. 'Contested Developments: Enduring Legacies and Emergent Political Actors in Contemporary Urban India', in G. Shatkin (ed.), *Contesting the Indian City: Global Visions and the Politics of the Local,* pp. 39–64. Chichester: John Wiley and Sons.

Wilcox, W. 1965. 'Politicians, Bureaucrats and Development in India', *The Annals of the American Academy of Political and Social Science,* 358(1): 114–22.

Wirth, L. 1938. 'Urbanism as a Way of Life', *American Journal of Sociology,* 44(1): 1–24.

World Bank. 1997. *India Achievements and Challenges in Reducing Poverty.* Washington, DC: World Bank.

———. 2010. *The Karnataka Urban Water Sector Improvement Project: 24×7 Water Supply is Achievable.* Washington, DC: Water and Sanitation Program, World Bank. Available at https://www.wsp.org/sites/wsp.org/files/publications/WSP_Karnataka-water- supply.pdf (accessed on 12 April 2015).

———. 2014a. 'PPP Conversion Factor (GDP) to Market Exchange Rate Ratio'. Available at http://data.worldbank.org/indicator/PA.NUS.PPPC.RF (accessed on 18 June 2014).

———. 2014b. *Running Water in India's Cities: A Review of Five Recent Public-Private Partnership Initiatives.* Washington, DC: Water and Sanitation Program, World Bank. Available at https://www.wsp.org/sites/wsp.org/files/publications/Running-Water-in-India-Public-Private-Partnership-Initiatives.pdf (accessed on 12 April 2015).

———. 2015. *Project Information Document (PID): Appraisal Stage.* Washington, DC: World Bank. Available at http://documents.worldbank.org/curated/en/745381468041650545/pdf/PID-Appraisal-Print-P130544-03-30-2015-1427712934942.pdf (accessed on 12 April 2015).

———. 2015. *Eastern Dedicated Freight Corridor – I.* Washington, DC: World Bank. Available at http://www.worldbank.org/projects/P114338/eastern-dedicated-freightcorridor?lang=en (accessed 16 January 2016).

Zhu, Y. 2004. 'Changing Urbanization Processes and In-situ Rural–Urban Transformation: Reflections on China's Settlement Definitions', in T. Chapman and G. Hugo (eds), *New Forms of Urbanization: Beyond the Urban–Rural Dichotomy*, pp. 207–28. Aldershot: Ashgate.

Index

About the Authors

Sandeep K. Agrawal is Professor and inaugural Director of the Urban and Regional Planning Program at the University of Alberta, Canada. Prior to moving to the University of Alberta, he was the founding Director of the Urban Development Program and a faculty member in the School of Urban and Regional Planning at Ryerson University in Toronto, Canada, for over 14 years. His research works in Canada have focused on the effects of human rights and multiculturalism on urban planning practice and policies. His most recent international works are on high-density rural regions in India, human capital migration between China and Canada, and exploring effects of tall buildings in Colombo, Sri Lanka. Agrawal is a recipient of fellowships from Shastri Indo-Canadian Institute, Canada, Sri Lankan Ministry of Higher Education, Indian Institute of Technology, Roorkee, Uttarakhand, India and Jawaharlal Nehru University, New Delhi, India.

Shishir Mathur is Associate Dean (Research) in the College of Social Sciences and Professor of urban and regional planning at San Jose State University, California, USA. His research program spans the fields of public finance, housing, urban and real estate economics, international planning and development, smart growth, transportation planning, and emergency management. Mathur has strong working relations with several regional, national, and international organizations active in the field of urban development. He recently advised the Federal Transit Administration to identify ways to encourage the use of land value capture to fund transit-oriented developments and transit infrastructure and also the United Nations Human Settlements Programme (UN-HABITAT) for input on strategies to encourage land value capture in the Global South. His recent book is titled *Innovation in Public Transport Finance: Property Value Capture*.

Sanjeev Vidyarthi is Associate Professor, Urban Planning and Policy and a senior fellow of the Great Cities Institute at the University of Illinois, Chicago, USA. His research interests span the fields of planning theory and history and globalization and development studies, and his recent book *One Idea, Many Plans* tracked how the American planning concept of the Neighborhood Unit shaped post-Independence planning in India even as many urban actors changed the concept itself. Exploring planning efforts in a wide variety of cultural settings, Sanjeev has lived, worked, and studied in the Middle East, Western Europe, and the USA while maintaining a strong research agenda around the spatial planning and development of independent India.